Praise for *All I Ever Wanted*:

"This absorbing memoir is so much more than a story
about a band that rose to the top. It's the story of a strong,
wounded, driven woman who found her way, like so many
of us, against the odds. Go-go get it. (Sorry—I couldn't
help myself.)"
—Cheryl Strayed

""A vibrantly self-aware rock memoir buzzing with music,
drugs, sisterhood, and blissful redemption."
—*Kirkus/Rolling Stone*, "Best Music Books of 2020"

"An open and often surprising read."
—*Billboard*

"⌊A⌋ vibrant new autobiography."
—*Washington Post*

"[An] entertaining and eloquent memoir."
—*Forbes*

"Kathy Valentine takes us on an epic tour of honest
storytelling. *All I Ever Wanted* is a raw look at the highs
and lows of being high and low. Long live the Go-Go's!"
—Amy Poehler

T0001046

"This book is the equivalent of the best concert I ever attended, possibly better. I was utterly sucked in and immediately devoured it. Honestly, just read it. SO GOOD. You're welcome."
—Jenny Lawson, *New York Times* best-selling author of *Let's Pretend This Never Happened, Furiously Happy,* and *You Are Here: An Owner's Manual for Dangerous Minds*

"Like a scorching guitar solo emerging from the prettiest pop song, Kathy Valentine's *All I Ever Wanted* blows away every other music memoir out there. It's the raw, real story of a Texas girl who raised herself and became a legend through sheer grit and talent, from raucous rocker to pop princess and back again. In prose that is powerful and relatable and unsentimental and funny and scary, Valentine takes readers from the depths of a dark childhood to the electric heights of superstardom. It's a stunning journey, masterfully told."
—Augusten Burroughs, *New York Times* best-selling author of *Running with Scissors* and *Toil and Trouble*

ALL I EVER WANTED

A ROCK 'N' ROLL MEMOIR

KATHY VALENTINE

UNIVERSITY OF TEXAS PRESS ᗄ AUSTIN

Requests for permission to reproduce material
from this work should be sent to:

Permissions
University of Texas Press
P.O. Box 7819
Austin, TX 78713-7819
utpress.utexas.edu/rp-form

♾The paper used in this book meets the minimum requirements
of ANSI/NISO Z39.48-1992 (R1997) (Permanence of Paper).

Library of Congress Cataloging-in-Publication Data

Names: Valentine, Kathy, author.

Title: All I ever wanted : a rock 'n' roll memoir / Kathy Valentine.
Description: First edition. | Austin : University of
Texas Press, 2020. | Includes index.

Identifiers: LCCN 2019032318 | ISBN 978-1-4773-2466-0 (ppb.) | ISBN
978-1-4773-2074-7 (ebook) | ISBN 978-1-4773-2073-0 (library ebook)

Subjects: LCSH: Valentine, Kathy. | Bass guitarists—United States—
Biography. | Go-Go's (Musical group) | LCGFT: Autobiographies.

Classification: LCC ML419.V19 A3 2020 |
DDC 782.42166092 [B]—dc23

LC record available at https://lccn.loc.gov/2019032318

doi:10.7560/312339

*This book is dedicated to Audrey and Margaret,
my daughter and my mother.*

*Audrey, I would trade anything and everything to
be your mom. "Pennies, sand, leaves, atoms."*

*Mom, you are so much stronger and braver than you know.
Thank you for your blessings upon this book.*

CONTENTS

PREFACE

When my teenage daughter asked why I was writing a memoir, the answer was surprisingly elusive and difficult to articulate. I mumbled something about wanting to connect with people, maybe inspire some, which felt like a dull and half-assed reason. And yet I was driven. I *had* to write it, moved by a force very different from the one behind all the songs and music written and played throughout my career.

At first, I thought this was sufficient: I had a story to tell and thought it was important. It's a story that hasn't been told enough, the one about the young girl who decides she wants to be in a rock 'n' roll band and then does just that. There aren't many of us, and there are even fewer who stick with it their whole lives. Rare birds. Rock 'n' roll had saved me, soothed me, shown me there was a world of outliers succeeding in life. But when I picked up my first guitar and started learning to play, it never occurred to me that I could plug it into an amp and get onstage like Keith Richards or Eric Clapton. Why would it? Women occupied a narrow space in relation to the music I loved. They might be hysterical fans, sobbing and pulling at their hair while the Beatles stood onstage calm and cool, tapping their pointy boots, playing music that could be barely heard over the screams and wails. Women might be singing in rock bands—fronting the band, not playing *in* the band. Or they might be groupies on a mission to be close enough to a rock star to be his lover, girlfriend, or muse.

I would have likely stepped into a different future if I hadn't been in England in 1973 with my British mom, watching a music television show. I was fourteen years old, and there she was: Suzi Quatro, a bass player fronting a rock band of guys. Seeing her doing what I had seen only men do changed everything. From that moment, I had one goal: to be in a kickass band with a gang of like-minded girls and claim the life I wanted for myself.

There was just one problem: no clear path or program to follow existed. I encountered unexpected obstacles that popped up like weeds. But I also found unlikely allies and support. And then I landed in the most successful all-female band in the world, making a record that became the first and only one written and performed by an all-female band to hit the top of the American charts. *Ever.*

The Go-Go's made history in the field of popular music.

There's sex, drugs, rock 'n' roll, and redemption—but as it turns out, that wasn't the whole story. Keeping my daughter's question of "why" in my back pocket, the memories unfolded, and I shook out the chapters. Some parts of my life felt so discarded it was as though someone else had lived them. Writing this book allowed me to see clearly how desperately I wanted my dream to take me far away from where I had started. How I used ambition and success to make me forget the loneliness, longing, and sadness of my youth. And how my past not only compelled and motivated me but also shaped my responses to achievements, failures, and everything in between. We all have to find our ways through adolescence and into adulthood, but doing it all alone, without being parented and guided, can be especially painful. I learned how to self-preserve, but at great cost.

The following pages tell a rock 'n' roll coming-of-age story. It takes a candid look into the alchemy of a band, both the hard work and the inner workings. It's about refusing to give up despite facing skepticism and opposition at every turn. It's a chronicle of an era and pop culture spanning two decades of music in two renowned music cities, starting with my discovery of rock 'n' roll in 1970s Austin, Texas, and continuing on through the heights and depths of my twenties in 1980s Los Angeles. And with all that good stuff, the most important bits are woven in; this is a story celebrating resilience and survival. Because some of us need to lose what we love—all we ever wanted—in order to find what we need.

ALL I EVER WANTED

Prologue
HULLABALOO

When I turned twenty-one at the beginning of 1980, Los Angeles had been my home for close to two years. I had moved from Austin, Texas, with the single-minded purpose of making it in a band. My first band, called the Violators, had broken up before we even booked a rehearsal room. Then I started the Textones with my best mate, Carla. Two women guitar players from Texas fronting a band seemed promising at first, but after a while I started to feel we hadn't risen in the ranks or built a solid core of fans fast enough. I wasn't sure we would get there. Other people might move to LA and fret about not having what it takes or end up watching their dreams stall out in the middle of the 405 freeway, but not me. I was ready to kick things up a notch; I just had to find the right band.

After moving into a friend's Hollywood Hills house late in the fall, I kept working on my own: writing songs, going out and meeting people. By the end of 1980, I was ready for a new year and a new start. My mom had come from Austin to spend the holidays with me, just the two of us, like it used to be before I had left Austin. On Christmas night, after we exchanged gifts and ate dinner, she got in bed with a book. Bored and restless, I drove down Sunset Plaza and up Sunset Boulevard to see the band X at the Whisky a Go Go, the famous club on the strip. X ruled the scene, and rightfully so. Their debut album, *Los Angeles*, was slammed with so much originality and intensity it could make some musicians think they should've kept their day jobs. X had a romantic fury; they played and sang like the devil was

1

chasing them. The Whisky had a full house, packed with people happy to burn up alongside the band if the devil caught up.

Pushing my way through the crowd to the graffiti-covered toilet, I found it empty except for one chick. Coming out of the stall, she stood there still, waiting.

The girl introduced herself. "I'm Charlotte, from the Go-Go's."

I thought she'd looked familiar. Charlotte Caffey. I knew her band; I had seen them a couple of times, when I first moved to LA in 1979 and a year later at the Starwood. The Go-Go's were happening.

"Oh, hey," I said.

I liked how she looked: comfortable with herself, not trying to be rock or punk. Just hip and cool like a beatnik or a mod might be, neat and composed. X pounded through the walls, so we had to yell to keep talking.

She got to the business pretty quick, asking if I could play bass. She knew of me from the Textones—we had even shared a bill at the Whisky once: Lydia Lunch, the Go-Go's, and the Textones. Girls who played in bands took notice of each other, a silent affirmation of sorority.

"Sure," I said, without pause. I had never been the bass player in a band, but I figured with five years of guitar playing under my belt, how hard could it be?

Charlotte said they had a four-night gig, two shows a night, starting New Year's Eve, and their bassist couldn't play. Sick or something—I didn't need details. Alongside the muted blitz of X, I felt a surge of hope and possibility revving up like a motor going through a reverb plate. I caught Charlotte saying their roadie thought I might be good for them. I had met him back in Austin when he worked for the Runaways, and we'd hung out some when I first got to LA. I hadn't played a live show since leaving the Textones, and I missed it. I thought about the last time I had seen the Go-Go's, back in October. The crowd had gone nuts for them.

"I can do it," I said.

We searched for a pen and a scrap of paper, then exchanged phone numbers. I got out of there. I couldn't hear X anymore, couldn't talk to anyone, couldn't stand at the bar and get a drink. No room for anything else.

The next morning, I woke up early, wasting no time, not one minute. I called Charlotte and made a plan for her to bring a recording of the Go-Go's so I could learn how to play bass on their songs. One of my musician friends loaned me a bass—the perfect bass. Fender Mustang, small bodied, with a slim, scaled-down neck. Charlotte dropped off the tape. We didn't visit or hang out—I had work to do. Popping the Go-Go's into my cassette player—a basic, cheap unit—I pressed the "play" button. It pushed a thin stream of muddled sound through the tiny speaker. Charlotte had given me a rehearsal tape, probably recorded on a machine as primitive as the one I used. With the borrowed bass plugged into my guitar amp, my left hand circled the neck, the strings thick under my fingers. I used a pick, like I would with a guitar, and played a little, just like it was a guitar. There, this part, easy. Deciphering what the hell I heard on the recording, not so easy. I listened to the first song over and over: play, rewind, play. Before I could get a handle on what to do on the bass, I needed to work out the chord changes and learn the melodies. Making my way through the tape, one thing became clear through the distortion of the cassette player: the Go-Go's had some really good songs. I hadn't realized that in my limited exposure to the band. Each tune had a distinct personality and sound, all of them powered by great drumming and melodies. They blended punk, pop, surf, and rock like no one else.

For the rest of the day and through the night, I played the nineteen songs. The next day I did the same. I had never sustained such an undiluted, deep focus. Getting some blow helped. Mom hung out with a friend and left me space to do my thing, like she had always done. Supporting my music ambitions, not worrying about my proclivity for getting drunk and high—that was her standard MO. It wouldn't have been unusual for us to go on a little bender, get high together, but this was different. The coke was a tool to keep going. I practiced for three days and nights—I must have played that tape hundreds of times. I didn't want to fuck up one thing, not one note. The repetition committed the songs to memory. Finally, some bass lines came through. The ones I could sort out were good and I kept them. I made up the other ones and hoped the band wouldn't notice.

Charlotte came over and brought the rhythm guitarist, Jane Wiedlin, to meet me. After a three-day coke binge learning their set, my vacant, glassy stare probably didn't make the best impression. All I remember is Jane being elf-like—and I mean dressed-like-an-elf-like, not impish and mischievous elf-like. She wore green with a felt hat, the whole deal.

The following day I went into Stone Fox rehearsal studio in the Valley, alone, using every ounce of cool and casual I could muster. I had met the drummer, Gina Schock, once before, but she didn't act like she remembered me. She didn't seem convinced about this whole idea of playing with someone new. Ready to get down to business, anxious to hear if this could work, she wasn't interested in chitchat or pleasantries. Belinda Carlisle, the lead singer, thought we had met before and mentioned being at my twenty-first birthday bash gig with her boyfriend at the start of the year. I appreciated the attempt at a connection, a polite and friendly welcome. She had moved on from her heavy, dark makeup and punk tart fashions of the band's early days and adopted a retro feminine look. It suited her curves and uncommonly pretty face, a face you didn't forget. Jane, the guitarist I had met the day before, struck me as shy, maybe even a little nervous. Charlotte took charge of the room.

Ampeg SVT amps are fairly standard for a bass player. The equipment stood taller than me, set up close to the drum kit. I assumed it belonged to Margot, the absent bassist. I plugged in and turned up, and Gina launched into the tom roll intro of the '60s surf-inspired "Beatnik Beach." Everyone relaxed and played their parts. "How Much More," which had become one of my favorites, was next. It kind of reminded me of the Elvis Presley song—the one with the Bo Diddley beat—where he sings, "Marie's the name of his latest flame." No matter how much you practice to tapes or records, it's completely different playing the same songs and parts with the musicians. It can throw you sometimes, adjusting. In this case, being with everyone made it way better. Playing bass quietly through my guitar amp with the awful cassette had been a drag. When I got up the nerve to glance up, I saw looks being exchanged between the Go-Go's. They liked it. Belinda smiled.

When it comes to playing music, feel is an indefinable thing. Two musicians can play the exact same notes, but they're going to do it differently. Maybe the Go-Go's didn't even know why they liked the way it sounded or felt with me, but they knew it made a difference, and the difference was my feel, the way I played. Playing bass might have been new to me; it was an instrument I hadn't thought much about before. Keith Richards had always been my hero, not Bill Wyman. But having no experience on the bass didn't matter with the Go-Go's. What mattered was that I understood exactly what the Go-Go's should sound like. I knew when to swing. I knew when to drive. I knew what to listen for, and I had good timing.

Ginger Canzoneri, the band's manager, showed up. Ginger was a whippet in red lipstick. If she stood in a lineup with the band, no one would pick her out as the manager.

"All eight shows have sold out!" She delivered the news with breathless, manic energy; the four Go-Go's whooped and yelled in response. I tried not to look like a deer in the headlights. All those sold-out shows at the Whisky carried some serious weight. Only a handful of LA bands could draw those crowds.

Gina cut the rejoicing short: "C'mon guys, we gotta work! We gotta sound tight!"

After band rehearsal, I went back home to the tape player and did more on my own. We only had one day left to play together before the first gig, so every time I reviewed the songs counted.

On show day, Charlotte picked me up, a much-appreciated kindness. "SOLD OUT" the Whisky marquee blared, red on white. Seeing it gave me a little electric buzz.

I had never played a sold-out show in my life. Already, fans were hanging around the front door, forming a line. At sound check, Kent, the roadie I already knew, added some familiarity; I thanked him for his vote of confidence and suggesting me. The only other crew was a gal named Lydia who mainly helped Gina. I liked that the Go-Go's had a female drum roadie and a female manager. Staying after sound check, we waited in the dressing room for our first set. Jane and Belinda went onstage to introduce our opening act, the Raybeats from New York City, with an endorsement: "Hey, the Go-Go's like these guys and so should you." I heard a cheer from the crowd, magnifying the anticipation and excitement in the dressing room. As our time neared, Gina practiced furiously, her sticks speeding through rudiments on a rubber pad. The rest of us paced, bounced on our feet, and made pretend-scared faces at each other. It had already started to feel like my band.

Walking onstage, it was hullabaloo. A collective ardor had energy rising like vapors off the crowd. There were only five hundred people in the club, but they had double the power; everyone crammed together with the same purpose. They were here to experience the magic of music from a band intent on delivering escape and simple fun. I told myself to focus: *Get set up, strap your instrument on, be cool, be calm, but feel this—because you have never felt this before.* It was an approval so absolute and certain that nothing could stop it crashing toward the stage.

Planting my feet in front of the bass rig, I fixed my eyes on the neck of my bass, making sure my hand and my fingers moved to the right place at the right time. I hung back next to Gina, who made her presence known with every beat. We were a rhythm section, right and solid as a wall. Her drumming made it easy, and I just let the band carry me.

The audience was infatuated with Belinda. She sang with her heart and danced good-naturedly, unconcerned, like the most fun chick at a party. She had no artifice. In time, she would cultivate a persona that fans were no less enamored of. Jane looked nonchalant and buoyant, considering she did a lot of heavy lifting entertaining the crowd. As animated and cute as a cartoon girl come to life, she twirled and skipped, strummed her SG, and made the choruses soar with her harmonies. Charlotte studiously dispensed with guitar lines and melodies intrinsic to each song. She had been involved in writing nearly all of them. Most of the time she doubled up on rhythm guitar and stayed stationary and contained, her blond hair and bangs like Nico from the Velvet Underground.

"Where's Margot?" someone in the crowd yelled after a few songs.

I was mortified. Belinda introduced me, saying I was filling in for Margot, who was sick. Once the next song started, I forgot about the interruption, and anything else. This—right then, right there—was the reason I had come to LA, why I'd started bands, why I'd picked up a guitar and learned to play. Now I got to experience the only part that had ever been missing. People loved this band. Playing those songs, making that crowd happy, was the best time I had ever had on a stage or as a musician. I could hardly believe I would get to do it again later for the second show, and for three more nights after.

Everyone showed up for the Whisky gig—so many LA musicians. Hanging out in the cramped dressing room with the band between the two sets helped with my nervousness. My mom had been there for the first set, somewhere in the crowd, and had probably left by now. I hadn't given her a thought. In our little family, you took care of yourself. Ginger had natural gatekeeper talent, knowing who to admit and firmly turning others away. One notable person came in: new fan John Belushi. A backstage photo with him is my only memento from my first gigs with the Go-Go's. It's a classic.

During the second set, cream pies appeared out of nowhere. If a fan got overly excited and jumped on stage, our crew planted a pie right on their face. People hardly noticed. We were five girls barely into our twenties propelling the crowd into near delirium with our music. People started throwing money on stage, and it just kept coming. Belinda scooped up a handful of bills and stuffed them in her bra. Jane egged them on for more. "C'mon! Is that all you got?" Charlotte and I swapped grins, bright with the tacit acknowledgment of a new synthesis. Maybe we knew before anyone else that I was there to stay. By midnight, the Whisky walls could barely contain the energy of the show. Everyone—band, crew, staff, and audience—joined in to shout out 1980. It felt like a rocket ship countdown, and I was ready to blast off.

1

THE STARS START FALLING

When I was a kid, my mom used to tell me I could credit my existence to a sandwich. I made her tell me the story over and over. She was born and raised in England and had gotten an office job in London when she was eighteen. On a rare sunny day, she took her lunch break outdoors in a nearby park and happened to meet a handsome American Air Force serviceman. Two years later, in 1957, she married him at the neighborhood church in Stanmore, where she had grown up.

"So," she would say, "if I hadn't gone out to eat my sandwich in the park, I'd have never met your father, and you wouldn't be here." And I'd make her tell it again, trying to see my life as a magical coincidence not predicated on a random whim.

My mom is Margaret Valentine, and the guy who became my dad, Clifford Eugene Wheeler. Their traditional wedding was documented in a huge, white album I pored over as a child, the only proof of their marriage I would ever see. It chirped a music box tune of "Here Comes the Bride" while I examined my parents' smiling faces trapped behind the translucent, filmy paper.

None of my dad's family was at the wedding. He had been born in Athens, Texas, before moving to Lubbock, where he grew up in a two-room house. Cliff, or "Brother" as they called him, was the second oldest of nine siblings with an alcoholic dad and a stoic mother. He was a practical, no-frills guy. Rightly determining that the military would be the only way out of the

West Texas poverty surrounding him, he enlisted as soon as he could. Despite dropping out of school twice, in the fifth and eighth grades, he was one of a handful of literate recruits and granted office duties. A captain noticed an intellect my dad hadn't considered and encouraged him to use his military service as a springboard for college.

By the time the young newlyweds arrived in Lubbock in the summer of 1958, on a courtesy stop for Mom to meet her new in-laws, she was newly pregnant with me. In a faded photo showing her in stilettos, pencil skirt, and ten-gallon cowboy hat, I can see the bewilderment in her tiny grayscale face. This new American life didn't look much like the romanticized version she had imagined, inspired by American movies. Margaret had always felt special and expected great adventure and privilege to be hers for the taking. My dad was four years older than his new bride, and he had a plan: military service, college, a secure future, and a family. His English wife helped create the distance he wanted from his impoverished upbringing. Margaret was beautiful: glamorous in that way so many young women in the '50s were, with a classic wave of blonde hair and a luminous, pouty face. She had an insouciant British charm that made her shine brightly—even more so in Texas. Perhaps, she thought, Austin would be better than Lubbock.

The young couple arrived before the fall semester, and Cliff set out to get the education he had earned in the Air Force, enrolling in an economics degree program at the flourishing University of Texas (UT) campus. Austin was, in fact, way better. It looked like paradise to Margaret after driving for six hours across dreary landscapes. While it couldn't compare to the rolling green meadows and forests of England, the hill country capital was surrounded with lakes and a river running through the small city—quite lush in comparison to Lubbock. She began to acclimate to her new home, growing large with the only child she would bear. When I was born, on January 7, 1959, my mom was twenty-one years old.

University student family housing provided a cheap apartment, and my parents squeaked by. I don't remember these years, but a collection of photos depicts me as a baby and toddler, always with one parent, the other presumably snapping the picture. In each, it's clear that I'm the joy of their life. My dad holds me as a newborn with tender love. I'm with Mom by my first Christmas tree, both of us beaming. Outside, I'm caught mid-waddle, then learning to walk at ten months, riding a tricycle, on the swings, at the pool with my dad at Barton Springs. At three years old, in 1962, I blow out candles on a cake. Then the family photos stop.

New opportunities came for my dad: he accepted a scholarship for graduate studies in Philadelphia. Margaret hated it there; she was lonely and unsympathetic to Cliff's responsibilities and struggles. In the winter of 1962, a charitable friend bought her a plane ticket to London. She took me to visit her family, leaving my dad in Philly for nearly a month. Upon our return, he had landed a job in New Jersey, planning to leave school to try and give her a better life. My mom hated it there too. She had decided to divorce him. My dad was devastated. I have no recollections of them fighting or splitting up, or how it felt to be a little girl newly without her daddy. I didn't ask my mom how I took it until my mid-thirties.

"It was so sad," she said. "You sat on the steps watching cars drive by and would jump up when you thought you recognized his. As the car kept going without stopping, you would cry inconsolably." She paused, then said, "I felt terrible!"

I wondered how decades could have passed with me unable to acknowledge that childhood grief.

Margaret might have been done with Cliff and being married, but she wasn't done with America. Instead of going back to her homeland, Mom chose to live in Austin. College hadn't been part of her plan as a young woman in England, but in Austin she applied to UT and enrolled as a psychology major. My dad moved to Missouri to work on his economics doctorate and teach. A few times, he made the drive to visit me. He never came to the door, just waited at the curb until my mom sent me out. I don't remember these visits, what we did or where we went. They stopped as suddenly as the childhood photos. My parents didn't see each other until my wedding day, forty years after they divorced. Once, as a grown woman with my own family, I asked my father why he had stopped coming to see his only little girl in the world. I couldn't imagine it. He said he had figured Margaret would marry someone else soon and it would be easier if he was out of the way.

"Easier for whom?" I wondered.

With my dad gone, it began to seem like "us versus them." At first, "them" could be anyone making things tough for my mom. It might be my dad, always too broke to send more than a pittance of child support. Or it was the bill collectors—for years, each month she frantically told me that we might be going to the poorhouse, as if we lived in nineteenth-century Dickensian London. "No, we're not," I finally started responding when it never came to be. UT administrators, professors, or her boss also caused problems for my mom—but before too long, she got a social conscience, and the main "them" became the establishment. America didn't have the class distinctions of her native England, but poverty, prejudice, and unequal women's rights disturbed her. She admired radicals like Madalyn Murray O'Hair, an outspoken atheist who got prayer removed from schools. When US involvement in the Vietnam War increased, my mom marched in protest, even getting her picture on the front page of the *Daily Texan* (UT's student newspaper)—not for protesting, but for wearing the first miniskirt seen on campus. Fueled by Virginia Slims and Lipton tea, she socialized in late-night get-togethers with friends while I kept busy in my room. I had learned to read from a caregiver who watched over me after nursery school while Mom took classes and worked in the anthropology department.

She remained stunning in her beauty, and a growing confidence in her intellect added mystique. Within her first year of divorce, she had a boyfriend, Ronald, a psychologist with the charisma and looks of an American movie star. On weekends he played jazz drums at the Villa Capri. My mom obsessed over Ronald. She would ditch anything if she had a chance to hang out with him. She even ditched me once, leaving me as I slept in my bed. After waking up and realizing I was alone, I raced with rising terror from room to room. I pulled at the front door, panicked at how it stuck in its frame, reaching into my five-year-old reservoir for the extra heave-ho to fling it open. I ran across our weedy yard and pounded on a neighbor's door, ashamed that I needed something from these adults.

"She must be with Ronald at the Plantation," they said. The twenty-four-hour coffee shop on Nineteenth Street by UT was her favorite hangout. Hearing the familiar name calmed me down. I had sat in a booth there with Mom many times, playing my favorite Beatles and Herb Alpert songs on the table jukebox. After a muffled phone call, I was assured she had been found and was coming to get me. Mom appeared, hugging me, saying how much she loved me and how sorry she was. I was so relieved to have her back I barely heard the words. But the feeling of being left in the night by the only parent I had left a residue of fear and uncertainty.

Besides her boyfriend, my mother hung out with a circle of academics and bohemian intellectuals. I was the only kid around. I instinctively became self-sufficient, not needing much tending to. Sometimes her psychology friends gave me IQ and personality tests and raved at my answers and scores, Mom looking pleased and proud at how smart her little girl was. It's the best vestige from my childhood. Today, every time I want to tell my daughter how beautiful she is, I try to stop myself and tell her instead how smart she is.

I read constantly or escaped into an imaginary life crafted with elaborate but mundane fantasies about normal families, best friends, and romances. I could gaze out a window or stare blank-faced at a wall for hours replaying recurring, tedious storylines. Sometimes I wonder if the neural pathways for addiction might have started with my penchant for checking out to daydream.

Occasionally, I got to experience what it was like to be part of a bigger family. My mom didn't speak to my dad, but one summer she and her boyfriend Ronald drove me to Lubbock and asked my dad's mother—my grandmother—to look after me for a few weeks. I hid in the closet for an entire day until they coaxed me out and I discovered I had a surplus of colorful aunts and uncles with nicknames such as "Baby Gal," "Shorty," and "Red," and cousins of all ages. Then I liked Lubbock, and I even thought it was kind of exciting to be there.

The summer of 1968, I was nine years old and spending my third summer in Lubbock. My sixteen-year-old cousin AJ stopped by my grandmother's house and headed right into the teenage Baby Gal's girly bedroom. I still couldn't believe I had actual guys as family members. Deprived of brothers and a father, I was enamored of AJ's male-ness, easy assurance, and cockeyed cast. I remember the afternoon, listening in the hall outside the door. On the other side, AJ played one song, "Sunshine of Your Love," over and over. Picking up the needle and setting it back at the start, again and again. I didn't want him to ever stop.

Music had calibrated the imbalances of my life for as long as I could remember: listening to the table jukeboxes, dancing the twist with my mom, singing along with bouncy bubblegum melodies. I discovered pop music on AM radio and had a record box with a solid collection of singles. But this sounded nothing like the 45s I had collected. Years later, I would have the vocabulary to describe it: six notes on a blues scale. Arranged and phrased in a way that unlocked something inside me I didn't know existed.

"I'll be with you when the stars start falling," Cream's Jack Bruce swore with woeful desire before the song peaked at the jagged power of a B chord, the melody tumbling over the last word, "lo-uh-oh uh-oh-oh-ove," back to the driving riff, Clapton's tone cutting through the door like a thick blade. In one afternoon, I learned how a song could have the potency to elicit a deeper response than I had ever experienced. Cream opened a portal to an unexplored hidden self, making my heart ache with anticipation of what might be waiting to be discovered. Now, music held something to look out for and recognize. I didn't know what "sexy" or "subversive" meant; I couldn't have defined those elements in the rumble of drums or the slides and bends of guitar. The concept of a song—of a sound—being raw and dirty but so pure wasn't one I could formulate or distinguish from the music I was familiar with. I definitely had no idea what the "sunshine of your love" was, but I couldn't wait to find out.

2

MAGIC CLOAK

The English relatives on my mother's side couldn't have been more different from my father's in Texas, but our trips there also gave me a sense of belonging to a family. In 1970, when I was eleven years old, Mom took me for my second visit. My grandmother, also named Margaret Valentine, came from Lancashire; she was a handsome lady with a lush headful of solid white hair. My grandma hugged and fussed over me a lot, which I liked. My mom's relationship with her mother dictated much of what she didn't want in ours: my mom wanted a pal, not the distance and formality she'd had with her mother.

My grandpa wrote letters with little notes and pictures to me every few months. He had been ill for years, slowly dying from what my mom said was a disease called "hardening of the arteries." Despite this illness, his heart stayed soft and open. It's too bad he didn't get to see me become a musician, because among his many interests and jobs, he played violin and stand-up bass in a jazz combo. He seemed to be unusually full of life for a dying person—nothing depressing about hanging out with him.

Mom and I escaped on day trips, taking the tube into the city to roam around without a plan or destination. I had read every book about English history I could get my hands on. English history seemed vastly superior to American history, as far as I was concerned. We giggled at Henry VIII's armor at the Tower of London, with its big steel bubble to encase his penis. I got a kick out of the mummified cats in the Egyptian section of the British

Museum, their shapes wrapped in decayed brown linen, all the way to the ear triangles on their heads. In Trafalgar Square I fed pigeons breadcrumbs until their frantic flapping got scary. Best of all was Carnaby Street, filled with tourists but still enough mods and rockers to make it nothing like you would see in Austin. Everywhere, Mungo Jerry's "In the Summertime" and the Guess Who's "American Woman" blasted out of shops and trendy bars. I might have been miles away from being hip, but I knew the words, melodies, and guitar hooks as well as anyone else.

At the end of the summer, Mom and I went back to Austin and moved for the fourth time in as many years. We didn't own much and could transport our belongings in two or three drives back and forth across town. My self-assigned job entailed making a list of things to pack and checking them off one by one. Always first was the wooden box from Kraft Korner sitting on the coffee table. A few years before, we had glued glass tiles in rusty oranges and emerald greens on the lid in an orderly design. I remember leaning over the table with our heads together, the tiles reflecting little prisms of light. My hair fell thick and brown, like my dad's. I got his green eyes, too, not far off from the green of the tiles. He had been long gone by then, for seven years. Living across state lines, dug down deep with his second wife and her two daughters. The Kraft Korner box followed us every time we moved. It was the one constant in a life of variables.

There wasn't much more. The miscellany of our cookware got tossed into a crate: plates, cups, utensils, burned pans. One prized possession—folded with pride—was a set of four washcloths. I saved babysitting money and got them for Mom's birthday, thinking they might be like what I would find in the bathroom closet of some nice, elegant house. These washcloths were the only matching things we owned, and I had bought them. Two bigger pieces summed up our belongings: some planks of wood and bricks to dismantle and rebuild for bookshelves, and a Zenith black and white television with aluminum foiled antennae.

Mom rented one of two conjoined units in a duplex, supposedly an upgrade from an apartment building. It was second in a short row of rentals on Gloucester Lane. No one but us pronounced the English name correctly. The rest of the neighborhood houses were well tended, traditional brick, stone, and frame Neocolonials with good-size lots and yards.

Mom had traded in her sporty Fiat Spyder for a white Ford Maverick. It looked like a flattened washing machine, a clumsy clunker of a car with barely more than an ignition and speedometer on the instrument panel. Parking in the shared carport, we unloaded the last of our belongings into our new living space. The brown-paneled walls of our new home made it gloomy and dark. There was an open kitchen and dining area divided by a counter with an inset electric stovetop. A split-level step from there led into the living area, where sliding-glass doors led to the back yard. Like everywhere we had lived, the place came furnished.

Mom had noble intentions: moving to this suburb gave me the stability of staying in one place. For the first time, I would be able to make neighborhood friends. The wide streets allowed kids to weave bikes on and off the sidewalk. Nearby, a big park and public pool provided a hangout spot. I would hit sixth grade two blocks away at the elementary school, then move over to Pearce Junior High a short distance away. If I squinted my eyes at the house, it looked sort of like the other homes in the neighborhood. Maybe I would walk in a cluster of girlfriends to their homes after school, where their stay-at-home moms would give us cookies and milk. A new way of living seemed possible here, around real families, instead of living by the UT campus or in remote apartment buildings.

A year later, I would know better.

Here, in this middle-class Northeast Austin duplex, the diffused sense of "us versus them" became a hard reality. We would never fit in, and that was fine with my mom. We were different. They were all ordinary, by-the-book, pillars of propriety—the ones who got married and stayed married, the ones who got jobs and kept them. They were churchgoing, sports-loving, sitting-at-the-table-for-home-cooked-meals regular folks. To my mom's thinking: squares. She had evolved into—or perhaps had always been—a self-governed individualist anarchist, taking whatever action she deemed best for her at a given moment. I thought she was fearless. Mom didn't like convention or rules. The way she acted, you'd think she wore a magic cloak of exception, an impenetrable wrap shielding us from consequences. The only problem was, her magic cloak didn't protect me.

In the three years we lived in this duplex, I grew up fast. Here, I used my first tampon, my mom shouting outside the bathroom door: "If you can feel it, it's not in there right." In my room, I plastered the wood-paneled walls with black-light posters and got my first real stereo, a portable one with speakers that clamped onto the sides. This is the house where an intruder got frightened off by Mom swinging an iron at high speed from its cord, the place where prowlers and peeping toms and cruel teenagers made home not a safe place. This is where the police brought me home, too drunk to walk. These were the years I spun out in the turbulence and confusion of living with a mother who allowed anything. The duplex is still there, with its stone veneer and carport, and when I drove by decades later, in my fifties, my hands turned clammy on the steering wheel and I pulled over to cry.

3

LIQUID FORGET

Sixth grade had the flush of a new beginning. As a straight A student, I found the schoolwork easy and had little to worry about other than trying to find my place in the social hierarchy. Each month, the kids got to bring our favorite records to play for music class—back then, still considered part of education. The records you chose made an overt statement about your identity. I obsessed for weeks about my turn, finally deciding on "Na Na Hey Hey Kiss Him Goodbye" by Steam and "Mississippi Queen" by Mountain. Both seemed to cover the swing of my taste pretty well. From the get-go, I'd always appreciated a good pop melody; but since the Cream discovery, I required equal doses of riff-centered heavy blues rock.

Maybe my English grandpa had said something to stir up my interest, or it might have just been in my nature, but when the option to join the school band or orchestra presented itself, I chose the violin. I practiced with discipline and enthusiasm for hours each day. Neither makes a beginning violinist bearable to listen to, but my mom beamed with pride at my scratchy, screeching musical talent. Letters kept me in occasional contact with my dad. After finding out I had a violin, he urged me to learn some fiddle songs. He had gotten into bluegrass music and started playing guitar and banjo. I dutifully tried to learn the "Cotton-Eyed Joe," hoping to impress him should I ever get to visit.

Latchkey kids weren't common in the neighborhood, and divorced moms who wore bell-bottoms and miniskirts like mine did were nonexistent. Finding a friend who was off-brand like me took a while, but in the summer of 1971 I met Jenny at the neighborhood public pool. Like two magnet poles in a misfit field, the two of us were simultaneously pulled together and repelled by each other. Jenny's house was run-down, and her mom was divorced too. Jenny had dark skin, dark hair, and dark eyes that looked suspiciously at everyone. She just escaped being pretty. My new BFF was troubled and crazy, up for anything. Neither of us was the leader. We were each other's sidekicks.

That summer, baby doll bathing suits were all the rage and my favorite song, "Maggie May" by Rod Stewart, played constantly on the radio. But our friendship had nothing to do with bonding over music or fashion trends. It was built entirely upon becoming fuckups together, beginning with smoking cigarettes. We went straight for the hard-core Marlboro Reds, the boxes smashed flat in the pockets of our cut-off jean shorts, slit up the sides to the top of our thighs. Pocket tees and halter tops, wild knee-high socks, and suede desert boots completed the uniform. Jenny refused to wear a bra. I felt embarrassed by her loose swinging breasts. "Banana titties," the boys said, but she didn't give a shit.

We got drunk together for the first time on Boone's Farm Strawberry Hill wine, taking chug-a-lug turns on the bottle. I wiped my mouth on my shirt sleeve after every retching gulp. We laughed until tears streamed down our flushed cheeks, dizzy and giddy, bonding with this new secret knowledge. We had found something important, something incredible, something with the power to make you forget the discomfort and awkwardness of not fitting in. Forget that you live in a crummy rent house. Forget that you don't have a dad. Forget those imaginary too-fat thighs and large pores. Booze was a bottle of liquid forget.

By the time seventh grade started, I could smoke like a pro but drank like an amateur—as if I did it for the express purpose of throwing up. I didn't keep the smoking hidden from my mom. As a kid, I had hassled her to quit; the warning labels had started in the mid-1960s. You'd think people would have found that alarming, but no one seemed to care. Smoking gave me and Jenny a built-in peer group in junior high. The delinquents met in the mornings, maybe five to ten kids slouching and sprawled on the steps at the back door of a church across the street from the school.

Our little group of outcasts made easy targets, an exploitable source that drug sellers tapped. High school boys began to zoom up in the mornings on their whiny motorcycles, Yamaha 180s. Over the curb they would bounce, swerving up a donut in the dirt before stopping. At first, they sold us little joints or matchboxes of weed. I got high for the first time and laughed my ass off. Never a paranoid stoner or weepy drunk, I felt like a good-time girl out to have some fun. Once the pot started, the proverbial gateway opened, and through it poured the first wave of drugs. In my case, it was LSD named like crazy candy: Orange Sunshine, Windowpane, Clear Light. We could pool our lunch money to buy a few hits, dividing up shares of the paper or tiny pills that held the acid. The dose made me feel silly and brave enough to try more next time. Students who didn't smoke or do drugs got branded as "narcs," despised by my lowly gang. The only approval that mattered to me was from the kids I got stoned with. For the first time, I didn't care what teachers thought, and my grades plummeted from straight As to Cs.

The world stayed busy. The Vietnam War dragged on, Apollo 15 launched and landed. There was the Concert for Bangladesh, the first of the big-name benefit concerts. Manson and his sicko followers got sentenced. The events of the year didn't go unnoticed by me but seemed far away. The societal ill making it down to my world involved racial discord. Like many schools in the country during this era, race riots had become routine at my school. The black kids sharpened the points on their afro combs to use as weapons, and the white boys hurled inflammatory insults. Mobs of scuffling students clogged the hallways, spilling out onto the sidewalk. You haven't lived until you've been on LSD when a race riot starts in your stupid school. The chaos was terrifying, but most of the stoners rejoiced, knowing that bells would start ringing and the PA system would be blaring threats from the principal. Everyone who lived close by took off for home, the sirens of approaching cop cars in the air. Looking back from today, with guns and shootings as the norm, the violence seems quaint. Even the overt and open racism seems like a relic far removed from the pretend-tolerance of subsequent decades.

Sometimes I skipped school because of doing acid, but before too long I didn't need any reason other than I just didn't feel like going. My parentless home became one of the houses where truant kids could hang out. Playing hooky united kids in a conspiratorial goal; we were all avoiding school and trying to not get caught. I thought of myself as a tomboy, one of the guys, so I was surprised one afternoon at Kerry Sadler's house when her cute brother Kevin, a fourteen-year-old eighth grader, cornered me as I exited the bathroom. His blond hair hung over pleading eyes, his full lips whispering for me to touch his wiener. I giggled and squirmed my way out of that one, but he certainly got my attention. I went over there more often, trying to get noticed by him and avoid him at the same time, which somehow made sense.

Around the same time, I rode my green sparkle Sting Ray over to Frank Ryan's house in the early evening. He and another guy had holed up in an RV in the driveway with a bottle of Jack Daniels. I gamely tried to keep up and chug it the way I did with cheap wine and beer. After each turn, they tried to cop feels, saying, "C'mon, gimme some," then roll back howling when I yelled and fought back. Whatever discomfort or fear I felt was soon obliterated when I passed out. Whether they "got some" or got scared, I don't know. I woke up in the front yard, laying by the curb, the headlights of a police cruiser blinding my confusion. The patrolmen escorted me home. Mom answered their persistent knock, stepping aside as I crawled on all fours through the door. She didn't seem worried that the police had brought me home or that I couldn't walk. There were no consequences, no lectures, no punishment except for saying she hoped I had learned my lesson—presumably that getting drunk was a stone drag. I hadn't learned any lesson except no more whiskey. That stuck. For the rest of my drinking days, if the party dried up, I'd rather call it a night than drink Jack.

One afternoon, the inevitable happened. Playing hooky again at my friend Kerry's house, her brother Kevin called me into his room. He asked if I loved him. I stood there dumb and uncertain. He wasted no time and pulled his pants down. Backing toward the door, I half-heartedly tried to escape. He gently took my hand and pulled me toward him. He whispered, his breath sweet and warm in my ear, "Let me be the first; let me be the one." I wanted to leave, but I wanted to give in. I wanted to be important to him. He pulled me to the floor, pushed my shorts and panties to my ankles, spread my knees apart, and poked at different spots between my legs while breathing hard in my face. I lay there with no idea what I was supposed to do. It was over quickly. Was that sex? He knelt above me and I looked up at him, not sure what I would see. Would he be embarrassed? Tender and loving? Smiling and happy? Contempt was the last thing I expected. My bewildered face must have tickled him, because he started laughing.

"Get up, slut," he sneered.

That humiliation was the first deposit in a new, unwelcome account. At school the next day, he tossed the news of his exploit around. Like a match to kindling, it caught fire and spread. Walking through the halls that day, I could feel the flames on my cheeks, a gauntlet of smirks and elbow nudges paving my every step. Overnight, I was reborn as a girl with a reputation. Running to my mom in tears, I told her everything. She listened sympathetically, hugged me close.

"You didn't do anything wrong," she said. "You did it with the wrong person."

I'd never gotten the self-respect talk about saving my twelve-year-old-self for someone special, and I didn't get it then either. My mom was visibly distressed to see me so unhappy. But most importantly, she wanted to make sure that I didn't get hung up about sex. That's a 1970s deal, *hung up*. The worst thing you could be after the '60s sexual revolution was uptight or hung up.

So off I went to school the next day with the notion that everyone else had a problem, not me. They didn't get it. Mom had assured me I'd done nothing bad.

Her affirmation didn't help with what followed. Guys I'd never even seen before would yell at me, asking for blow jobs or "poon" or "nookie." Guys I had thought of as friends tried to get me alone and force me into sex. I always got away, but they lied and said it had happened anyway. Mom was wrong. I couldn't outrun the shame or abuse. It wasn't getting better, and it wasn't going to get better. I did the only thing I knew how to do: project confidence and strength, and pretend none of it bothered me. The one time that moving to a new home and school would have made life easier instead of harder, it didn't happen. I cranked the attitude knob up, all the way. Everything was fine. I drank more and drugged more and toughened up.

4

VACATION

I hadn't completely caught up to my new debauched-lite life-style. Empty Dr Pepper bottles and troll dolls decorated the window ledge of my bedroom. A pile of stuffed animals sat on a giant fur pillow. Black-light posters of neon waterfalls and psychedelic designs covered the walls. I still had a schoolgirl crush on a Beatle. I can connect the dots of my childhood by the order of my favorite Beatles. First was Ringo, then Paul. John was next, until he married Yoko. George stayed number one forever after.

Despite these vestiges of innocence, there was evidence I was in transition. I stopped riding my Sting Ray and instead tried to get rides on the back of guys' motorcycles, or stuck out my thumb and hitchhiked. Getting stoned and putting on head-phones, all my uncertainties and the trash talk of school were drowned out by the few albums I owned. I played each one over and over and can sing every lick and note of *Led Zeppelin IV* to this day.

The neighborhood, junior high, and high school made a very small world. By the end of fall, high school boys got hip to the duplex on Gloucester Lane where the "wild" girl lived and where delinquents could ditch school. My being a twelve-year-old was irrelevant to them—here was a funky house they could hang around and act like big shots. I knew better than to think they were friends, but the older boys were marginally more mature and seemed less interested in rumormongering. Their frequent presence curbed the ostracizing that gave guys in my school such glee. Henry was a good-looking sixteen-year-old high school junior with greasy hair, big lips, and bulging eyes with a twitchy tic in one. You had to be there, I guess, to see his appeal. Despite making fun of my lame stereo, he spent many hours at our house, arriving with an armload of great records by T. Rex, Alice Cooper, and David Bowie.

Rock 'n' roll, the superhero to a new generation of misfits, was my lifesaver. A magical conduit to a celebration of outrageousness, sexuality, and decadence came through the music. I could hear it, see it, and feel it. I knew Bowie or Marc Bolan would never have fit in where I was either. The same guys who dug their music would have tortured them as schoolmates. The rock stars were inseparable from the music, just as important as the songs. Liking the same music, the same bands, was the first bond I ever felt with other people.

The Stones' *Sticky Fingers* had come out, its cover with the blue jean crotch and actual zipper practically screaming, "This is what it's all about!" Henry would put on "Brown Sugar," lip-syncing along while he strutted like Mick Jagger, back and forth in front of me all knock-knees and gyrating hips. One afternoon, with much difficulty—it took nearly all of *Sticky Fingers* side one—I had sex with Henry. It hurt a lot and made me realize I couldn't have had sex before. After that day, he stopped coming over and I rarely saw him. He was in high school; I was a seventh grader. Maybe he thought I would tell my Mom and he'd get in trouble.

A month later I was at the doctor because it felt weird when I peed. Mom hoped it might be an infection, but instead we got some unexpected news: I had gotten pregnant. Hearing this, both my mom and I kicked into our own sphere of *oh shit oh shit oh shit*. Unwanted pregnancy in 1971 Texas meant big problems. This was two years before *Roe v. Wade*. It never occurred to me that I should, or even could, stay pregnant. I didn't know of any other girls my age having sex; I had never heard of abortion. While I went back to school with my secret, Mom found a clinic in California that the doctor had recommended.

"Let's make a vacation out of it," she said.

Her cousin Doris lived in San Diego. We could take care of our business in LA, then go visit Doris.

Mom moved fast when she had to. A week after finding out, we were on the sidewalk at LAX, looking like sisters in hip-hugger jeans and wide belts. Across the street, planted right in the middle of the airport parking lot, was the Theme Building, its space-age arches crossing over a flying saucer–shaped dish. Awestruck, I ached to explore it—then reality jolted me back to why we were there and who I really was: a scared and tired twelve-year-old in town for an abortion. Forty-three years later I would look at my own twelve-year-old daughter, thinking of this time. I cannot imagine her having to deal with the sex, the shame, and the mistakes of my childhood. I both grieve and marvel at the difference in our twelves.

A dirty, dented white van pulled curbside to the terminal. A guy in scrubs hopped out and welcomed us, no attitude or judgment, and drove us to the clinic. Like a series of snapshots, I remember images: a low, brick building adjacent to a motel. Glass doors swinging open to a green-walled waiting and reception area. A Planned Parenthood social worker wedged behind her desk in a cramped office.

We sat across from her. She stared me down from behind large eyeglasses. A helmet of frizzy, permed hair encased her head. In response to her quiet, earnest questions, I shrugged my toughness at her.

"I want to deal with it," I said. "I want it to be over."

Frizzy turned to Mom like I wasn't there and told her I must be repressing my feelings. Maybe so. I felt nothing. Here I was at the abortion clinic, after having sex two times. Except now I was sure nothing happened with Kevin Sadler. Still, his big mouth blabbing had inflicted a far-reaching torment on me. Now it was like his bullshit stories were writing my life.

I braced for a lecture or some "counseling," but Frizzy didn't have time for deep sessions to unearth repressed feelings. She moved on, teaching me about the pill, all business and procedure, spinning the top of a sample Ortho-Novum dispenser. It looked pink and feminine, easy, a spiffy little invention. My mom jumped right on board, noticeably relieved that I had officially crossed the border into compatible friend territory. The mysterious and uncharted land of single parenting a lost, unhappy daughter wasn't a place she'd ever wanted to be.

Moving from a changing area to a curtained cubicle, I disassociated and became an observer. I looked down on myself lying on a gurney, my hair in a plastic shower cap. One girl waiting in a row of women exposed under the florescent lights like mistaken, forsaken Jezebels of conception. The doors swung open, one rolled out, another rolled in—an efficient and effective assembly line. The McDonald's of abortion. My turn came, and a nurse tsk-tsked over her surgical mask and murmured to her colleague.

"So young."

My mouth and nose covered, I heard instructions to breathe and count backward from ten. Nine, eight . . . and I was flung far, far away.

Waking up from oblivion is like being born again. It's a revelation. For a minute, nothing but a blank slate of pure consciousness without memory or knowledge. Then I came to, drifting back into myself in a woozy mix of cognizance and shame.

"You have a filthy mouth. Cursed like Cain when you came to." The nurse talking to me softened at my confusion and embarrassment.

"It happens," she said. "You ain't the only one."

I couldn't stop shaking. She pulled a blanket up to my shoulders.

"It's from the anesthesia."

Relief flooded me. Knowing it was over felt better than anything I could remember.

From then on, I had an unspoken mantra: Got a problem? Deal with it. Expel it. Chop it off. Abort it and move on. It took me a long time to understand or cultivate compassion. The evidence of the abortion was there, on the bloody pad I had to wear, in my cramping uterus, in my desolated capacity for grace. But more than that, I had lost my childhood, vacuumed out with the zygote, and with that loss, my mom and I had become like a couple of girlfriends getting out of a jam. And of course, the feelings—there was no time for inconvenient feelings. It wasn't a secret; it just didn't happen. I knew intuitively I needed to be A-OK. Mom worked full time, barely making ends meet. She still hadn't been able to finish her degree. If I didn't keep my shit together, I would tilt our whole precarious balance over the precipice into chaos.

We checked into a new era, beginning in an Inglewood motel room by the clinic. With its two single beds, paper-wrapped plastic glasses, tiny squares of soap, and nubby towels, it still had an aura of the exotic to me. After all, we were in California. With a Trailways bus ride to San Diego, a visit to the zoo, and one to the beach, the abortion had been erased under a fresh, tacky gloss.

5

TEENAGE BABYLON

Birthdays didn't get fussed over when I was growing up. There were no parties, no cake, no presents. As a brand-new thirteen-year-old with a license for promiscuity through the pill, the course of my teenage years was charted: sex, drugs, drinking, and bad grades. There was only one person who had the authority to redirect me. But Mom was immersed in her own life and either didn't see what I was doing or didn't find anything wrong with it. Food and shelter, love and acceptance she could handle. But when it came to boundaries or protective guidance, she practiced free-range parenting. Because my mom didn't see my vulnerability or needs, I didn't see them either. We were a perfect pair. Since I didn't break down or fall apart, she thought everything was good with me.

I wanted to matter so much that I wouldn't be left behind ever again. More than anything, I wanted to feel safe. Without rules or consequences, home can feel unsafe, like a town without laws would feel uncivilized. It kept me in a perpetual state of unease. I fidgeted and picked at my cuticles nonstop. At the same time, my mom was literally all I had. I needed her to be fine just as much as she needed me to be. And the way to make her OK was for me to parent myself. The two of us did this dance for my entire childhood and adolescence.

After ten years, she finally got her degree in psychology. It had taken a long time because of her full-time work and being a single parent. Now she worked for the City of Austin, implementing childcare programs for mothers on welfare to help them get jobs. When she came home our driveway was often filled with teenagers' motorcycles. Seeing her, the boys dragged their departure out as long as they could, hiking up their shoulders, puffing out their chests, reluctantly putting on their helmets. They would meander around, finally straddling their bikes with an aggressive kick-start and then roar off with a wheelie down the street. Hovering at the edge of this display, I relished the acceptance. My mom didn't seem to notice the preening. She'd never had to flirt, be suggestive, dress provocatively, or come on to men. Just being herself did the trick.

The guys who came around were a mixed bag: troublemakers, ringleaders, super stoners. Some just wanted somewhere to go. Only one felt like a friend. James, two years ahead of me in the ninth grade, came over more than anyone else. He would saunter in, laid-back and easygoing, tall and filled out—nothing gangly or teenage about him. He could have passed for a man, a baby-faced man with a headful of bushy hair who said "indubitably" a lot. He wore his pocket tee like every other teenage boy, Marlboros over his heart, easy to reach, Zippo lighter in saggy jeans. James liked hanging out with both my mom and me. He poked fun, teased us, and cracked up at my jokes. One evening James told me my mom smoked pot just like us. I didn't ask how he knew that, but once I knew it, weed became a part of my family life.

Crumbling tightly packed buds onto an opened double album jacket (*Wheels of Fire* or *Eat a Peach*), rolling the leaves off and sifting the seeds out, I could roll a perfect joint. Passing it around, inhaling my lungs full, hanging on, James and I taking turns wheezing and coughing until we had to spew out the smoke. My eyes stung, but the immediate stone relaxed me into a slump of good humor. Mom was more ladylike and took her hits neatly, declining the roach when it got small.

One night I sat with a group of friends in the sunken living room of our duplex, high on synthetic mescaline. Cigarette butts spilled out of ashtrays; crunched and folded empty beer cans were scattered on the floor like it was a low-rent teenage Babylon. I rolled my head from side to side, studying the wall art that melted like Dali clocks into rubbery walls. A couple of older guys I barely knew disappeared outside for a bit, then returned to the living room. When the world outside the curtains turned a bright dancing orange, we snapped to attention, delighted in the shared hallucination we were having. Until someone yelled "fire." Then the good times stopped rolling. *Whoa. Fuck. Motherfucker.* Fire trucks came screaming up the neighbor's driveway, men in yellow coats yelling as they swarmed the identical duplex next door. I saw an old couple—the neighbors—outside, the woman pulling her robe around her tightly, their faces stricken in the moving shadows as their home burned. Fear and a gnawing guilt dissolved the effects of the drug. I wondered if the unfamiliar guys who had sped off on their motorcycles had caused this.

My mom came out of her bedroom, where she had been sleeping.

"What's going on?" she asked, confused by the noise and commotion.

"The neighbor's house is on fire," I told her.

The pals who were left slipped out the door, one at a time, until just my mom and I sat together. I waited with dread and fear about what would happen when the firefighters were done. It didn't occur to her that there was any connection between the fire and the teenage party in her living room.

It was a free pass. The investigators didn't even come to question us. I never knew who started the fire but couldn't stop feeling responsible. Every day I saw the burnt remains of the neighboring duplex and thought about their lives being nearly destroyed. I knew that some of the boys finding their way into the edges of my life were terrible people. I'd heard stories of gangbanging, crime, and vandalism. It added to the pervasive feeling that there was no safety in my home. I wanted to have friends to get high and laugh with but had no way of keeping the wrong people away. I knew if mom had a husband, if I had a dad, they wouldn't be coming over.

That summer before eighth grade started, my dad decided I should come visit. I flew by myself to Oklahoma, where he, his wife, and the two daughters he had raised since marrying her lived. Everything about them was typical: intact, happy marriage, sweet sisters, a romping Labrador that obeyed and did tricks. They had a rambling, ranch-style house with matching towels and dishes, curtains, and bedspreads. My stepmother's eyes were like shiny black stones, even when she smiled at me. I made it my job to try and warm them up, make them sparkle—to make her like me. My stepsisters were shy and friendly. Maybe this visit would make me a part-time member of a "real" family.

They had a boat, and we spent time on the lake. I learned how to water ski pretty quickly. I had forgotten what good, clean fun was like, and the pleasure of mastering something new. The girls, Laurie and Elly, had minibikes, little motorcycles with actual clutches and gears. Jealousy dug into my gut. I pried it away. No use for feelings that wouldn't land me where I wanted to be: in this case, part of the wholesome family my dad had made for himself.

Laurie sidled up to me late one day. "Have you ever smoked?" she asked.

I had packed some cigs but hadn't once thought of sneaking off to smoke one. Maybe the respectable life was rubbing off on me. Then again, maybe not.

I shrugged. "I've tried it."

She huddled next to me, a co-conspirator. She knew she had me on a hook.

"What about marijuana? Do you smoke that?"

Bouncing the volley back at her. "Do you?"

A smile crept across her face. I couldn't believe my good luck.

I said, "I brought a couple joints. We can get high on the camping trip!" I went to bed that night thinking maybe I wasn't so different after all.

The next morning, Laurie and Elly were at the table eating breakfast, a box of Corn Flakes on the table. The room felt silent and heavy. I heard my dad come in and then his voice, serious and low, speaking in a flat monotone:

"You know that song 'We Don't Smoke Marijuana in Muskogee'?"

He was a big Merle Haggard fan. He couldn't wait to deliver the punch line and rushed it: "Well, we don't smoke it in Tahlequah either."

I looked up to see him holding my cigarettes in one hand, two reefers in the other. I continued eating, reading the cereal box intently, my whole insides churning. The realization of Laurie's betrayal seeped in. I decided I would never look at her again.

"I'm calling your mother," my dad said. And he did.

"Send her home," my mom said. "I'll take care of it."

That seemed fine with him, my visit being over. If he had kept me there, if he'd tried to be the parent I didn't have, I don't think it would have changed anything that followed. There really wasn't any turning back. Rather than think of him as a dad who cared about what his daughter was doing, I saw him as a square. Rather than be my dad, he chose to protect his family and get rid of the problem: me. I understood. I didn't belong with him or his family. I belonged in the dumpy duplex in Austin, with Mom and our cats.

I came back to find my friend James hanging out with my mom. Somehow, they had decided this was cool even if I wasn't there. At the time, I didn't think much about it. My mom was cool and my friends liked her.

Fifteen years later James came up in a late-night conversation with my mom. We were both high on cocaine. She confessed that they had been having an affair. She told me he wrote her, drew pictures for her, was madly in love. It was a shocking and completely unexpected revelation. How could I not know? Maybe because it was unthinkable that she'd do that. By the time I learned of the affair, our relationship was in full-on best buds mode. We were mother/daughter only in biology. You don't get mad at your pal for having an affair with your other pal. I was too cut off to generate feelings about it and had no place to put them.

I brought it up again twenty-five years later. By then, I was a mom to a fourteen-year-old daughter. And I was writing a book. I thought the subject needed another visit and asked her about James. Maybe it had been a bad idea to have sex with a teenage boy, I suggested. Not to mention all the pot smoking.

"You could have gone to jail," I told her.

"I know," she said. "I was scared."

"I could have been taken away, put in foster care," I said.

"I know," she said, looking around nervously, like Child Protective Services might burst in and drag her fifty-eight-year-old daughter away.

I tried again. I wanted to hear her say she was sorry.

"You were smoking pot with us and having an affair with a teenage boy."

"I know! I was scared," she said again.

"But not so scared that you decided to stop," I said.

Why was I doing this? I knew she did what she wanted, when she wanted.

"Those rules weren't my rules," she said, finding her bearings, getting some steam. "I lived two lives. My friends and I, we were free thinkers. We were ahead of society. We didn't belong there, in that part of town." Decisive now, her convictions coming back, her voice growing more defiant, her eyes narrowing slightly and lips pressing together. She wasn't going to back down.

I didn't tell her how it made me ache, how it felt like a hole in my gut. What was the point? She would be sad that I hurt but unable to accept that her actions caused the pain. By then I'd learned that I couldn't expect more than anyone, even my own mom, was capable of.

That was a lifetime later. At the time, my friendship with James continued for several years. To his credit, he didn't blab about what he was doing with my mom. The one guy who had a real story said nothing, while all the rest spread lies, rumors, and malicious fantasies. Guys said they had sex with both my mom and me at the same time, orgies in her bedroom. I heard we were prostitutes and incestuous lesbian lovers. Acting like everything was fine had become my best skill. Only one thing to do— hold my head up and ignore them. The lies added another layer of hardened protection, but that tough shell didn't stop me from hating the people who talked about us. I wanted nothing more than to be as far away from them as I could get.

6

JUST DO IT

How do you misbehave if nothing is off limits? When the young rebellion stage kicked in, acting out against Mom proved to be a challenge. I tried stealing her weed and leaving the useless debris of stems and seeds, like she wouldn't know any better. It worked, making her mad: "You think I don't know the difference?"

I had done a lot of drugs by the time I reached fourteen, smoked a lot of good, cheap pot—ten dollars an ounce in a baggie called a "lid." I'd also had sex several more times—really bad sex. Before internet porn, teens had ways of getting info, so it's not like I didn't know the difference. Books including *Fear of Flying* and *The Happy Hooker* taught me about good sex, how there was supposed to be foreplay and the woman was supposed to have orgasms. But the guys I had been with had no idea about it other than getting off. When I asked my mom what an orgasm felt like, she responded coolly, happy to help out.

"It's kind of like when you think you're going to sneeze and finally do, and it feels good."

Satisfied with the answer, I went back to my bad sex.

My first best friend, Jenny, moved away after seventh grade, never to be heard from again. I found a Jenny replacement in Melody, a mousy girl who impressed me most with the way she would arrange herself on a chair, placing her drink and her smokes on the side table, leaning back and putting a cushion on her lap. Every single time she sat down she did the routine.

The friendship ended when her mom didn't let me come into their house one day, making me stand outside in the front yard because of my "bad influence" on Melody. Except it had been her daughter's idea to drink a quart of Southern Comfort together, making us reel all over the neighborhood, falling down and vomiting in someone's driveway. As a screwup, the compulsive Melody outpaced me. As soon as I told my mom what had happened, she called up Melody's mom and hammered her: "Your kid runs away from home—not mine. Your kid is failing school—not mine."

The confrontation blew me away. My mom raged at that lady like I had never witnessed before. I pictured Melody's mom with her flipped-up bob and pantsuit, pacing in little half circles, attached to the wall by the coiled phone cord, her hands shaking too much to light her cig. The incident marked the end of my friendship with Melody, but I basked in the glow of my mom standing up for me.

Then I found another caliber of girlfriend altogether, a worthy friend. Dusti Robbins lived in a nearby apartment building with her dad. He gave us rides in his white Cadillac with red leather upholstery, a six-pack of beer on the seat next to him, a sloppy wet cigar smoldering in the middle of his mouth. That Dusti even wanted to be my friend made everything better. With her blond hair, a laugh like ringing bells, and a low, throaty voice, she reminded me of Cybill Shepherd's Jacy Farrow in *The Last Picture Show*. I'd read the book by Larry McMurtry and seen the movie. It made me proud to be from Texas, even the bleak Texas they depicted. The hopeless resilience of the characters and their casual sex, fueled by boredom more than lust, romanticized my own encounters.

With Dusti's friendship, I could put some of the past, the part where I always felt out of place, behind me. She and her sisters were beautiful and cool and didn't care whether they fit in or not. Sometimes in the middle of the night, we would steal my mom's white Maverick while she slept and drive around until right before the sun came up. Dusti did the driving and I supervised, tired but buzzing with the weird combination of the night being both boring and thrilling at the same time. If a cop drove by: *Oh shit. Stare straight ahead! Don't make eye contact!* Most nights dragged on with little to do and no place to go. We were damned if we were going to stop before we had to. Up and down we cruised, circling around Airport Boulevard, two girls in the dead of night. Shooting games of pool at Moyers Pool Hall, open twenty-four hours, helped pass time. Bikers, speed freaks, night owls—no one paid much attention to us. People weren't looking for girls in the middle of the night at Moyers. Down the road Mrs. Johnson's Bakery opened a drive-up window at 4:00 a.m. with fresh donuts for sale. A dollar in change bought plenty and the car filled with the smell of sugar glaze, our sticky hands leaving evidence my mom never discovered. I was pretty sure stealing her car would have made her mad. It felt kind of normal to do something that I worried about getting caught at.

One weekend we hitchhiked to Houston. I'd never hitchhiked so far away before. Dusti's big sister Linda lived there, and Dusti said we could meet her at a club, then stay the night with her. After getting dropped in the nightclub parking lot, we were stuck. Without IDs there was no getting in—we hadn't thought the plan through too well. Dusti had some quaaludes, the new happening drug high everyone liked. I had tried 'ludes before and didn't like them. They gave me no manic energy or buzz; I just sloshed around like a raw egg in a bowl. Also popular were black beauties, which I didn't like either; the speed capsules made me scared my heart might thump itself right out of my chest.

The night went on and we hung around, leaning on a car like it was ours. Trying to make it seem normal to not actually enter

the club as others parked and went in. We wore matching cor-
duroy hip-hugger jeans, with extra wide belts and teensy crop
tops. Dusti assured me her sister Linda would come out eventually and get us, but the whole trip had started to feel like a full-
on bummer. The two college-age guys who started talking to
us were nice enough. They offered to take us to wait at their
apartment instead of the parking lot, saying they would bring us
back at closing to meet up with Linda. Dusti slurred her words,
saying, "Let's get out of here." Afraid to leave, but more afraid
to stay on my own, I tagged along, uncomfortable in a strange
city with older guys.

We sat in a row on a nubby brown couch in their stale-smelling
apartment. I asked about watching TV, thinking it might make
the atmosphere more familiar. When Dusti started making out
with one of them, the other put his hand on my leg, squeezing
my knee. When Dusti went into the bedroom with guy number
one, I braced for what was sure to come. He stroked my leg. He
leaned in for a kiss and I turned my head. I didn't want this.

"C'mon. Let's have some fun too. Like your friend is in there,"
he said.

He looked pasty with fleshy, pink overtones. Little swirls of
sand-colored hair stuck in sweaty formation across his forehead.
Sideburns flanked his face nearly down to his chin. I retreated
further into the corner of the couch with each advance.

"No. I don't want to." A whine, not a statement—without force
or certainty. I could feel his impatience and annoyance. He'd
gotten the dud girl. He pushed his hand up my top. I whined
some more.

"No. Stop. No."

He stood and pulled my legs straight out and went for my
belt.

"No. Stop. No."

I didn't struggle. I felt like wood: rigid but movable.

It occurred to me that if I just let him, he would stop. He would leave me alone.

"Just do it," I said.

I lay perfectly still while he invaded my body. He is a stranger, I told myself. It doesn't matter. I turned off, shut down, tried to leave my body. It didn't work. I couldn't detach. My eyes overflowed. Still he pumped—fast, slow, fast. My nose ran, my face shining wet with tears and snot now, and what had been silent became sobs. He paused. "Stop crying," he commanded. "Cut it out."

Sniffles on bottom, grunts on top, it had to end. I'd had enough sex to know it would end soon. It would be over, and this stranger would take his alien penis out of me, leaving his gooey sperm between my thighs, and I would be free again. Uncaptured.

Dusti was passed out in the bedroom and wouldn't get up. Humiliated and miserable, I left her there. Outside the apartment building, the hum and drum of nearby highway traffic guided my exit route until I found the bottom of an on-ramp. The night felt peculiar and sharp. My thumb was lazily out, afraid of a ride, afraid of no ride. Cars ignored me, in a hurry, accelerating down to merge on the freeway. Eventually a roughed-up El Camino pulled over. Next to the passenger window, a young boy sat. He had no interest, didn't even look at me. In the driver's seat, a man stared, or leered; I couldn't figure out his expression. The steering wheel pressed into his belly, his overalls straining. Mottled cigarette butts spilled out of the ashtray.

Sometimes your options are so slim, you just take what's in front of you and hope it's not a disaster.

"C'mon, get in," said the man.

The boy slid to the middle, leaving room for me beside him. The man turned out to be kind. He came up with the idea to take me to the bus station downtown, even gave me a dollar to buy a soda. My mom didn't know I'd gone to Houston until she answered my collect call. Without questions, she wired money for a bus ticket home. The bus had an early-morning departure, so for a couple of interminable hours, I waited in the Houston Greyhound station. A man wandered close, sat by me; I moved with frozen fear to a new seat.

Overcome with shame, I turned on myself. I didn't like the frightened girl back on the cheap apartment sofa, the one who had let this happen. Being violated left me feeling disgusted. The word *rape* didn't enter my mind. I had let him, after all. I had said the magic words: "Just do it."

After I got on the pill, sex as a teenager was always unmemorable. But I never forgot this time.

7

GREENBRIAR

My friendship with Dusti survived the Houston debacle. We were tough little cookies and had all the arrogance of youth— nothing bad could happen to us, and if it did, well, another day of misadventure waited. A few weeks later, the two of us hitchhiked a few miles outside of Austin, where one of my favorite bands, ZZ Top, was headlining. Other cities—tough, hustling places like New York and Detroit—had bands like the New York Dolls and Iggy and the Stooges blasting out of the streets. I didn't know about all that, only that Texas had ZZ Top. The show, my first rock concert, took place in a huge outdoor field called Kings Village and featured five bands. It had rained the day before, and I ended up blasted drunk, falling around in the mud, and throwing up next to a row of reeking portable toilets before ZZ Top even made it to the stage. I thought it was one of the best days ever.

Right before ninth grade something I had always wanted happened: Mom moved us into an actual house. It was a rental on a cul-de-sac and—huge for us—had two stories, four bedrooms, and a fenced back yard. And a den! I lived in a house with an entire extra room for no reason. Mom bought a used pool table to put in there, and I decided I would be a woman pool hustler. I fantasized about all the places I could casually saunter into, never having my own stick, only using the shitty ones on the wall of the joint so no one would suspect me as a pool shark. Then a crowd would gather around, watching me make triple banked shots, elaborate ricochets, sinking balls. I practiced fiendishly on our pool table. It proved to be a good training foundation: the rudiments of repetition, learning how patience and commitment could build into competence.

Mom got a new job working for the City of Austin, more grant writing work to get government funding for childcare centers. Later in the summer I found work with a ginger-headed carpenter named Benny, who taught me how to use a nail gun and cut angles, paying me well to be a trim carpenter, putting down baseboards and cabinet moldings. My mom thought he was creepy, but her fourteen-year-old daughter liked the job, so she put up with him. I felt important and independent, grown up, getting up at 6:00 am, putting on my hardhat and carpenter's belt, waiting to be picked up and taken to the construction site, being left alone with the radio on, and doing something right.

One night, Benny and a bunch of his friends included me in one of their parties. We got drunk and convoyed to Port Aransas—a four-hour drive south. I woke up on the beach when the sun rose in a circle of cars with the doors opened, people crashed everywhere. An eight-track blared from someone's tape deck, stuck, blasting "Livin' in the USA" over and over. "Stand back. Stand back. It's my freedom, don't worry about me, babe, I got to be free." Steve Miller, nailing it to the wall, every word, every note, every beat of the song telling my story, telling me how it should be. Free to take off down the highway and wake up on a beach. Free to make some money and take care of myself. Free from trying to fit in with a bunch of suburban school kids. Hungover and exhausted, something let go that morning, got released. A big chunk of sorrow broke away and floated off. Breathing that fresh and salty air, I felt like good things were coming my way.

There's always a crack in the wall of bad where the good can start to seep in. You just have to notice it and let it happen.

Our best friends were a couple my mom had met who were involved in the drug business. They thought we were the coolest mother-daughter duo ever, and I thought they might be the best people I'd ever known. Susan and Rob lived in a super nice house, high on a hill overlooking Lake Austin. Dinner parties involved playing cards and getting stoned, all of us, laughing and talking until way after midnight. I was treated as an equal— all my comments, jokes, and opinions listened to and taken seriously. This backdrop affected how I started high school. Finally, I didn't give a shit about any of it: being popular, having a social life, going to football games, joining clubs, whatever. The only thing I enjoyed was getting As again in all my classes. All the books I had read paid off—being well read is always an educational ace in the hole. It makes you think better, write better, figure stuff out better. But even with my academic improvements, I missed a lot of school due to my late nights and apathy.

Mom always wrote a note to excuse the absence, so we thought we were beating the system. But a couple months into ninth grade, the attendance office called me in to question why I had missed two-thirds of the school session. I pointed out that good grades and parent-excused absences didn't indicate a problem. The school bureaucrats saw things differently. If things didn't change, they said the school would make a report to authorities to investigate our home life.

The last thing mom wanted was any kind of authority checking us out. When she needed to stay out of trouble, she could take care of business. Fortunately for both of us, she found me a new kind of school, and I dropped out of the public school system in the first semester of ninth grade.

Located on 170 acres near Bastrop, Texas, about forty miles from Austin, Greenbriar provided an unaccredited alternative to conventional education. If only we had known about it sooner. Greenbriar started as a commune and later developed a school for kids who lived with their families in homes they built in the woods. By the time I started, many students commuted from Austin, joining the residents of the commune. Each day an old school bus drove the town kids there and back. Greenbriar's education philosophy boiled down to: leave kids the fuck alone and they'll figure out what they want to learn. This matched and validated mom's parenting style. In her view, I existed as a fully formed individual completely capable of discovering my own way.

At Greenbriar, most of the teachers held graduate degrees and were qualified to teach in different fields and skills. Students ranged in age from four to seventeen and numbered about fifty when I started in the fall of 1973. From the second I stepped on the grounds, I loved it. No one ditched school here. Every morning began in the main building. It looked like an overgrown fungus in the woods with the roof dipping and swelling in orange polyurethane waves over the irregular-shaped structure. Concrete floors were partitioned into sectional rooms, filled with mismatched cozy furniture and the smell of fresh baked bread throughout.

A large blackboard had announcements chalked in: who taught what and when. "Judy is teaching literature and English in the library, 11:00 a.m." Or "Dave is having a nature walk at 1:00 p.m., meet at the creek by the dome." Or "Herb is teaching math at noon in the A-frame." Just like that. You either went or you didn't. If a kid didn't go to class, there were plenty of other commune activities available, such as working in the garden or repairing and building things. You could dress up in crazy outfits or take off your clothes and run around in the woods. Kids swam in the cow pond, wandered the land, got stoned, read books in old armchairs. It sounds weird, but the Greenbriar kids I knew back then have grown into well-adjusted, self-realized people: professors, researchers, business owners.

I embraced the commune hippie environment. Under Greenbriar's influence I stopped eating meat and learned how to make a compost heap. Long camping excursions, taking canoes down the Rio Grande in Big Bend National Park, sleeping out on the Guadalupe River, the adventures kept coming. Nights were a different story, the other extreme: high rollin' and hanging out with our friends Susan and Rob. We smoked hash oil, and my mom and I did cocaine for the first time. I thought drugs and money and a nice house were all interwoven things.

I had no concerns about my future, nor did my mom. There weren't conversations about graduation or college planning. I kept up with the basics at Greenbriar, some math here, some literature there. One morning, the blackboard at school read, "Dave is giving guitar lessons today." I liked Dave, and I hadn't played an instrument since quitting the violin when I stopped caring about regular, typical school.

Dave and I sat on chairs in the woods with the sun splintering through winter branches. The guitar neck felt like a two-by-four with strings stretched a quarter inch off the fret board. I played my first chords: D, A, and G. Dave didn't ask if I was right- or left-handed, so I held it like a righty. Being a lefty helped me master the chords quickly; in the first session I pushed the shapes on the neck to make sounds and music. The simple songs he taught, "Wildwood Flower," "Blowing in the Wind," and "This Land Is Your Land," gave me a way to practice my new chords.

I doubt that I knew my hands on that guitar would forever shape my life. But while I strummed those songs, the diaphanous thread that tugs us down any given path fastened to me like a strand of spider's silk. It would stay intact and attached forever, with music on the other end pulling me forward.

8

EARTHQUAKE

Mom and I went to England for a month, including Christmas, at the end of 1973. I was nearly fifteen but thought I was an adult. I got a job in a boutique and met a grown man at the pub who became my lover. He must have been in his late twenties or even thirty. Finally, I could see what the fuss about sex was, feeling passion and actually caring about the guy. Teenage boys never interested me again. My aunt Anne didn't like her older sister's parenting protocol. The last time we had been there, Anne had known me as an eleven-year-old kid. Now, three years later, I was drinking at the pub in my wraparound skirt and cowboy boots and having a fling with a man twice my age. Years later, Aunt Anne told me they argued about it a lot, but I never heard anything and thought she was fine with the program.

At my grandma's house one night, I turned on the TV in the front room. One of the three BBC channels was airing a Christmas special of *Top of the Pops*, a popular music show. Lazy and bored, I slumped in a corner armchair. Mom curled up on the sofa with a book and a cigarette, leaving it to burn a long ash in between puffs. Grandma knitted, her hands moving at warp speed, seemingly producing nothing from the ball of yarn. Outside, the winter cold tried to draft into the row house. Inside, warm and cozy, the smell of dinner mingled with antiseptic. Occasionally, my grandma looked up from her hands, checking to see if there might be something to worry about. Three generations of Valentine women, each as different in character as the era she came into. One of them about to get shock waved into a new galaxy.

On the television screen a figure appeared wearing head-to-toe leather, posed in a classic rock stance: legs planted firmly in front of an angled mic stand, leaning back on platform-heeled boots. I caught my breath and slid off the chair to the floor. The music chunka-chunka-chugged along the verse, drawing me closer, on all fours now, crawling toward the TV. Across the groin of the black jumpsuit, a bass guitar slung low, hips pumping in rhythm behind it. The face framed in perfectly shagged brown hair, the voice high pitched, the eyes defiant. Just like countless other rock 'n' rollers—with one major, mind-blowing exception: this was a female. Doing what I had only seen men do before. All my synapses were processing at once, transfixed on the screen.

She wailed at me: "Put your man in the can honey—get him while you can!"

Chunka chunka chunka went the band. She held down the low end and screamed the hook: "Can the can! Can the can!"

If the ground I had been walking around on consisted of music, if it were a foundation, it had been built by the Stones and Hendrix, the Faces, the Who and the Beatles. Bowie, T. Rex, Deep Purple, Cream, ZZ Top, and Led Zeppelin, like strata, added layers upon layers to the terrain I knew.

Suzi Quatro split that ground wide open. She was a fucking earthquake.

I knew women existed in music. They sang in bands, they held acoustic guitars or sat at pianos. Years later I would learn that women had even played electric guitars in rock 'n' roll—but I'd never seen or heard of any of those women. Seeing Suzi Quatro had the same effect as lightning bolts shooting through my grandma's house, with thunder blasting along. Where do I go, what do I do, who am I? Every question had an answer. All paths and possibilities suddenly pointed in one direction.

Back in Austin, mom and I were at Susan and Rob's one evening, when a guy named Jim joined our card game. He sat by my mom, giving her sexy squinty looks from under his cowboy hat. His short, sandy hair and mustache accented a face defined by bony features and guarded, hard blue eyes. Tall and slouchy, twenty-four-year-old Jim had a distinctive presence and a shadowy mystery. You didn't want to mess with him. I had met several big-time dope dealers at our friend's house and figured Jim was one too. It turned out he had escaped from Leavenworth prison the year before. Despite feeling like he was beneath her, and maybe a little dangerous to boot, my mom started dating him.

Jim had a heroin habit he kept under control and drove a chopper with a few other guys who had flashy bikes. Cool and detached, disdainful of everything, he made you feel special if he liked you. He was exciting to have around but left abruptly and often. A week or so later he would be back, maybe in the middle of the night, insistently knocking on the door. He returned once in a massive Pontiac station wagon. I was surprised he wanted to drive something so conspicuous around, considering he was a fugitive. He asked me to give him a hand, saying he hoped we didn't mind because he had to leave some stuff at our house.

Fortune must have been shining her spotlight right on me, because now—along with the two-story house, our pool table, and my cool hippie school—now, besides all that good shit, my mother's drug-dealing, heroin-addicted, prison-escapee, biker boyfriend was bringing a huge amplifier and an electric guitar inside. He set it up in one of the spare bedrooms. I tried to act cool. Just an amp and an electric guitar and my ticket to rock stardom.

Jim's the one who taught me how to plug in the cord, one end in the guitar, the other in the amp. He showed me where to turn on the amp, what the standby switch did. I hit the strings with a pick he pulled from his jeans, a perfect blasting E chord that made the walls shake. The sound was raw and dirty and loud. It eclipsed every bad thing that had ever happened to me, things forgotten and pushed away, every sad, hurtful betrayal nuked by the grit of circuits, pickups, and tubes. It was the most empowering thing I had done in my entire life. From that moment, I knew.

I was never going to not do this.

Slowly and reluctantly, I passed Jim's guitar back. He could play. Seventh chords accented a funk rhythm, riffs thrown in like drum fills whenever he felt like it. Each time, something was different and yet something was the same. Notes and sounds were put together in infinite ways: different, alike. Like people, like nature, like everything.

"What's that? What is that?" I begged him to show me.

He went on playing in his own world while I sat and stood, paced and watched, impatient and reverent, waiting for my next turn. He had made the guitar, a double cutaway hybrid mutt, with a stained wood body and one pickup. Finally, Jim looked up. He asked if all I knew were open chords and showed me how to hold my index finger across the fret board and make a bar chord. Get that down, he told me—practice it until every string could be clearly heard. I had it down by the next day, making him smile, and say, "Well, then, time for this." The first song I learned was "Jumpin' Jack Flash." Then, "Johnny B. Goode." I had plenty to keep me busy with those two, and I spent hours trying to sound exactly like Chuck Berry's rhythm—mop-em mop-em mop-em mop—coordinating my right hand to hit the strings right, my left to stay strong and firm. Same with the Stones song: I had to get the rhythm and sound just right. Having a naturally good ear that picked up on subtleties and being left-handed gave me a jumpstart; I could play chords without tiring for a long time, and my fingers shaped up quickly. The right hand had a little more trouble. When people ask why I didn't switch to playing left-handed style, with my right hand on the neck or the guitar upside down, I say that it just didn't seem important. Either way, one hand is going to be a little better off.

Either way, my whole being was better off. I had found my thing.

9

CARNATIONS

A velvety roar outside the living room window got my attention. The finest car I had ever seen idled in the drive: a candy apple red Maserati. Jim's aviators and grin barely cleared the window of the passenger seat. I fell for the driver as soon as his boot hit the ground. Charlie wore head-to-toe western-cut denim, a long ponytail, and a mustache—typical '70s dude attire and appearance. He had a friendly face with a big Roman nose between crinkly edged eyes and deep smile lines. Because he was naturally laid back, talking in a slow drawl accompanied by languid, effortless movements, it was hard to tell when he was on dope or straight. Charlie was Butch Cassidy to Jim's Sundance. He had multiple girlfriends, owned a ranch in Kansas City, and always carried a briefcase full of money. I became his designated Austin girlfriend even though he was thirty-eight and I was only fifteen. Mom was thirty-six, and her boyfriend, Jim, was twenty-four. We hung out as two couples. We went on road trips to the Gulf of Mexico, stayed in fancy hotels, ate at expensive restaurants, and went to concerts: Willie, Waylon, Dylan, the Grateful Dead. When he left town, Charlie's Maserati waited in our garage for safekeeping, a shiny promise that he would return.

Running around with drug dealers came with seductive perks, but occasionally reality raised its voice, so harsh and raspy you couldn't ignore it. One of Jim's biker friends overdosed on heroin in our living room. Hearing the commotion, I came in to see a girl on the floor, still and gray as a statue. Mom and I hovered in the doorway, hand-wringing and wide-eyed, while Jim miraculously went to work and resuscitated her.

Dating the two outlaws bonded us; my mom felt like my best friend during that time.

I saw our dealer boyfriends as harmless characters, the drug use casual and friendly—aside from the chick overdosing in the living room. After a couple months my affair with Charlie came to an abrupt end. One day the Maserati was gone, and he just stopped coming around. I shrugged it off and refused to be bothered. He was old after all, and I had my whole future ahead of me. Besides, there were better things to do than mess around with men. The best thing in my life was playing guitar. Jim taught me a "box" of scale notes that I practiced stubbornly and slowly, determined and patient to train my fumbling into finesse. If it got tiresome, I played the few songs I knew or posed in front of the mirror practicing Pete Townshend windmills.

I should have seen it coming: my mom was bored with Jim and broke up with him. Now the gear was gone like the Maserati had disappeared when Charlie took off. How would I keep up with my playing? Fretting about getting my own guitar and amp, I dispatched a letter to my dad in Oklahoma. I had never asked him for anything in my life, and I begged for an electric guitar and amplifier to help me in my chosen career. The reply he sent nearly scorched my hands: "No, I will not buy you those things. I will not support this in any way. Being a musician is a lifestyle of little substance and worth. The only financial help you will get from me is for college."

The letter also said, "Girls don't do that." The rebuff, and the fact that he barely knew who I was and disapproved of everything he did know about me, left me feeling more cut off than before. I hadn't seen my dad since the pot-bust visit, and now, with this rejection, I didn't care. It hurt deeply, but I scoffed at the letter, laughing when I told people what he had written. I beat the sadness down and kicked it off to the side. Feeling hurt doesn't help anything.

When you want something badly enough, you figure out a way to get it. I worked selling carnations to cars stopped at red lights, then landed a job with the Internal Revenue Service. It required form-stuffing envelopes and preparing mail-outs in an assembly line. It was a mind-numbing and tedious job, but it paid six bucks an hour, three times minimum wage.

By July, I had enough money to go shopping, and Mom took me to a music store. I'm sure I was the only fifteen-year-old girl who had ever walked in that store wanting to buy an electric guitar. I picked out a blond wood Telecaster with a couple of pickups in it, thinking it looked like the guitar Keith Richards used. The sales guy sold me a Peavey amp, solid state—a real dog of an amp. I didn't know I'd actually bought a Deluxe, not a Custom like Keith's. I didn't know that the Peavey amp would never sound good, no matter how much I turned knobs and practiced. I only knew how it felt leaving the store, solemn and exhilarated, like I had passed some exclusive formal initiation rite. Silent tears of joy streamed down my cheeks. Mom looked at me, concerned, and asked what was wrong. The amp's wheels rattled over the parking lot, my guitar in its case held steady on top while I pushed my very first gear to the car.

I beamed at her, tasting salt, stopping to wipe my face with the back of my hand.

"Nothing, Mom. I'm just so very happy."

Two dreamers are better than one. I made a new friend at Greenbriar. Marilyn had outrageous good looks and collected admirers with a toss of her long, stick-straight hair and a goofy giggle. The combination of being a brunette with blue eyes and clear porcelain skin is already a genetic jackpot, but Marilyn's slight frame came packaged in an extra translucency. Delicate wisps of tiny blue veins traced just under the surface where she was palest, adding a vulnerability that made you want to wrap her up and protect her. Guys fell for her hard and fast.

We bonded over the Stones. I had discovered my favorite record of all time, *Exile on Main Street.* Hips, heart, head— every part of my being responded to those songs. The double album seemed like a full-on musical expression of doing whatever the fuck you wanted, how you wanted. I imagined the guys insulated, catered to, in an exclusive club having the best party ever, needing nothing but each other, guitars, bass, and drums. The fantasy fueled my vision of what being in a band would be like. The vision had already been shattered by the time I learned the making of *Exile* had been pieced together with whoever showed up, nothing at all like a celebration of solidarity and unity. Still, magic.

Seeing the Stones in San Antonio during the Tour of the Americas was the biggest, most anticipated, most spectacular concert I had ever been to. Jagger and Richards were at the peak of their sexually charged, swaggering glory. Any human discomfort or conception of where I stood in space and time was nulled and voided. It could have been just the Stones and me in the Hemisphere Convention Center for all I was aware. This marked Ron Wood's first tour; both he and Keith were filling the hole Mick Taylor had left, or trying to anyway, and the guitars seemed fluidly intertwined, sharing lead parts. I couldn't take my eyes off Keith, watching how he moved and played. His signature rhythms were like algebra, the reduced essence of each song.

Keith and Chuck Berry inspired me more than any other guitarists. I loved Hendrix, Clapton, Page—all the greats, and living in Austin schooled me on a regular basis with players. I aspired to be in the pantheon of trailblazing guitarists. Uncertain how to transform from a wannabe into an actual musician, I jumped at any chance to play. I knew it would take lots of practice to get some nuts-and-bolts skills. Taking piano lessons from a Greenbriar associate taught me music theory and some sight reading, but after a year I just wanted to play guitar.

My first band with Marilyn included her younger brother and a couple of other students, John and Kenny. Kenny's dad was a professional musician, and he supplied us with a couple extra amps. Marilyn's brother had a drum kit, and Mom let us set up everything in our house to play. Marilyn wanted to sing. I'd worked on my mop-ems relentlessly, as a disciple of the Chuck Berry school of rock. I tried writing songs, basically putting lyrics over twelve-bar chord progressions. I didn't have the nerve to show the band my first composition, "My Man," about a junkie boyfriend, or the other gem, "Black Widow Spider (Don't sit beside her)." We had to think of a name fast because a gig at a Greenbriar benefit had come up, and we picked the not-so-great name Childhood's End. I know.

No egos, no competition, no lobbying, no power plays. There's nothing like your first band, and you kind of spend the rest of your music career wondering why it has to ever be any different. If someone wanted to play a different instrument on this song or that song, that was fine. Go for it. If someone had an idea for a song to learn, *yeah, great, learn the song, play it. No problem. I wanna sing this one. Really? I wanna sing that one too. What do we do—let's both sing it, taking turns. Or you can do it—I'll do this one instead.* It was so fucking easy then.

The debut of Childhood's End at the Greenbriar benefit took place in the afternoon, with many bigger Austin bands following. I worked diligently on making my first stage outfit, swirling colored glitter glue on a black tank top and adding a snakeskin hatband and peacock feather to a fedora. Walking onstage to a crowd of nearly a hundred—mostly families and kids cheering and screaming our names—I felt proud and embarrassed at the same time. Draggy, ragged versions of "Foxy Lady," "All Along the Watchtower," and my mainstays "Johnny B. Goode," "Little Queenie," and "Jumpin' Jack Flash" followed. Everyone switched around instruments for different songs. I sang "Wild Thing" without a guitar and decided right then and there I didn't like being the focal point. After our set, I obsessed over figuring out how to get onstage again, to do it better. We got the chance at a second Greenbriar event, held at an actual popular Austin honky-tonk called Soap Creek Saloon. I had seen John Lee Hooker there the month before and couldn't believe I was performing on the same stage. This felt like the beginning.

10

CLUBLAND

Austin in the 1970s was a mecca for music—a very lax mecca. I became an underage regular with my pal Marilyn at all the best live music clubs and venues. The concerts I saw at the legendary Armadillo World Headquarters made a world of difference in my formative musical framework. While other teen girls shopped for prom dresses, I gazed up at Freddie King onstage, sweat pouring off his face, taking me on a tail-spinning ride of hot rod, gutted guitar playing. While standard issue high school sophomores cheered for varsity football games, I got to cheer for Ray Charles. While other students were picking electives, I stood front and center as a guy named Bruce Springsteen scorched the Armadillo.

As music became more important to me, Greenbriar began to lose its appeal. The long bus ride to and from town, especially the getting up early in the morning part, had grown tiresome. Most of the kids were younger now; the older teens were getting jobs, finding things in life they wanted to do. Marilyn and I wanted our own band. I pressured her to get serious about drums. We needed a drummer and I wanted our band to be all girls—all instrument-playing musicians. Girl singers were common, nothing new, but girl *musicians* weren't. Marilyn jumped right in and started practicing.

In the world at large, plenty was happening. The year 1975 was chaotic: Nixon left in disgrace and Vietnam left a permanent ugly stain. Patty Hearst got kidnapped then drove a getaway car for the Symbionese Liberation Army. An Eastern Airlines jet crashed at JFK airport, freaking me out about flying, and Irish nationalist/unionist bombing and fighting made us worry about our English family. Charles Manson returned to the news when Squeaky Fromme tried to kill then-President Ford. The mob appeared everywhere, in the movies and in real life. I devoured anything mafia, Manson, or murder, shuddering over Vincent Bugliosi's *Helter Skelter* and Truman Capote's *In Cold Blood* and whipping through Mario Puzo's *The Godfather*.

Then came *Saturday Night Live*. It has been with us so long, it's easy to take *SNL* for granted and hard to describe how it astonished us all to see a show on television defining a sensibility and generation so outrageously. It had been done in comedy, in rock 'n' roll, and in movies, but nothing on television had the balls of *SNL*. It seemed like times were changing and the world had shifted—my world certainly was.

Mom now worked at Austin Community College. I left Greenbriar to take classes there, lying about my age and high school education on my application and easily registering for college with courses in music theory, psychology, and English. Those were my day classes. At night, class happened on the streets, in the clubs. Hitting multiple spots several times a week, I was a full-time student.

At the brand new Antone's, Austin's "home of the blues," I wandered in one night and was transfixed by the guitar player. Jimmie Vaughan had slicked-back hair with a loose forelock falling over his eyes, like Elvis's after he got less squeaky clean. I took in the rest of the band, the Fabulous Thunderbirds. The singer wore a turban and played harmonica. The bass player had gold teeth and tattoos. The drummer looked like a kid. All of them were sharp dressed. Jimmie became the object of my every desire, a bit easy to assess because I had only one desire: to play in a band. While beautiful hippie girls and sexy women in vintage dresses danced seductively in front of this beta version of the Fabulous Thunderbirds, I stood to the side of the stage. I didn't want to fuck Jimmie Vaughan. I wanted to be him.

He stood onstage with comfort and confidence, and no self-consciousness. Surveying the club, a gleam in his eye, he would draw in a breath and then just go somewhere else while he soloed. No one uses tone, space, and phrasing like him. It makes what he plays so raw and to the point and . . . prominent. It seemed as though his choices, his notes, were like a magic door to just feeling things. I had learned to get by via checking and stuffing my emotions, but in that moment, stripped of context and association, it was exhilarating to feel.

I impressed myself by landing a job working in the Pabst Blue Ribbon distribution warehouse. I was still a kid of sixteen years old, playing at being an adult. But I knew where I wanted to go in life, what I wanted to do. I had gotten my first car, paid fifty dollars for a bronze 1962 Rambler Ambassador.

At night, Marilyn and I moved through clubland with precise timing, like gears shifting, from one club to the next. Catch the Bowie covers set at one club, head to Antone's, finish up with some dancing at another. Everywhere, we networked. It paid off when we met a guy who told us his girlfriend, Donna, played bass. Nervously—Donna had more experience than us—we went over to her house to jam. Man could she play. Donna was the first girl in town I had found as serious as me. Sometimes a Fender Precision Bass can dwarf a girl, but Donna looked like she had been made to hold her bass. Standing there in her flip-flops and unhemmed bell-bottoms, big, smooth, and tanned, Donna instantly elevated our vision. Since we were a trio, we learned a couple of ZZ Top songs. I had the riff to "Francine" down cold and didn't think twice about its content: lusting after a thirteen-year-old girl. Same with "Tush," a song about guys gettin' some action. Big Donna stepped up and sang both of them as well as holding down the bass, an eighth note pocket with some passing lines. Marilyn sang "Little Queenie," and I sang "Carol."

We were girls singing songs that men wrote about girls.

My mom finally ditched the suburbs, and we moved into a ramshackle house on a dirt road close to downtown. I was glad to leave the part of town where so many bad memories had been made. The floors and walls of our new home creaked and swayed—my room was an addition on stilts over an overgrown ditch—but it matched us and our lifestyle.

Finding someone in Austin who knew how to give a proper shag haircut in 1975 wasn't easy. Not feathered Farrah Fawcett wings, but actual rock star English-looking Ron Wood, Keith Richards, Rod Stewart hair. One night at Mother Earth, a club featuring Texas rock bands, I nearly fell over laying eyes on the two best-looking rock stars I'd ever seen up close. Both guys wore printed long scarves around their necks, flared jeans, skimpy T-shirts, and form-fitting jackets. And they had perfect hair. Jesse Sublett and Eddie Munoz looked like they could actually be in the Faces. They had a band called Jellyroll. Jesse and Eddie completely validated me as a musician. When someone you look up to buys your whole deal, it's equal to a year or so of drudging experience. Besides becoming my lifelong friends, they told me where to get a good haircut. That first one started a lifetime of good rock 'n' roll hair.

Another exceptional guitarist named Van Wilks took a liking to the idea of our little rock trio. He thought up the name Lickedysplit for our band. It may have lacked subtlety—for teenage girls, it sounded pretty nasty—but we loved it. Van got us our first gig, too, in San Marcos, a little college town about thirty minutes south of Austin. Eddie from Jellyroll stepped up, saying my lame Peavey amp had to go. We went amp shopping and wandered around to music and record stores, Eddie in his giant sunglasses and platforms, walking around Austin like it was London or New York. I followed him like a puppy dog, scarfing down every little crumb of credibility falling in his wake.

At one music store I saw a guitar hanging on the wall that I couldn't get out of my head. It haunted me for a week. None other would do. Trading in my Tele Deluxe and an extra hundred bucks got me the 1962 Stratocaster I felt destined to play. I curled up with my new guitar and slept with it that night. I still have it, and it's still the best guitar in the entire world. Years later, my idol Keith Richards would hold it and play a few licks on it, and I would promise to give it to him if I died.

I had my band, Lickedysplit, and my new gear, and I was trying hard to feel legit. The first gig didn't quite get me there—the short, six-song set had no original tunes. As much as I had watched guitar players onstage and practiced in the mirror, I didn't come out of the chute rock-star ready. The couple times I had played before had been in front of friends and family at Greenbriar benefits. Marilyn and I didn't even invite our families to this first real gig. Music was for me, my thing, my world I intended to create far from where I started. My mom had given me the freedom to pursue whatever I wanted, and she kept her hands-off policy with my dreams too. It's not that she lacked interest or didn't feel proud. She just let me do my thing—whether it be fucking up or achieving greatness.

I was fucking up a lot less and fucking a lot less too. Drinking and drugs weren't any big deal. And the only thing I really wanted from a guy was for him to sit still a minute and show me something cool on the guitar.

11

THROWING SHAPES

At Austin Community College, I loved being a student. I got straight As and thought about majoring in English. But they wouldn't allow me to register for a third semester without providing high school transcripts. The jig was up. You'd think that after a year of classes with a 4.0 GPA they might have let me slide, but bureaucrats play by the rules. With college taken away, I zoomed in fully on rock 'n' roll in concerts and clubs. Radio had become a wasteland: bloated, bombastic rock and disco. Soft, soulless, and smooth, no rough edges anywhere. There might be exceptions—Bowie's "Station to Station" came out, after all—but many of the bands I loved had sunk to a low level, causing releases such as "Squeeze Box" by the Who, "Hot Stuff" by the Stones, and the worst offender, "Tonight's the Night" by Rod Stewart. How could the singer of the Faces come out with a song like that? It was weird, like all my idols lost their voice right when I was trying to find mine.

A little club opened called the Rome Inn. I went regularly to see Stevie Ray Vaughan and Doug Sahm's bands. When Doug found out the seventeen-year-old girl who stood in front of him at the Rome Inn played guitar, he invited me to sit in with his band at a future gig. I worshipped Doug. Few could match the range of his music, incorporating ballads, country honks, straight-up rock, Tejano, R&B. He led his great band through all the paces. To me, he represented the human form of everything cool and hip about growing up in Texas. For a week, I sweated about this "sitting in" business. Either I didn't do it and was a coward or I did it and might suck. Both options terrified me. I had to try.

I requested "Carol" by Chuck Berry since I knew it well. Approaching the Rome Inn stage, my heart pumped a double speed pulse. The crowd thrum sounded like the ocean. Doug handed me his Telecaster, slipping the strap over my head. It hung low, making it hard to reach my hand around the neck. A four count from behind the drums, and we launched into the song.

I couldn't tell you one thing about what happened in those three and a half minutes, except nothing in my entire life had made me prouder. Powering past fear, risking humiliation and failure, and doing so alongside Doug Sahm. His support equaled a stamp in the passport, access to a new place, and I never forgot his kindness.

Stevie Ray Vaughan always attracted a crowd. The chemistry between him and Lou Ann Barton in Double Trouble made a perfect yin and yang; they burned together like wind and fire. Lou Ann had so much cool style and glamorous sass, I couldn't imagine talking to her. Stevie had an unexpected sweetness and humility to him, a little at odds with the intensity of his guitar blaze. In one conversation, I mentioned how much both his and his brother Jimmie's guitar playing inspired me.

"I'll tell you something," he said. "When I play, I'm playing everything I know. When Jimmie plays, he's playing about a tenth of what he knows."

I joked with him that if I played only a tenth of what I knew, I'd just be standing there holding a guitar, which made him laugh. Stevie's revelation helped me appreciate and understand what it meant to put my personality into my playing. It takes a while to get there.

Austin was giving me the best music education I could have asked for. I saw B. B. King, Bobby "Blue" Bland, and Clarence

"Gatemouth" Brown at Antone's. The Armadillo offered up shows from Frank Zappa to Toots and the Maytals. The Kinks came through town, along with Dr. Feelgood and Todd Rundgren. Little Richard played the Ritz theater, his orange chiffon cape emblazoned with reflecting mirror squares. Adding to the fun, a Saturday night ritual at the best party in town picked up some slack, too, with midnight showings of the *Rocky Horror Picture Show*.

An all-girl teenage band came to play in Austin at the Armadillo. The Runaways were my exact age, actual peers. I knew very little about them; they weren't on the radio and I hadn't seen an album. I took a place on some steps at the back of the hall for an unobstructed view of the crowd—a good-size crowd—and the stage. Conflicted and torn, I ricocheted from jealous to excited, dismayed to curious. How had they already achieved this level of success?

The Runaways took the stage, posturing and strutting like rock caricatures with hypersexualized stances and stage presence. The audience pressed in, dubious spectators. I didn't think the jailbait gimmick would take them far in front of an Austin crowd. Men leered, laughed, or veered uncertainly in between. Women gawked, slack-jawed—hopefully some of them having their minds blown just like Suzi Quatro blew mine. Wishing they weren't so contrived, I nevertheless found myself rooting for the band.

A few songs into the set, the Runaways began to win over the crowd. By the end, they owned the place. Lita Ford shredded on lead guitar—I had never seen a woman play lead so proficiently. Drummer Sandy West meant business—powerful, charismatic, and way beyond capable. Jackie Fox solidly held her own on bass. I related to Joan Jett most, the one I would want in my band. The Runaways were living the life I wanted: making records, touring, and performing. As their renown grew, I eventually learned that the forced sexuality they projected had been an unnecessary machination of their mentor and manager, Kim Fowley.

How had they gotten to where I wanted to be? Seeing the Runaways made me think if they could do it, so could I. That show lit a fire under my ass. I decided Lickedysplit needed a star to lead and front the band.

I'd always had a general fixation on being the "first" something: first woman scientist to cure cancer, first woman president, first woman in space—that sort of thing. Apparently, my band might not be the first all-girl rock band, but I could hope we might be the first to be big, really big, maybe even like the Stones.

The Runaways would never have to worry about competition from Lickedysplit. Our band had a short run, even after finding a lead singer and playing a dozen more gigs—always due to the kindness of male bands letting us open. Getting the encouragement and support of Austin musicians kept me going. When our bass player, Big Donna, moved on, I knew it was time to start over. I had no idea what the next band would be like, only that I needed one, and the sooner the better. Being an only child of a single mother, growing up as one of a pair, I longed for close familial connections. I had the idea that a band would be a surrogate family. With Marilyn, I began a long habit of finding a sisterlike friend to bond with and be my partner in music.

I also looked for a brother figure in Eddie, the guitar player from Jellyroll. He had rented a room in our house, and I was thrilled to have ongoing proximity to my very own rock 'n' roller. Eddie played guitar all day, and every night he went out gigging or seeing bands. I followed his lead, practicing and going to all the shows I could. Eddie had major stage presence, really had the whole thing down—not just looking perfect, but as he would say, "throwing great shapes" as well. That meant stage moves.

The shortage of young, female musicians in Austin was frustrating my ambitions. Turning eighteen held no new landmarks for me; I'd been going to bars and drinking for several of my underage years. I wasn't against going to college like anyone graduating high school might do, but it meant studying and taking the GED test. Giving that much attention to something else might even mean I had given up on my dream, and that was unthinkable. No, college could wait. Guys were playing in bands all over town. The Runaways were on freaking tour. Now was the time to make this happen.

12

VIRTUOSITY

Mom had stuck with her job for several years, working on programs and grants for education. It gave her a sizable retirement check to cash out when she got antsy to leave and visit her family in England. I thought of Suzi Quatro and figured I'd better take my guitar—maybe I would find my band there. The plane had barely landed in London before I headed straight to the newsstand for a copy of *Melody Maker*, scouring the musicians-wanted classifieds. It jumped out, my destiny in tiny newsprint:

"Painted Lady—All female band seeking guitarist."

I hadn't heard a note or even made the call yet, but I knew it must be fate, bringing me full circle back to London, to fully light what had sparked there three years before. Kim McAuliffe answered the phone when I called, and after a brief talk we made plans to get together.

The day had turned cool and rainy when I met Kim at Waterloo Station, holding my guitar wrapped in a Hefty bag—my flight case was too heavy to lug on the subway. We hit it off right away and headed to her row house, where I met her parents—nice Londoners with thick accents. We talked about music, her band, and what songs we knew. She took me down the road to meet her musician friends, girls who had inspired her. Kim's neighborhood crawled with female musicians—a gorgeous rocker with a massive strawberry blonde afro that matched her Orange amp stack, a killer guitarist, a tiny powerhouse drummer. They all exuded confidence and seemed to be in a different

league than me. This display of hip chick musicians made my
head spin. I hoped I would be good enough to play in Kim's
band. We met up with her bassist and went to play, finally over-
coming our nervousness about plugging in. It felt like a good
match.

For the next month I went back and forth from my grandmother's or aunt's house to Kim's, sometimes sleeping over after
a late night at a pub. New music came at me from every direction. They turned me on to Tom Petty, already big in England
but unknown in America for another year. I turned them on
to ZZ Top and showed them "Tush," which they kept in their
set long after I left and they became Girlschool. We learned
songs by Ultravox and Thin Lizzy and AC/DC. When I wasn't
at Kim's house, I went back to my aunt's, said hi to my mom,
found a place in the house to plug into the tiny Pignose amp I
had brought, and practiced. I had joined as the lead guitarist
and needed tons of work to fill that job on these songs.

Something else had been happening in England—punk rock,
full on. The Sex Pistols were everywhere, shock machine in
full-tilt mode. Their disposition of nihilism and anarchy didn't
resonate with my optimism and drive to rock 'n' roll and have
a good time. Even worse, besides the drummer, they weren't
cute. By the end of the year I was a fan, though, after the release
of the perfect *Never Mind the Bollocks*. Kim took me shopping on King's Road, and I saw my first punks in person, all
over the place. I tried not to stare at the fashion and makeup
that the girls and boys wore. I'd just started to feel pretty hip
back in Texas, but the King's Road punk rockers made me feel
like a hick. We walked to the end of the road and ended up
at Seditionaries, Vivienne Westwood and Malcolm McLaren's
shop. Always a quick study, I bought a black T-shirt with zip-
pers in the shoulders. Kim took me to the Marquee, to the 100

Club. We saw the Vibrators, the Boomtown Rats, Eddie and the Hot Rods. These bands skated punk—more like standard rock bands in terms of their music and image. But the whole vibe started rubbing off on me. The road to being in a successful band looked a hell of a lot shorter with the advent of punk rock. No one played like Jeff Beck or Jimmy Page. The attitude and image, the energy and message carried these bands, not virtuosity.

Rock 'n' roll still had the best heroes and icons, though. When T. Rex's Marc Bolan died in a car crash, we were stricken with the tragedy. It made huge news in London, the cover of the dailies showing pictures of the crash site, the whole thing made more dramatic because his girlfriend had survived the wreck. Elvis's death a few weeks before had been my first jolt of what it feels like when someone you've grown up with dies—the bubble gets pierced and all the air rushes out of your innocence. Then it happens over and over again, and life goes on, and you start to understand that we're all erasable blips in time.

My English band played some songs at a local pub, still using the name Painted Lady. I have one fuzzy picture to commemorate my illustrious UK debut. Their friends, the girls who were really good, came. I went through all the motions, trying not to let on how fraudulent and uncomfortable I felt. My eyes fixated on my hand moving on the guitar neck, nowhere close to being able to "throw shapes." Despite my awkwardness, I still got off on feeling Marshalled up in amplification and locking in loud with other musicians on a stage *in London*. Within days we booked a real gig, and we practiced daily to get ready.

A few days before our first gig, a pain came from the center of my stomach, boring through me from front to back like a cylinder of constant agony. When it didn't let up, Mom took me to a hospital. After a day of X-rays, ulcer tests, poking, and pills, it passed, undiagnosed. As soon as the stomach ailment rolled on its way, I hightailed it over to Kim's house.

Her poor mom had to tell me they were practicing with my substitute at the church activity center. When I walked in, they were blasting. One look and I knew I was out for good. In my place, in front of the Marshall half stack I had been playing through, I saw through a dizzy blur of dismay and awe a girl with long lanky legs, casually tilted and resting her weight on one hip. She wore a tight, cap-sleeved T-shirt and played a Goldtop Les Paul, her shaggy blond mane hiding her face. Her presence alone made me want to slink out of the room. But on top of looking like she should already be on an arena stage with a spotlight, Kelly Johnson was fucking ripping, note for note, the entirety of Led Zeppelin's "Rock and Roll." She was legit to the core—a star. Like so many inherently bestowed stars, she was humble and shy. "Rock and Roll" staggered to an end, Kelly playing the last guitar lick by herself perfectly. No one really needed to say anything at all, but Kim wasn't the type to shy away from the hard jobs.

"Hey Kaff. Feelin' better now? Um, we've decided to play with Kelly from now on." *No shit.* I took it like a good stoic, holding it together on the train and walking from the station, saving my tears for the upstairs bedroom at my grandmother's house. Flopping on the bed, overcome with despair, the loss cut to my core. The antiseptic scent of Grandma's house hung in the air among the muted, striped wallpaper, the soft velour of the bedcover. The moment condensed into a full stop, and like a reboot, I un-flopped off the bed, determined and resolved, charged with a new focus. Getting fired by the band left a hole that quickly filled with a plan: I would go back to Austin and start the first punk band in town. I didn't have to be able to play "Rock and Roll" note for note to be in a punk band. I didn't have to play like a whiz virtuoso. I didn't have to look or act like a rock star. I didn't even have to look like a punk—there were plenty of variations on the theme. People took what they liked or needed from punk and fused elements with their own sensibilities, and the music world already had started exploding with the freedom it brought.

13

RED HEAD

One day, our housemate and my friend, Eddie from Jellyroll, casually mentioned that his girlfriend played guitar. What? I couldn't believe he had kept this from me.

I made him call Carla and put me on the phone. We agreed to meet at her parents' house, where she kept her equipment. After answering the door, she led me into a bedroom. Carla flipped on the light and there, in front of the window—it looked ten feet tall—I saw a Marshall stack. Not just any Marshall stack (two speaker cabinets and a hundred-watt head)—a RED Marshall stack. As if that weren't enough, she pulled a beat-up guitar case out from under the bed. Opening it revealed a 1954 blond wood Les Paul Junior.

I had never met anyone like Carla Olson. One generation removed from her father's Swedish homeland but Texan all the way through, with a moral compass like a cast iron skillet. Carla made it clear right off the bat that she didn't do drugs or smoke—never had, never would. Anyone else I would've written off as a straitlaced square, but not Carla. She seemed like some kind of superhero. I thought I was tough, but I could tell this Carla chick out-toughed me by miles. I made sure I didn't let her know that. Some women are pretty, but something else stronger and indefinable eclipses the physical. Part of her confidence came from being way too cool for Austin at the time: she wore stiletto boots in metallic pink patent leather. All her jeans had seams down the back, where she had converted flares into straight legs, way before anyone else gave up their bell-bottoms.

Carla had the longest, blondest, straightest hair—it covered her slight frame and went all the way past her butt.

As I came to know her, I observed that she kept a very neat and organized life: she had a full-time job for the travel agency but could get off work and have a home-cooked meal on the table within an hour. Carla had a natural feminine and nurturing talent and would have made a great mother. The only mothering she ended up doing was to the men she loved—and for a while to me, the little rocker chick she started a band with. Carla lived a fully functioning twenty-five-year-old adult life when we met.

Coincidentally, she had just gotten back from London, too, and was hip to Elvis Costello, Nick Lowe, and loads of Stiff Records new wave and punk music. Both of us were fired up by the London scene and ready to start a band in Austin.

The three of us—Marilyn, Carla, and me—played without a bass player at first. I tried to find Big Donna from Lickedysplit again, but she had disappeared. Anxious to keep the band moving forward, we asked our friend Jesse Sublett to play bass with us. Even with the contrast he brought—being taller, and, well, a guy—he fit in. I think it was because he's one of those men who truly loves and admires women. Jesse had a soft-spoken voice and a gentle, quiet strength. In terms of the whole punk thing, Jesse had more than a foot in the door, way ahead of us, as a longtime fan of Lou Reed, the New York Dolls, Patti Smith, and John Cale.

Playing cover songs is always a good place to start, a way to filter what everyone likes. Carla suggested Mott the Hoople's "Death May Be Your Santa Claus." It sounded punk to me, ahead of its time in attitude, and the chorus shouted "I don't give a fuck anyway," so good enough. We worked up a speed-demon version of "Let's Spend the Night Together," snarling the words and eliminating what little melody the chorus had in the first place. If we could play the song fast enough, it fit. The first song I wrote with Jesse for our new band, "Gross Encounters," had chords matching the five-note cue recurring through the film *Close Encounters of the Third Kind*. It told a story about a girl meeting a guy in a bar and the guy turning out to be an alien. Not exactly "Anarchy in the U.K." or "White Riot."

Van, the guitar player pal who had thought up the name Lickedysplit, came up with this band's name too: the Violators. I haven't thought up very many great band names in my life. The Violators was a name to live up to. We added more songs; Jesse brought in another original for me to sing, and we learned "Shake Appeal" from Iggy and the Stooges' *Raw Power* album.

Life seemed to be moving as fast as the music we played. I found a decent job at a gym for ladies called Elaine Powers Figure Salon. I had to make sales and help the clients with the equipment, including those machines with a band that went around your butt and shook it as hard and fast as "Shake Appeal."

I still needed to move out on my own. My mom and I hung out like pals sometimes, seeing a movie or sharing a meal, but she had her separate life and I had mine, centered on music. Carla's friend Lois moved from San Antonio and became part of our pack. We found a four-bedroom apartment for me, Marilyn, Carla, and Lois. Lois and Carla—the together, mature ones— had one side of the apartment; on the other side, the wild side, were my and Marilyn's bedrooms. In the living room we set up our music gear and equipment.

Marilyn's drummer boyfriend had helped her get better on drums. Like all the musicians we knew, he encouraged and sup- ported our band. The support had no patronizing elements, no "aren't they cute" mentality. The guys we ran around with were rooting for us and wanted us to do well. A couple of years ago, I met and talked with both Suzi and Patti Quatro, the

Detroit musicians who started playing in bands in the '60s, and they'd had the same experience: most all guy musicians took them seriously. I would find this to hold true as I continued in the music business; the skepticism and sexism came from the non-artists, whether the audience was hootin' to "take it off" or suits in the offices were telling you there was no audience for your female band. I'm indebted to those guys I looked up to in Austin. Jesse and Eddie were the real deal, alongside me every step of the way. Van Wilks, Eric Johnson, and Bill Maddox were consummate musicians who went out of their way to help with tips and gigs. Jimmie Vaughan, Keith Ferguson, and Doug Sahm were already Texas royalty. They welcomed me singularly, and us collectively, as musicians with every right to be in the same musical landscape they inhabited.

Me and my gang were the hipsters of Austin now. We figured if our band played some gigs and got out in the world, other people would probably agree. No one else in Austin played music like we did. The cosmic cowboy thing was old news. All the rockers were dated. Blues players were perennially cool but not exactly fresh. Our first gigs were at Mother Earth, a rock club where I'd spent many nights watching bands. Jesse cut his hair off, and I made T-shirts with rips and tears and painted pink skulls, crossbones, and the jagged Violator logo on them. We did a photo session, posed on a pile of rubble, mustering up all the menace we could fit into our expressions. I thought we would run the town.

The Sex Pistols were coming to Texas. We sent the promoter a demo tape and picture to get on the bill. He offered us the slot, with a caveat saying Marilyn had to fuck him in return. He could go fuck himself we said back and bought tickets like everyone else. Everyone buzzed with anticipation for the Pistols' San Antonio show, scheduled for the day after my nineteenth birthday. Playing Randy's Rodeo, a cowboy bar, made the concert a combustible choice—by design. The band's manager, Malcolm McLaren, knew shit would get stirred up like nobody's business.

Piling into Eddie's van and Marilyn's Galaxy, the hour drive to San Antonio passed amid loud singing of Sex Pistols songs as we guzzled cans of beer. At Randy's Rodeo the marquee read, "The Sex Pistols in Texas Tonight" framed in neon stars and spurs. Everyone milled around outside—mostly San Antonio metal heads, longhairs, and freaks. When the doors opened, people went in to see the opening band—a group who presumably didn't have to fuck anyone for it. Marilyn and I meandered around the band's tour bus, taking our time to light cigarettes, hoping a Sex Pistol might wander out. Probably for the best, we failed to be noticed and headed into the gig. I found the idea of befriending the most notorious band in the world appealing, but I sure didn't want to be mistaken for a groupie.

Way before they took the stage, the mixture of boorish and unsettled energy in the room made me cautious. The crowd had more than a few troublemakers, thick with the types who would pay money to enjoy a dogfight. No one knew what to expect. I clutched Marilyn's hand and we shimmied our way into the mob, about a quarter of the way back from stage left.

On stage Johnny Rotten wore a T-shirt with a graphic of two cowboys jerking each other off. Sid wore no shirt and had "gimme a fix" carved into his chest. When Sid got hit by one of the endless projectiles hurled at the band from the audience, he proceeded to bash the guy with the big end of his P bass. "Oh, Sid's dropped his bass," taunted Johnny. Throughout the show, Johnny baited the crowd as the frenzied horde howled back in fury or hysteria. I watched it all from my place on the floor, amazed when another song started and played to the finish. They sounded great. It didn't matter that Johnny Rotten couldn't carry a tune or Sid Vicious could barely play. Paul Cook

and Steve Jones carried the music, a sonic and molten cater-
waul, and the songs carried themselves. They were like wild
animals fighting for their own destruction instead of survival.
Whether theatrics or real, it was brutal. In my mind, anarchy
had to do with socioeconomic and class issues in England. I
understood punk as an antithesis to arena and radio rock, but
not why a band would try so hard to be hated.

The chaos caused a lot of distraction, but after a few songs
the musicians and music fans formed a loose layer behind all
the antagonists' food and beer throwing. I spotted a cute punk
boy with ripped T-shirt and arms. We jostled each other, bump-
ing shoulders and bouncing to "Holidays in the Sun." He stuck
close by for the rest of the concert, putting his arm around me
when the Pistols started chugging into their love song "Sub-
mission." Just like that, we were a couple. The show seemed to
go really quickly, like a tornado shearing through the venue,
leaving a swath of stunned people and debris—and a lot of us
satisfied because we had just seen rock 'n' roll get completely
reinvented. I brought my new boyfriend back to Austin to live
with me after the show, but being a girlfriend lost its novelty
quickly. It got in the way of hanging out with my friends and
my band, and he was gone in less than a month.

The smallest handful of bands launched punk and new wave
in Austin, centered at Raul's, a struggling Tejano bar near the
UT campus. The owner took a chance when he booked Project
Terror and the Violators. Overnight, his club repurposed into a
new scene. Project Terror couldn't be called a punk band; they
were a trio of three superb musicians, but they were cool enough
to want to be in on the new sound. Raul's had a foot-high stage
in the front and a bar in the back: your basic dark, dingy dive.
Our gig had a crowd, largely due to the Project Terror fans that
lingered after their set, somewhat confused as we slammed
through a short list of songs. I had no idea how jarring it was for

men in the audience to see cute girls breaking out of the boxes those men had apportioned for us—a prototype experience I would see replayed over and over in my career as a musician.

The Violators were booked right away for another gig at Raul's, this time with the Skunks, Jesse and Eddie's new band. Jesse would have to play double duty. In short time, a batch of new bands sprouted up in our wake. Punk and new wave had a home in Austin, and the Violators and Skunks, along with the Mexican-American owners of Raul's, had made it happen.

14

NUT WHITES

The Runaways came back to Austin, opening for the Ramones at the Armadillo. I had a smile on my face for the entire Ramones set, which was my reaction to the dozens of their shows I saw over the next eighteen years. The Runaways had changed—Joan Jett sang lead now and Jackie Fox had been replaced with Vicki Blue. Heading backstage with my own actual band cred, I felt sure I would connect with them. Meeting the Ramones wasn't on the agenda—I had no idea what to talk to a Ramone about. I wanted to hang with girl rockers. I met new bassist Vicki first. She invited us in the dressing room, telling Joan we were Kathy and Marilyn from the Violators. *Yeah.*

From the backstage visit, we were invited to go back to their hotel.

I'd never hung out with a touring band on the road. Up the elevator, a circular wander through the hotel corridor, knock on the door, shave and a haircut. We sat on the edge of the bed and lit cigs, a familiar ritual to dispel shyness. Joan went out to the ice machine and filled her bathroom sink with ice, spinning some beer cans in the ice to chill them quicker. I made a mental note and repeated her ritual three years later on my first tour, like I was some seasoned pro. The atmosphere felt low key, with Joan and Vicki glad for the company. Their roadie Kent joined us. He had black, spiky hair, pasty white skin, and sleepy, sullen eyes. I blurted out that the Violators were moving to LA in the summer—a future plan I made up on the spot, and Kent offered his phone number. I would've rather had Joan and Vicki's number but didn't want to push it. We left in the middle of the night and met up for lunch the next day.

The Violators had no big message or vision, but that didn't stop us from thinking great things lay ahead. We played some out-of-town gigs in Dallas and San Antonio. Someone put on a punk Battle of the Bands in Austin, and we got second place—I still have a cassette from it, a distorted ruckus of a relic. We'd had a little press but hadn't thought about recording and didn't know how to move forward. The idea I'd blurted out in Joan Jett's hotel room, that the band was moving to LA, started to take root. We also considered New York City—mainly because I had a full case of Blondie-mania.

Blondie mesmerized me. I pounced on anyone who called Debbie by the band name: "Blondie is a band; Debbie Harry is the lead singer!" Not only were the aesthetics of their fashion appealing, musically they bridged the energy and edge of punk with the melody and drive of the radio pop and classic rock I had grown up with. The whole package was tied together by a gritty New York City urbanity and worldliness unlike anything I'd seen in Texas or England. With their mod suits, tousled dark hair, and Ray-Bans, the guys made a classic background to showcase Debbie, who had an unparalleled flair for mixed-and-matched styles. She was malleable: morphing from glamorous retro movie star to girly tomboy to sex kitten. When they showed up at Raul's after an Armadillo World Headquarters concert, I got to see Debbie close up on the sidewalk outside the club. She seemed untouchable, like a work of art. The guys in the band were down to earth. My teenage fan-girl crush centered on drummer Clem Burke, but I didn't get to meet him. Other band members came back to our apartment, where we drank and jammed until the sun came up—no one trying to get laid, just musicians hanging out.

Carla managed to keep her life totally together despite living with kids like Marilyn and me. She took her work seriously, showing up every day poised and competent. I needed to keep my job at Elaine Powers and often had to lead "Team Time," the group exercise class at eight in the morning. After a late night of rock 'n' roll, getting up the cheerful energy to do jumping jacks with a bright, shiny smile became too ambitious even for a nineteen-year-old.

As talk about moving the band heated up, Carla surprised me with her willingness to leave family, career, and her boyfriend, Eddie. When she landed a job at the Beverly Hills American Express office, it sealed LA as our destination. One added bonus about LA came from Marilyn, who had a friend in West Hollywood promising to put us up a while.

While the Violators continued to play, my head was already out of Austin. Jesse had left us to stay in his band with Eddie, the Skunks, so it would just be me, Marilyn, and Carla making the move. I bought a 1968 Oldsmobile Delta 88 four-door and hoped like hell it could get me to California. The Olds was a monster of a cruiser, nineteen feet long and nearly seven feet wide. A blue machine forged in steel with a 455 V8 to power it. Working extra shifts helped me save money for the move. I made a few more contacts when the Plugz, a punk band from LA, played Raul's. The Plugz solidified my feeling that LA was the place where the real shit happened. They were pros, right on top of the heap with their own sound.

The year 1978 brought bizarre violence and killings. If Larry Flynt being shot by a sniper or Sid Vicious killing his girlfriend, Nancy Spungen, didn't shake you up, there was always the ghastly John Wayne Gacy or the mass of people dying at

Jim Jones's temple in Guyana. That same year, the Son of Sam killer was convicted and Ted Bundy was apprehended. The Bundy killings really took root in the cultural consciousness; his nonthreatening demeanor proved that any normal Joe could be a psychopath. I got scared to drive halfway across the country. Finding an English tourist who needed a ride to California allayed my fears. In late August, I made the move.

The Delta 88 was packed from floor to headliner, from trunk to the back of the headrests: Marilyn's drums, my amp and guitar, our clothes, and whatever house items we could wedge in between the gear while we sat thigh to thigh in the front seat. Determined to make it to LA in two days, the Olds shot across the desert like a torpedo, hitting one hundred miles per hour until we merged onto my first six-lane freeway. Pomona, El Monte, Pasadena: each sign a giant beacon of hope. At three in the morning, we ended up lost in downtown LA, a ghost city of empty buildings, dark and sinister. Cardboard lean-tos, vagrants, trash, and bottles lined the curbs. *Where was the fucking freeway?* Marilyn, our big LA expert with her one visit, had no idea how to get to West Hollywood, where her friend Ally lived. We pulled over to cry through the panic and burnout.

Eventually, we hit Sweetzer Avenue in West Hollywood. For decades, whenever I drove by that street, I remembered trying to park my huge car on the crowded street right as the sun was rising. LA conjures those throwbacks for me—every street, every corner, every shop and building holds two perspectives, proximate reverses: the present and the rear view, the memory of being there the first time. Pulling suitcases out, trying to figure out the outside buzzer to Ally's apartment building. No apartments had buzzers in Austin.

For $116 a month I found a one-room studio in an old building on Orange Avenue in Hollywood. It wasn't nice like West Hollywood, and it was a lot less like Texas. On a few occasions, gunshots cracked and popped in the night. More often there was the unfamiliar, low rumble of low-riders and screaming, drunken fights on the street outside. A Murphy bed screeched out on rusty springs and hinges. Marilyn never stayed there, choosing to stay at Ally's nicer apartment instead. She had brought a fake ID with her and they were hitting the clubs. Alone at night I listened to the strange new sounds or watched helicopter searchlights lighting up the bare room as they swept through the windows. I lived in isolation until I had a phone line installed after a couple of weeks. Trying to stretch my meager savings, I walked to the Mayfair Market and bought mac and cheese. Adding a stolen can of tuna could turn the ingredients into a "casserole" to eat for days. Feeling lonely and abandoned, I called Marilyn and heard about the places they were going: the Rainbow, the Whisky. Ally liked mainstream LA rock, bands with dudes who wore white Capezio shoes and high-waisted bell-bottoms that were so tight they got what I called "nut whites," where their balls rubbed the denim into faded spots by their crotch. I would have been happy to go see any band, but I was still a minor in California. After years of hanging out in Austin clubs, it felt frustrating to be shut out. I didn't understand why Marilyn, my best friend in the world for the last five years, had ditched me. Hadn't we come out here to seek fame and fortune in our band?

I wrote long letters to my mom and joined the library, checking out a book every few days. And then, in the absence of the things I thought I was missing out on, something better came to me. In the isolation and rejection of my first month in LA, I turned to songwriting.

Trying to start bands and practicing guitar had been my priorities before. Now I needed an outlet. Those first weeks in LA, sitting on the edge of that creaking Murphy bed with no television, no money, and nowhere to go, my beloved guitar became my best friend. The first song I wrote, about not giving up, I called "Can't Stop the World." The lyrics weren't the best, although there are a few great lines and the hook is pretty close to perfect. In my head I heard how it should sound, how it should be played. Like a stream of consciousness, the song came in order. By the time I had finished a second verse, I knew it only had one place to go. The simple refrain expressed exactly what I wanted to say. More than anything else, more than satisfaction or feeling proud or contemplating whether my song might be any good or not, I felt better. I followed it up with my next song, putting all my disappointment in my best friend into verse and calling it "We Don't Get Along."

In those days, writing these first "real" songs, I became a true musician. Not because I was proficient or well-practiced, but because I'd found how to merge what was going on with me internally with what I wanted to create musically.

15

TROPICANA

Writing songs was empowering. I blew off Marilyn and reached out to the Plugz, the band I'd met in Austin, and Kent, the Runaways roadie. It turned out there were plenty of places for underage folks to see shows. On one of my first nights out in LA, I rode with one of the Plugz to his gig in the Valley at the Rock Corporation. I was thrilled to be going out, even if it wasn't on the Strip. The Valley felt weirdly alien, all squat buildings in strip malls and half-dead neon signs flickering in front of motels and used car lots.

Inside the Rock Corp a band played—girls. Hmm. The singer, a round-faced kewpie doll, swung her arms and danced, the guitarists barely able to look up from the necks of their instruments. They didn't hold my attention for very long. The Plugz' drummer, Charlie, found me at the bar and asked what I thought of the band playing, the Go-Go's. I shrugged; "They've got a ways to go." He agreed and said they were his good friends and were beginners, but he thought they had something. I didn't think so and didn't give them another thought for a year.

I couldn't wait to get a band together. Carla got to town finally, coming in like a hundred-pound version of the freaking cavalry stampeding over the desert from Texas to California. Ditching what remained of the idea of the Violators along with drummer ex-best-friend Marilyn, we decided to start fresh. Not long after, I heard Marilyn moved back to Texas, but we didn't speak again until forty years later. On a mission to find musicians, Carla and I went out nearly every night. One of the things people who aren't in bands always wonder is how bands get together, how the members find each other. There's not a band or musician alive who hasn't been asked in an interview, "How did you guys get together?" The answer is: going to hear other bands is how bands get together. Hanging out with musicians. Maybe looking in music magazines for ads. There's nothing mysterious or magical about finding people to play with. The magic happens with lucking into a winning chemistry.

Getting a musical foundation and education in Austin gave me an appreciation for a wide spectrum of music. This era in the LA music scene had it all too. Great bands of every genre played in clubs from the beach to downtown. Smart, artsy, tongue-in-cheek punk bands and unpretentious bands like our friends the Plugz. Every band had its own character, its own story.

Power pop, new wave, whatever you called it—the guys in the skinny ties and suits had a big place in the scene, too, often playing at the flagship new wave club Madame Wong's, a restaurant turned club in Chinatown. Across the plaza, the seedier and more low-down Hong Kong Café hosted the rest. Crossing all lines, welcome on any bill at any club, were the Blasters, the OG Americana band. Completing the range were rockabilly bands and fashions like teddy boy jackets and creepers. Anyone paying attention could figure out the big lesson: good music can find an audience. I couldn't wait to figure out where we fit in the thriving LA scene.

Carla and I were a noticeable pair. We were opposites in many ways but came from the same place, had both been compelled to pick up electric guitars, had the same cocksure attitude, and had plenty of good humor to keep us laughing. There weren't all that many female musicians—more than in Austin, but women were still very underrepresented. We were looking for anyone to fill out our band, never mind the gender, but I hadn't ever let go of my true wish: to be in the best all-female band ever.

I knew who Kim Fowley was; everyone in Hollywood did. He had made the now-defunct Runaways a sensation and had a couple of new acts playing at the Whisky. I dragged Carla to see them, hoping to meet him and find out if he could be helpful to us. It took no time to spot him: he stood out in a crowd. Not just because he was tall, but because he could put an outfit together with flashy suits, boots, and scarves. As soon as we approached him, the shtick began. In minutes I had him pegged as a glam Colonel Parker huckster crossed with a game-show host. The guy reeked of bullshit to two Texas girls.

"See that dog up there," he said, pointing at the singer on-stage. "She does what I say."

I didn't give him the shocked reaction he had probably hoped for and instead asked about hooking us up with musicians. He told us we would never get anywhere in LA without his help. "Wait and see," I said, and that was the end of my first encounter with Kim Fowley. I never forgot the way he talked about that singer while she performed. I had always been around supportive and encouraging guys in the Texas music scene. People didn't label men as sexist or abusive in the '70s much, but his contempt for his own client made me grateful I never needed him for a leg up in the business.

The Capitol Records record-swap on the first Saturday of each month was the best event in Hollywood. After the clubs let out, hundreds of people gathered in a parking lot on Vine, across from the iconic Capitol Records building. Vendors set up stalls selling bootleg collectibles, memorabilia, and imports. People made connections, band lineups fell into place, and like-minded scenesters forged friendships. It was like the internet in a parking lot, the social without the media. Occasionally, a limo pulled up to the curb and discharged a real, live rock star to wander around. No one was starstruck. No one came here hoping to see the ones who had made it; this was where the upstarts and rising stars gathered.

A drummer answered an ad I'd put in the *Music Connection*, a local magazine. Over the phone, a strong accent that I couldn't place, kind of East Coast, kind of Southern. We invited her over to discuss. Meeting potential bandmates is exactly like going on a blind date. You want to see if there's any vibe before you take it any further. You need to judge their clothing choices. Eventually, after an overkill of awkward encounters, I would joke that I could save all parties a lot of time if prospects would just tell us on the phone what kind of shoes they were wearing. For our brand-new, very first LA band, we envisioned someone with edgy appeal and presence. The girl who showed up to our apartment on Hacienda Place didn't fit our vision any more than the baggy overalls she wore fit her tiny body. With her oversized, dorky glasses and a headful of permed hair, we didn't bother to take it to the next step of playing together.

The intrigues of fate sure seem to push and pull us, crisscrossing our lives and locking us into little orbits and revolutions. Like miniature stars in our own earthbound galaxies. The drummer we didn't think was right for our band was Gina Schock. Like me, she had come to LA to chase the same dream. Not long after I met her, the Go-Go's gave her a makeover and she returned the favor with her own makeover of the band.

Before long, the networking and showing up paid off. Carla and I got two guys, drummer Mark Cuff and bass player Dave Provost. Still clinging to our Texas roots, we chose the name the Textones. Our first demo tape included one of the songs I had written in my lonely first weeks: "We Don't Get Along." The Textones got lucky when Carla and I met Saul Davis. Saul managed

Phil Seymour, a great singer with the impeccable credential of having done the insanely great backing vocals on Tom Petty's "American Girl" and "Breakdown." Saul promised to listen to our demo. When the call came, it brought a windfall. Not only did he want to work with the Textones—he wanted to give "We Don't Get Along" to Phil to record for his solo debut on the new Boardwalk Records label. Scoring a cover song on a major label by a singer as talented as Phil and getting a manager who hustled like Saul was clear evidence that success in LA was a given.

We did a band photo session with Catherine Sebastian, a friend of Phil and Saul. For the first time in my entire life, when I looked at the pictures, I saw myself as pretty. My hair had grown out, full and spiky, perfect rock 'n' roll hair. Catherine did a few more photos of me, and those shots of me at twenty years old are some of my favorite photos.

Carla's friend married Jake Riviera, the curmudgeonly and charming cofounder of Stiff Records and manager of Elvis Costello, Nick Lowe, and the Damned. For the classic Nick Lowe "Cruel to Be Kind" video shoot at the Tropicana Motel on Santa Monica, Jake called on us to loan the band some equipment. We thought this might be the lucky break to bust things wide open for our band. Off we went to the hardware store, buying black letters to stick on the bass drum head. "The Textones," the drum proclaimed, clearly visible as the band played by the pool. I felt sure we would get a record deal from the video—not the last time I'd be wrong about the music business.

In Los Angeles the air is stained with smog and hazy with the dreams of aspiring actors, writers, filmmakers, musicians, and dancers. Possibility and chance woke us up, pulled us out of bed every morning, and sent us to rehearsals, classes, day jobs, errands. A world could change in a day. I thought every little thing might lead to some bigger, better thing. If it didn't, no big deal, just wait; another cool thing would come along and surely something great was right around the corner. I saw nothing but a series of good omens.

Saul booked a room for the Textones at LA's premier rehearsal space, Studio Instrument Rentals. As we ran through a version of "Second That Emotion," in walked Smokey Robinson. Saul bounced up and down behind him, all hyper with the sheer good timing and coincidental blessing that Hollywood had bestowed upon us. Smokey exuded smooth charm and smiles. We invited him to sing with us and then there we were, playing "Second That Emotion" with Smokey Robinson. His wife, Claudette, an original Miracle, joined in to sing along. Afterward, the room felt sprinkled in LA magic dust. Those little lifts and pushes are seductive and keep people going a lot longer than they might somewhere else. In hometowns, families and jobs win out over hopes for lucky breaks in the music biz.

The Textones started playing out at the "starter" clubs: Madame Wong's, the Hong Kong Café, Blackies, Club 88. Down the street from our apartment, a roller-skating "boogie palace" nightclub called Flippers opened and became a local favorite. Everyone from Cher to punk rockers liked Flippers. The Textones scored a gig playing in the middle of the skate floor. Hipsters obliviously roller-boogied through our set; anyone could have been playing. Still, we were a part of something exclusive and uniquely LA. Every gig and night out gave me cause to celebrate.

16

CHINO JAM

During the summer of 1980, I traveled home to see my mom. I entered the Austin airspace with a big-shot attitude and couldn't wait to bust through the doors of Raul's, where the Violators had started. Wearing Cuban heeled suede boots from downtown LA, black straight-leg jeans, and a vintage striped jacket, no one could mistake me for a local. *I'm Hollywood now and everyone should take notes.* It was the same bluster that helped me go to a new school every year as a kid, turned up to ten.

Being in Raul's was like being assaulted, with loudness, cigarette smoke, and unbearable heat. No one knew I had helped make this scene. It had gone on, gotten a life of its own; it didn't matter who started it. I leaned against the bar with a beer and surveyed the place like a returning homecoming queen anyway. My eyes settled on a gangly terrier of a boy, all spiky-haired and twinkling eyes. An electric current zapped between us, and we both knew in an instant we were going to have some fun together. Billy sang in a band called Boy Problems. He had so much affable charm, there probably wasn't a girl in town who wouldn't have followed him wherever he wanted to go.

Trying to talk over the noise, we stood close, pushed together into a vacuum, the music and smoke enveloping us. For the next five days Billy Problem and were I inseparable. We played pool, listened to bands, lounged around and talked. Like most guys I've liked, he didn't drink as much as I did and put up with my hard-partying ways. I got drunk but could handle it well. I didn't get sick; I didn't pass out. I drank and had a good time and felt like I belonged wherever I was.

Flying back to Los Angeles, I gazed out the window thinking about my time in Austin with him. I'd never had a real boyfriend before or ever felt like a guy cared about me. I wasn't his girl, and we weren't a couple, but my thoughts unfolded anyway with a rhyme and a rhythm:

> Now that I'm away, I wish I'd stayed
> Tomorrow's a day of mine you won't be in.

I scribbled all the lyrics out on airplane napkins and called the song "Vacation." I had been drunk, high, hungover, or asleep the entire Austin trip, but the memory remained in a fuzzy glow. The short romance had softened me, and the words, written from true-life longing, resonated forever.

Saul Davis, the manager of the Textones, put together a big shindig of a gig for my twenty-first birthday. It made up for all the years my birthday wasn't celebrated. For that night, the Blue Lagoon Saloon in Venice was the place to be, as cool as any Hollywood club. After the official lineup played sets, all the musicians who were there joined in on a spontaneous jam. Robin Zander of Cheap Trick, Phil Seymour, my band, the Plimsouls, and Moon Martin crowded the stage. I spent the whole night dazed and grinning.

Catherine Sebastian, the photographer who was now my good friend, captured the party. Click, click, no posing, all action shots. The next day Saul, a one-man buzz generator, made sure the photos and news got around. For a belated birthday present, *Rolling Stone* magazine's famous column Random Notes ran a news item on my party. My birthday party, my name, my picture in *Rolling Stone*! This would never have happened if I had stayed in Austin.

The exposure helped the Textones. Chiswick Records, an indie English label, wanted to release an EP. Saul worked some angles and got us an unreleased Tom Petty song called "I Can't Fight It." For the B side we recorded "Vacation," the song I'd written during the summer. Off we went to England to try and drum up excitement for the record—with paltry results.

Undaunted by England's disinterest in our Chiswick EP, I turned the rest of the promo trip into a holiday, taking a train to Rome with Carla. As a travel companion, she took charge, yelling and gesturing in Italian. We bought fringed leather jackets from Fiorucci, the most extravagant clothing item I had ever purchased. I had a fling with an Italian boy who could barely speak English—Carla waving and frowning like a worried mom when I sped off on the back of his motor scooter over the cobbled streets.

Back in LA, we had elevated our gigs, sometimes opening for bigger bands at the Whisky or the Starwood. The Textones were picked to represent Los Angeles at a concert in Michigan. It didn't exactly constitute a tour, but flying anywhere to play and getting paid for it felt like a prize. Then came an offer to play the California Institution for Men at Chino Prison. Riding into the desert east of LA, our band chattered and joked about stuff like cavity searches, causing a riot, and playing "Jailhouse Rock" to a captive audience. I harbored a morbid fascination about prison life and sat on the edge of the van seat, craning to get the first view. When we drove past the sign, everyone quieted down. Layers of razor-wire steel fences surrounded the facility. It looked lower to the ground than I expected, like barracks. Guards held rifles and paced a railed walkway circling a tower in view of the walls and yard. The locked-down atmosphere, ominous and suffocating, put an end to my curiosity.

Once searched and cleared, a couple of guys set up the stage in the cafeteria, folding the tables away and setting up chairs in rows. Only when we went on stage to play did the discomfort of being the only women in the place sweep over me. The audience was a sea of blue-shirted convicts—medium-security wards getting a concert as a reward for good behavior. A few songs into our set, a trustee gestured from the side of the stage. He wanted to know if we would let one of the inmates jam with us. I saw a large black guy wearing a prison-issue shirt holding an electric guitar. He looked eager to come up and plug in. What the hell, why not? The guy lumbered onstage to cheers. The trustee introduced him to us.

Wait, what? Are you serious? He'd just introduced us to Buddy Miles. Buddy-fucking-Band-of-Gypsys-Electric-fucking-Flag Miles. *How could this be happening?* How do a couple of girls from Texas end up jamming in a prison cafeteria with the guy who played drums with Jimi Hendrix? He probably wondered the same thing, opposite version. Buddy chose to play a slow blues in B-flat. Not my forte, but I faked along trying to look serious and bluesy. His voice rumbled out what sounded like "Red House." The song felt like it went on for twenty minutes. After our set, I asked him why he had ended up there. He came right out with it, no hesitation: "Drugs." And then, "Grand theft to buy more drugs."

The Textones recorded another single. The truth of how I felt was starting to dawn on me: none of our recordings sounded like I wanted them to. They lacked the power and edge of the bands I loved. The new record highlighted a divide that was becoming hard to miss—the Textones were two bands in one. Carla wrote and sang her songs; I wrote and sang my songs. Bands are like any relationship—if a creeping doubt enters, it's a fissure needing to be filled and sealed shut. If that doesn't happen, more doubts start piling in and the crack turns into a crevice. This is what happened with me in the Textones.

Lots of bands in the LA scene were getting signed or moving up in other ways. Saul's other client, Phil Seymour, had started recording his debut. Our pals the Plimsouls were about to sign a major record deal. They had started out exactly when we did but now could headline all the major clubs and get KROQ airplay. And that band I had dismissed when I first got to LA, the Go-Go's? They played all the time. I caught them again at the Starwood one night. They wore lots of colors and stripes and bounced around energetically, but what I really noticed was how the audience went nuts for them. I didn't recognize the new drummer as the same girl who had answered our ad when we started out. Another band's success didn't make me feel bitter or jealous, but it affected the way I looked at the Textones. Bad luck or lack of opportunity hadn't prevented us from getting further. I believed our direction had no cohesion.

Musical differences might have been one thing separating me from Carla, but since I had turned twenty-one, my excessive drinking got in the way too. In the early fall, I told my boss at Transamerica Real Estate Tax Service I needed to focus on music, explaining how working nine to five was holding me back. Actually, getting up early to go work cramped my late nights and drinking life. To my surprise, he didn't want me to go, said I had a good future at the company.

With me carousing every night and Carla going to work every day, we grew further apart. I knew I wanted to leave the band but didn't know where I would go. After confiding in Catherine, she offered to let me stay with her. Catherine was married to John Sebastian from the Lovin' Spoonful. They lived in New York, but she had rented a house in the Hollywood Hills for a year to build on her success as a photographer. She was glamorous and sophisticated, like a rock 'n' roll Faye Dunaway, beautifully symmetrical. She was always put together and well dressed in silk blouses, jeans, and leather boots. Catherine came to the rescue and helped me make the change I wanted to. Like a lot of guy musicians, I often seemed to fall under the wing of a mother hen. I don't know if I could have stuck it out in LA without them. Carla had loaned me clothes to wear to work, fixed meals, and kept our apartment decorated and clean. Catherine now let me move in and gave me a safe place to figure out my next move.

Carla showed a lot of grace when I quit. She's a matter-of-fact straight shooter and wouldn't let anything get in her way. My exit didn't break up the Textones—they went on for decades in several incarnations, always featuring Carla front and center. Later, I heard the Textones were glad I had quit because of my drinking. Like most alcoholics, the idea made me indignant and defensive. *Fuck them.* I had no problem and wrote to my mom outlining plans to get my drinking under control: "Nothing for two weeks, then only one beer or some wine with dinner."

17

REGULAR FORMAT

I didn't have much to move into Catherine's—a suitcase of clothes and shoes, my Stratocaster, and my amp. I'd been traveling light my whole life. Winding up Sunset Plaza Drive, I saw houses peeking out behind security gates with driveways edged in lush palms. Bougainvillea in clashing shades, pinks and oranges, tumbled off walls. The hillside was wedged with modern white houses like stacked boxes, Mediterranean stuccos, Spanish bungalows, chalets, even an A-frame house rumored to host Saturday night orgies. Catherine's house sat a third of the way up, a contemporary stone one-story with big windows. During my four-month stay, I got a taste of the high-rolling life, LA style. People in the Hollywood Hills rocked and rolled, all night long. I found an endless stream of parties overflowing with booze and coke. When everyone else wanted to call it a night, I would still be flying high, sitting with my guitar and trying to write songs, not wanting the good times to end. I was sure that people were more interesting and profound on cocaine. The conversations could ramble on till dawn—bug-eyed, tight-jawed philosophers solving the world's problems or revealing their deepest thoughts and fears. If I had nothing to say once the last line got snorted and the bottle went dry, it didn't dampen my enthusiasm for going another round with more revelers the next night.

When Catherine went back East, I holed up in the house, drinking by myself and filling spiral notebooks and cassettes with unfinished songs. As promised, Phil Seymour recorded

"We Don't Get Along," for his album, and I planned to release a solo single when it came out. Then I would have a double whammy of attention, put together a band, and be on my way. I missed having a gal music partner, someone to help shoulder the load of my ambitions, but living in Catherine's beautiful house and collecting unemployment was fine consolation. I'd grown up in crappy apartments for plenty of years and had made my own money since the age of ten. A temporary free ride felt long overdue.

Catherine's friend Leonard did all her photography work from his lab in West Hollywood. I liked going there with her and knew we would hang out in the studio for a long time. Huge portraits and artsy prints lay in stacks or hung from clips against the walls, sometimes a dozen versions of the same picture. Leonard told me they weren't the same at all—they were mistakes, prints gone wrong—but I couldn't see any difference. Chemical fumes from his darkroom infused the air. Leonard looked like he might be old, in his forties even, because he had crinkly brown eyes and a curly, grey beard trimmed close to his chin. He wore a loose, dark shirt, track pants, and sneakers. Tiny dreadlocks fell out of a wool cap; when he moved his head, they would bounce at the side of his face. Leonard had the gentle, quiet way of a loner, someone who liked his own company. He also had the best cocaine in the city, according to those who knew about such things. I went to buy but always ended up hanging out and getting high with him.

Most nights at Leonard's the radio was on. Background noise—we weren't listening, really. On this evening, the announcer's subdued and shaken voice cut through our conversation. Breaking news: someone murdered John Lennon. All reason shook from the rafters. Not many details, but each one, bloody and sharp, shards of glass. Shot in the back, at his apartment building, after a recording session. After the newsbreak, the station went back to its regular format. My regular format was destroyed. Catherine disappeared to call her husband. Then Leonard disappeared. Grief isolated us within minutes. From as far back as I could remember, John Lennon had been there. Every phase of the Beatles had a corresponding link with my life: from "Twist and Shout" to "Come Together," from cartoons and zany movies to bed-in protests and breakups. I thought about how narrowly he might have escaped death, just seconds and steps from the safety of his building. Never had the veil between worlds felt so threadbare. Alone, I cried for the hopelessness of having no choice or security or control. I cried for Yoko and Sean.

Leonard came back with a glass pipe I hadn't seen before. He lit the bowl with a lighter. After a few hits, he showed me how to inhale off the pipe. Freebasing now—what difference did it make? Freebasing could bring anyone to their knees, hard-core, right on the heels of hooking you. I didn't care. Catherine was still on the phone somewhere with her husband, so there was no one to talk me out of it. Freebasing felt like nothing; the high didn't have the power to snatch me from the shock of Lennon being killed. No one could escape that nightmare.

Eventually I dragged myself out into the dawn light, where the world looked harsh and colorless. John Lennon might be famous, but he was a musician, an artist. Far removed but one of us. Lennon's killer put the stalker-crazed-fan into the milieu, creating a template that would make many musicians and celebrities cautious and fearful. News of the murder dominated the last weeks of December, casting a nihilistic shadow. Catherine went home, leaving me in charge of the Sunset Plaza house. My mom came to spend Christmas with me. Our little family still stuck together on holidays.

There were seven days of 1980 left, but fortune doesn't need much time to work her favors. In that last week, I met Charlotte from the Go-Go's, agreed to play eight shows in four nights with them as a sub, borrowed a bass, and learned their songs.

If I hadn't been at the Whisky Christmas night, or gone to the bathroom right when I did, someone else could have likely been onstage with the Go-Go's on New Year's Eve in 1980. I wasn't the only girl whose name had come up as a substitute for their ailing bassist. Perhaps another girl would have done the job and made her exit, and the existing lineup would have stayed intact. Or maybe it was meant to be, preordained, and I would have seen Charlotte somewhere else and accepted her offer. Respecting the vagaries of random chance and acceding to the possibility of divine order is about as close to religion as I'll ever get. I can tell you this: I was on cloud nine, a dreamer's cloud. The biggest and fluffiest, the king of the cumulus.

I slept halfway through the first day of 1981; nothing mattered, not sunlight, daytime, breakfast, or lunch. Chores could wait, and day jobs—surely a thing of the past. The two shows each consecutive night at the Whisky filled my head. Settling in over the next six performances with the Go-Go's was enough to hit a rhythm, a new routine as easy as shifting gears.

Meeting Charlotte in the Whisky bathroom truly changed my life. The entire order of things flung into the air as free-floating parts, latching together and landing on the ground as a new system. Beyond pivotal, it became defining, and a part of me has always remained linked to the four women in the Go-Go's—girls then, whom I had known for less than two weeks. Possibly all of it pulsed with some newfound heartbeat from the start, beneath the surface: a push and shove of wills, dreams, and converging destinies. I was sure, like Newton's third law of motion, that the force I exerted upon them would match theirs upon me.

The day after our four-night stand, a music columnist in the *LA Times* wrote about my appearance: "Who was the brash young rockette on stage with the Go-Go's?" the story lede went.

Then he upped my cachet by calling me a "familiar figure on the local scene." The story said I would be playing with the Go-Go's on their upcoming tour. That was all right by me, but I didn't know where his info came from. The Go-Go's hadn't mentioned any tour. Sometimes you don't ask questions, just let things unfold. The next day came another *LA Times* Go-Go's article, this one with the headline "Why Can't the Go-Go's Get a Record Deal?" This story recalled the exuberant Whisky shows. Maybe the press mentions sparked problems in the band and brought a showdown with Margot. What happened behind the scenes didn't concern me. Lay low, keep cool—that was the only way to play it. But I couldn't help visualizing, fantasizing, and improbably manifesting my place in the Go-Go's.

Within a week Charlotte called to ask if I would consider sticking around. I had scripted the conversation over and over in my head: "Yes, I'd like to be in the band. But only if I could be one of the songwriters," I added. "Absolutely," she said, "Another writer only makes the band stronger and better." She also made it clear that they all felt my musicianship elevated the Go-Go's and could help their chances for success.

Our next gigs had been scheduled for the end of January. It was time to dive into rehearsals, this time with me as an official member. I liked to think I had willed my place in the band, but reality offered another probable cause. As is wont to happen in bands, Margot had landed on the hot seat with a target on her head. Ignorant of their history and the fact that Margot basically started the band, I didn't ask questions. I couldn't know what it felt like with her, but I sure knew the five of us felt irrefutably right together. Even the loyal drummer, Gina, wanted me. Taking the cowardly way, the band made Ginger do the dirty work of kicking Margot out. The Go-Go's blew off settlement terms with her, a big mistake that would bite us down the road.

Over the next several months of shows, the lineup change shifted the dynamics significantly. Our collective drive had an impetuous, devil-may-care veneer. Each night hundreds of fans lined up for show after show, refuting the record industry opinions that Ginger kept fielding. She had been "shopping" the Go-Go's to every major label in town. They had all sent representatives after the band had returned from England earlier that year, and all of them had passed on giving the band a deal. At our January Roxy show, only one record exec came. He'd had his eye on the Go-Go's. After seeing our set and the way the crowd responded, Miles Copeland decided he wanted to sign us to his International Record Syndicate, or IRS Records. IRS was the vanguard of a dynasty Miles had created, using his family history as inspiration. His parents had been secret agents. His brother Ian helmed the booking agency Frontier Booking International (FBI), and his other brother played drums in the band the Police, who Miles also managed. His management companies used the acronyms LAPD and CIA. It seemed kind of corny, but the businesses prospered, and there's no denying Miles had a certain genius to his schemes. He backed it up with unshakable conviction that his ideas were right. I thought Miles was interesting: handsome, opinionated, and charismatic, but a little like a combustible droid.

Coming into our dressing room dressed in his customary button-up shirt and jacket, his face a ruddy pinkish tinge, his hair so blond it appeared very nearly white, and giving us a penetrating blue stare, Miles acted like our signing was a done deal.

"Girls, let's make a record," he boomed, filling the small area with his certainty.

He may as well have been talking to a group of lemurs. Buzzing from our show, intent on some pressure-free fun, no one wanted to talk business with this guy. I had gotten high on coke with Char, Belinda had taken a 'lude, and Jane and Gina chortled over beers. Friends and Hollywood denizens squeezed their way through the door or waited on the other side. Ginger, rolling her eyes, shepherded Miles out of the way to butter up the elusive record industry catch who had landed in our net. A few days later, knowing she had Miles in her back pocket, Ginger hit the major labels again, smartly thinking one bite might attract some bigger fish. In meeting after meeting, the rejections came. All of the refusals were from men, all of them justified with the same rationale: there had never been an all-female band successful enough to warrant taking a chance on us.

Miles kept courting the band and making his case. He approached the music business differently than the big guys. Artistic freedom, smart business models, low expense, no debt—this was how he had built the career of the Police. Ginger took us to visit the offices and meet the president and staff—all of them young, enthusiastic, a little nerdy, and passionate about the Go-Go's. Their earnestness made for a nice balance to Miles's forceful bombast. Before the next show at Perkins Palace in Pasadena, our biggest venue to headline yet, Ginger huddled with us backstage. She laid it out: if the band wanted to move forward and record a full-length album, IRS had presented the only offer.

Since I had joined the band, my life had gotten so good that all this talk just meant icing on the rock 'n' roll cake. Not having a day job, playing music in a cool band I loved to packed clubs—all of it, one sweet deal. The Go-Go's even had a payroll: everyone got forty dollars a week and our rent paid. I had leased an apartment with a friend right off Sunset Boulevard, where I could stroll down the hill to the clubs and bars. Rockers and fans crowded the street; cars cruised with music from cassettes blasting from the windows. It was my time, our Strip, our town—easy to think the Go-Go's name could go from the club marquees to a record cover in the bins and promo posters in the windows of Tower Records and Licorice Pizza. But I couldn't have come close to imagining having an album in record stores across the country.

18

GOOD MOJO

The band and Miles gathered on April Fools' Day at Kelbo's, a lowbrow tiki joint on Pico. Over flaming tropical drinks served in giant coconuts, under backlit walls draped in fishnets, five signatures committed to the recording contract our lawyer, Emily, had vetted. Having female representation reinforced our sense of renegade girl power wattage. Marking the occasion at Kelbo's fit our off-kilter humor and approach, and the cardinal rule to not take ourselves too seriously. How could we? You couldn't have found a scrappier bunch of young girls. Patching and piecing things together, making up what we didn't know, and merging a spin-off feminist thrust just by doing whatever the hell we wanted.

Fuck big budgets, bloated excess and waste—our band was making a pop record with a punk rock ethic. In those days, big record companies gave lucrative record advances to bands. The money concealed and distracted grateful musicians from the reality that they would most likely get fucked and forgotten. Often, bands never got out from under the debt. The Go-Go's took no advance, and our producer, Richard Gottehrer, agreed to make the record for about forty thousand dollars. It was a modest budget for a signed group but a gold mine for a little band who had come up from the punk scene.

Miles came up with the idea to use Richard to produce the first Go-Go's album. I knew nothing about producers, had never paid attention to who had produced the music I loved. But I knew some of the records Richard had made, and the choice thrilled me. Just the Robert Gordon/Link Wray, Dr. Feelgood, and Richard Hell and the Voidoids credits alone were convincing enough—but the fact that he had made the first two Blondie albums? No one would be better for us. Learning more about Richard's background and career added more cachet: he had been in the '60s band the Strangeloves and written unique hits like "I Want Candy" and "Hang On Sloopy." Richard adapted his '60s throwback sensibilities and classic girl group experience to fit current, fresh music. He knew how to bring out the essence of a band.

My life felt complete. In addition to having my rent paid, the band I loved had a record deal and the perfect producer. But wait, there was more! Another bombshell to magnify all the greatness. We learned that the first Go-Go's album would be recorded in New York City. Every expectation I had dreamt up for my career had always been nebulous, a shape-shifting goal of "making it" in the music business by playing in a band. Living out my dream had a sharpness to it, like being catapulted into a hyperpresence, nowhere better than the immediate now. I felt fully awake, determined to enjoy every minute. The band left for the East Coast the day after our Kelbo's signing party.

The Go-Go's hit New York like we owned it. Our energy and excitement gave us the kind of edge Manhattan embraces. Checking into the Wellington Hotel at Fifty-sixth and Seventh Avenue, checking into the adventure of a lifetime and bonding like superglue from the get-go. Having the time of our lives came close to overshadowing our reason for being there—oh yeah, to make a record. We were hungover and distracted, impatient and cheeky, in love and in lust, indulgent and hungry, anticipating only what might happen later in the night. Everything about who we were and what we were living seeped into our record, stored to tape, adhering to oxide as readily as analog signals. Our youth and joy were the intangible and unprovable source informing our performances on the twelve songs that managed to get recorded in the midst of all the insanity.

Insanity headquarters at the Wellington was located in the one-bedroom suite on the fifteenth floor hosting Belinda, Gina, and me. Seven floors down, Jane and Charlotte shared their own suite. The recording sessions were booked for Penny Lane Studios, a small facility with a reduced price to go with our budget. There was no shortage on enthusiasm, though. Producer Richard and engineer/coproducer Rob Freeman made each of us feel important and essential to the record, treating every member with equal respect and listening to any ideas, opinions, and concerns. Richard chose eleven songs out of our repertoire, and the tracking started right away. The jokes started right away too. Nothing escaped our collective keen eye, no opportunity bypassed to make fun or give private nicknames to anyone drawing our attention. The studio tech guys had no idea why hiking up their pants and wiping their nose or name-dropping rock stars caused so much laughter. After a while, neither did we—but every joke sprung eternal.

Richard didn't want to change the band. He wanted the songs to be played slower, so the melodies and hooks had room to breathe. We understood his approach and agreed. When he could, he divided the guitars up, separating the two identical strumming parts Jane and Charlotte often played, getting one or both of them to do mechanical "stabs" on a beat instead, like on the song "Tonite." For bass, he told me to watch Gina's foot on the kick drum pedal and to hit a note every time she hit the drum. Following his advice, focusing on the notes and bass lines, worried about straying away from his formula, it took years before I began to bring more fluidity to my parts. I had borrowed a black Fender Precision from John Ciambotti, the bass player in the band Clover. Clover backed up Elvis Costello on his first album, *My Aim Is True*, so I thought it added good mojo to use the same bass from those songs. The basic tracks were recorded all together, while overdubs for solos, vocals and percussion, or simple synth lines happened right after or during a separate session.

We moved quickly through what would turn out to be a classic debut, not a clinker in the batch. I was proud of the varied subject matter of the songs, from insomnia on "You Can't Walk in Your Sleep (If You Can't Sleep)" to girl gang empowerment on several solid anthems. Even the songs dealing with relationships or romance weren't sappy love songs. "Lust to Love" and "Fading Fast" portrayed strong women who knew what they wanted.

When it came to "We Got the Beat," the band had misgivings about recording and including it on the album; a different version had already come out as a single in England on Stiff Records and had some traction as a minor dance club hit. Richard finally got us to re-record the song, double tracking the drums at Record Plant. Having trouble locking in as a rhythm section, we stopped and took a pizza break, then nailed the new version in a single take.

After finishing eleven songs, Richard decided the album needed one more. He didn't want any of the others from our set and surprised us with a cover song written by the legendary Ellie Greenwich. Richard tried to convince us with his usual excitement that the Go-Go's could have a hit with the song he had picked.

"Gone, gone, gone, gone; yeah, yeah, yeah," it went, in classic girl group style.

Most likely he could have done a great version with us. Richard has spot-on instincts, but the band took a united stand against him. Not because the song lacked anything—but because everyone felt strongly that only our own songs should go on the record. Discussions continued for a couple of days with no consensus, until Charlotte brought up a song she knew of. I had shown her my tune "Can't Stop the World" one night, and now she suggested it for the last track. I caught my breath and tried to be cool and nonchalant, as desperate to keep my hopes in check as I was to not let on how important it was. Having a song on our album would make me a full, contributing member and writer—more than a late addition, the last to arrive. When everyone agreed it belonged on the record, the Go-Go's became my family, the only thing that mattered to me. The stakes had never been high enough to matter, and now when they were, Charlotte had been my advocate and rest of the band had sealed the deal.

Still, there were insecurities. Working up "Can't Stop the World" right there in the studio, just before recording it, I worried. How could my song sound as good as the rest of them? The arrangement had a good flow, and Gina came through with killer drum parts, but it felt like the new kid. Plus, Charlotte and Jane had mined a songwriting vein prior to me joining and had written a consummate collection of songs. The band had been playing them for a couple of years, and they were tried and true, and tight. It was some time later, after hearing repeatedly from fans who told me "Can't Stop the World" had made it on their favorites list, that I started to believe my contribution held up alongside the rest of the album.

19

WILD JOKERS

In New York, the intensity of our camaraderie kept growing, a creation of its own force. Just breathing the air around each other charged the band chemistry. We were like newlyweds on a honeymoon, determined to inhale life together, filled with desire and euphoria. And drugs and alcohol.

Drinking had become my primary drug of choice, with cocaine playing a supporting role. I discovered that I could drink more if I did blow. My guy in LA, Leonard, sent packets of cocaine to the hotel via Federal Express. Each delivery was meticulously packaged; within cello-taped foam backing, I would find the little folded white piece of paper called a "bendel." They looked like tiny envelopes and held a gram or half-gram of coke.

Band dinners on the Go-Go's account kicked off in these early days. Our first took us to a swank Indian restaurant near the UN. The owner, Shenil, whom we nicknamed "Chenille Bedspread"—as usual, only funny to us—became part of our New York posse. The jolly restaurateur invited the entire band into the kitchen after a dinner in which he cooked up batches of a new drug called ecstasy alongside delicious curries. Chenille Bedspread turned us on to the crazy and unpredictable high. It felt like all drugs combined, wrapped up in a love fest.

In our Wellington suite, Belinda and Gina had the bedroom, with two twin beds in it. I got the living room, with a fold-out sofa bed. Some nights, one twin mattress would get dragged out into the hallway, a signal to stay out, the bedroom was being used—meaning a Go-Go was making out or passing out with a boy. The living room, where I slept, had no privacy. That didn't stop me from having a fling with a cute musician who I laid around with, scattering cans of beer all around my sofa bed like Wellington hillbillies. The carousing and debauchery escalated with goofy escapades and scenarios we thought up daily. I worked my ass off being the life of the party, with an endless enthusiasm and compulsion to be a merrymaking prankster. Enlisting my roommates to help me carry out "scientific" experiments, I bought a bag full of pink coconut-encased Sno Ball Hostess cupcakes and timed how long it took for one to land on the sidewalk. The drop had to be perfect to surprise distracted New Yorkers with a little cake explosion on the pavement a few feet in front of their stride.

A metallic roof spanned the inner square of the Wellington near the second floor, and many of the hotel rooms had windows surrounding the square. I hadn't gone on tour yet and would never throw a TV out a hotel window, but we held "sound contests" comparing the noise different items made when tossed on the metal roof below. Our kitchen had a view of a couple's bedroom across the gap; spying on them became a daily obsession, the three of us gathered around our window each morning to watch the woman charge around in a slip and bullet bra while her husband read the newspaper in bed. One morning Gina grabbed a grapefruit and took aim, landing it through the open window with the skill of a pitching pro. We cried laughing as the woman jumped in surprise, picked up the fruit, and failed to get the man's interest in the odd occurrence. She marched to the window just in time to see us in hysterics and slammed the window shut, pulling the drapes on our fun. Calling the prank an improvised play, Belinda and I were inspired to keep making up "plays" starring ourselves and performing them for the endless and recurring entertainment of our bandmates. Nothing got old; the repetition only made it funnier—to us. Onlookers or people who worked with us always felt left out of the joke, the circle, the fun.

My individual relationships within the band were fluid affairs, with constructs that changed over time and circumstance. In the years we spent together, I would come to know every facial expression and recognize each of my friends' singular quirks. The way Jane could flip like a switch from open and amiable to a steel-melting blowtorch if something violated her sense of righteousness. How Charlotte would seemingly retreat into her own world, then surprise me with a quick-witted one-liner—as if she were in her head and in the room, both places at once. And every single day, at some point Gina would reveal the sweet softness under her tough and salty shell. I discovered quickly that Belinda was careful about who she revealed herself to. The contrary shyness, at odds with her ambition, also kept most people in the dark about the fact that she was the most glamorous goofball I would ever know.

During my first year in the band, in Belinda I found an accomplice willing to get as wild and out there as I dared. If an occasion arose where the night could go longer and trouble could be found, with one look we would know the other was game. One night, dressed in sequins and stilettos, we staged a mock "catfight," rolling around on the floor of Bonds, a Times Square club where the Clash had just played. A normal guy would have been repelled by such antics, but not Danny Harvey, a young, hotshot guitar player with a blond pompadour who decided I looked like too much fun to bypass. Danny played with a rockabilly band, so for the remainder of our time in New York, Belinda and I hung out with a crew of baby-faced lookers with retro hair and clothes. Private, word-of-mouth after-hours bars where you could drink till dawn fed our young appetites to keep the party going. Danny didn't drink and usually ended up chaperoning me through the night.

Our cute rockabilly guys weren't the only ones who caught our eye. With Belinda, I was like a boy-crazed teenager, objectifying hot guys with the name "booty" or just "boot." It was the most reckless, silly, and consuming fun I'd ever had in my life. It more than made up for missing out on the joys of childhood and adolescence.

Depravity didn't keep the band occupied twenty-four hours a day. A few doors down from the Wellington, Carnegie Hall had a small revival house theater with great repertory programming. Belinda had an extensive knowledge of classic foreign films, directors, and actors, so we passed many afternoons sitting through double features. ("Booty," she whispered when Dirk Bogarde appeared on screen in *Death in Venice*.) Through Belinda, I got hip to the Italian classics from Fellini to Visconti. Gina knew all about art house and cult movies. She was full of stories about people she had known or grown up with in Baltimore, making it sound like they could all have been characters in a John Waters film. We were all avid readers; science fiction, biographies, classics, and bestsellers got passed around or discussed. Breakfast and walks to the bodegas near still-sleazy Times Square were taken in pairs or groups, as were shopping expeditions to scour the Lower East Side for thrift store clothes and shoes.

It was Belinda who came up with the name *Beauty and the Beat* for the album. It got a thumbs-up from everyone, no debate. From there, everyone brainstormed photo ideas, and we came up with the face masks and towel-wrapped bodies, the bubble bath shots inspired by an old Shelley Winters publicity shot. Ginger got towels from Macy's—and after the shoot, she folded and returned them for a refund. George DuBois shot us in Jane and Charlotte's less debauched suite. The face masks cracked and stung and looked weird; we tried a few products before we found one that worked for an extended time. For the bubble bath shots, each of us took turns sitting in the tub, wearing strapless bras and tube tops to reveal bare shoulders. Keeping the bubbles thick and high kept our manager, Ginger, busy. I posed with a champagne bottle, pouring it into a glass, doing it over and over until George got the right shot. The photos and artwork ensured our clothes or hairstyles could never date the record.

By this point the album had gone way over its allotted time and budget. Producer Richard put in his own money to finish when the money ran out. In the nearly two months the Go-Go's had spent in NYC, the quintessential spirit of the band had crystallized. Nothing would ever come close to matching the lightness and adventure we found there. Our wildness had a purity and simplicity, as if the band were conjoined and needed to go through a collective adolescence, pushing boundaries and cementing bonds. No responsibility dogged us: we had done our job, we'd brought the songs, we'd played them. In the Go-Go's I had found everything, an "us versus them" that had me on the winning side for once. An exclusive club with room for only five members. I was in the band of my dreams.

In New York, I had also found a romantic love. In between studio time, drunken nights, band dinners, and nights on the town, I had fallen for Danny. For the first time in my life, I felt loved by a boy. Asking how he could tolerate my drunkenness while being sober, he simply said, "Because you're sweet and smart when you don't drink." I thought I was pretty fucking great when I drank too. Danny's face looked like it had been shaped with a chisel: carved cheekbones, defined brows, and squared chin complete with the tiniest of dented clefts. Danny also got the bonanza of a gap in his two front teeth. It made his smile a mix of troublemaker and boyish charm. He could have won me over without the looks, though: hours of middle-of-the-night conversations at Manhattan diners revealed him to be Mensa smart and Bill Hicks funny. Danny's band, called Levi and the Ripchords, held its own on the club circuit in New York and London. Our romance started nearly equal as musicians. He held the edge in experience, but the Go-Go's could sell out LA.

That changed soon after finishing *Beauty and the Beat*. The Go-Go's broke a house attendance record with a gig at the legendary Peppermint Lounge. The difference between it and our last New York gig astonished me. The audience knew they were seeing a band destined to break out, playing bigger places next time. John Belushi, our new fan and one of the most famous and beloved names in America, introduced us, stamping his approval squarely on our heads.

The Go-Go's had to go home, back to LA. Moving out of our Wellington shared suites had a bittersweet burn. There had been a suspended unreality to our time in New York. That spring of 1981, countless young women enrolled in college, looked for jobs and started careers, moved out from their families, or chose to start families of their own. But only five had spent a couple of months in Manhattan making this record together. Only five were the Go-Go's, and none of us could predict how the carefree and unfettered joy of being five girls in a band would never be easy again.

20

UNFORGIVEN

Beauty and the Beat was mixed, mastered, and finished. All of the Go-Go's assembled for a listening session at the IRS office. Track after track, we listened in frustrated despair to the result of our hard work. The album had not turned out as expected.

The live Go-Go's sounded raucous, full of attitude and energy, not wimpy and clean like this. Some tracks had been recorded too slow, so they had sped them up, making the vocals sound higher and thinner. "I sound like a chipmunk," Belinda said, disgusted. Our shot had been blown, and I didn't even know who to blame. Surely not Miles—he had left us alone to make the record. Not us—we had shown up with a pile of great songs and a brash rock 'n' roll spirit. We blamed the producers. We put our trust in Richard, and then he had gone and turned us into a '60s lightweight watered-down pop group! Miles and the record company staff were unconcerned with our dismay. The letdown felt monumental, but I was in no position to do anything about it. None of us were. I rolled back my expectations for the record and focused instead on the upcoming national Beautify America Tour. For IRS the tour was all about promoting the record, but for me hitting the road meant I got to do what I loved more than anything: have the time of my life rockin' out onstage with my best mates. Night after freaking night. Yeah, the record was a disappointment. So what? I still got to go on tour.

The first single, "Our Lips Are Sealed," backed with a bonus track, "Surfing and Spying," dropped at the beginning of June.

Of all the songs, this one suffered least from what I perceived as the failings of the production. The song is a perfect pop tune with an atypical structure, unexpected chord changes, smart lyrics unlike any other song, and tons of hooks. Jane wrote it by herself but gave credit because of the inspiration: a love letter Terry Hall from the Specials wrote her. The Go-Go's put our distinctive stamp on the arrangement and music. The parts fit together like the links of a chain, from the chugging chord intro, solid beat, and rolling bass to Charlotte's chiming arpeggio guitar notes. Instead of a common stand-alone chorus, the key lines come as a refrain at the end of each verse. Belinda sang with authority and exuberance, and the lyrics told a relatable story—it could be about friends, coworkers, or lovers. The bridge is a short, shining interlude with guitar and bass interplay behind Jane singing. It sets up perfectly the soaring verse and chorus to end the song.

For nearly six months this song helped push our van, and eventually our tour bus, across the country. "Our Lips Are Sealed" brought us to Canada, the UK, and finally Australia, where it reached number two. In the United States, the song stayed on the charts for almost six months, finally getting to the number twenty spot on *Billboard*, the industry bible, by the end of the year. It took close to ninety live shows and countless interviews, concert and record reviews, radio station visits, television appearances, and photo sessions to get it there. After months of work didn't do the job, IRS Records hired an independent radio promotions guy to push it. They believed in the single too much to let it wither off the charts. Even with that extra push, enormous resistance from major radio programmers blocked every effort. It seemed like nothing was enough to prove our band worthy of radio airplay. If not for the college stations and rogue DJs, the public might not have heard the Go-Go's on the radio at all.

There were other places to hear and see the Go-Go's, though, the most significant being MTV. With much annoyance and reluctance, the band agreed to make a music video. I couldn't believe I had to spend a rare and precious day off on this dumb waste of time. The video had no concept other than Belinda behind the wheel of an old convertible Buick from Rent-a-Wreck, driving her bandmates aimlessly around and stopping at random places. I found it incredibly embarrassing and argued vehemently against pulling up in front of the "Trashy Lingerie" shop on La Cienega. What the hell did this place have to do with us? Parked in front of the store, the band is presumably shopping for lingerie while Jane sings her "hush, my darling" part sitting in the convertible. Belinda couldn't be bothered to exit the car and can be seen ducking down in the front seat—my favorite part. As the driving sequence continued, we had the idea to get out and splash around in the Beverly Hills fountain at Santa Monica and Wilshire Boulevards. If the cops or authorities interfered, then at least something exciting might happen. No one came to arrest us, so the band danced and got soaked while the camera captured every mindless minute. When the director set us up to perform on the stage of the Central (now the Viper Room) on Sunset, I felt better about the video. At least it would show us being a band playing and singing together.

All my doubts about the importance of videos were quickly erased. "Our Lips Are Sealed" went into high rotation at MTV, just as the music station grew powerful legs, about to stomp all over music business norms and break bands all through the '80s. The video cost practically nothing—Miles used the leftover Police budget from A&M Records. But for all it lacked, our video did the job it needed to do: present the Go-Go's to the public without any airs or gloss. With an MTV playlist heavy on Hall and Oates, Phil Collins, Journey, and Rod Stewart, the Go-Go's stood out. Even cooler bands like the Pretenders, the

Cars, and Blondie looked super slick next to our music video. The Go-Go's couldn't claim to sound like punk rock anymore, but we were a true indie band making records and videos void of excess and theatrics. When bands like REM, the Replacements, and Husker Dü became kings of an industry-tagged "alternative" genre, we could have easily gotten credit for helping to pave the way.

We were also the first all-girl band that countless kids, teens, and young adults had ever seen. I had been around for the Runaways; I'd played with the gals in Girlschool. There had been others before us, but we were the band MTV put in people's living rooms. We were five women having a good time like a bunch of girlfriends might do, except we played guitars and drums and wrote catchy songs. It was revolutionary. "Our Lips Are Sealed" also launched Belinda as a star, and not just for her photogenic looks. Our singer had the charm, magnetism, and voice to take us to the top. Our band had the songs and chemistry to make it an electric rise getting there.

The album came out a few weeks after our first single. The initial pressing had a weird peach-colored cover: par for the course, I thought—not only did our record sound bad, it looked bad. After we insisted on a new version, eventually all copies of *BATB* were blue. In time, what we thought had been a too-sterile production stopped bothering us. My opinion changed proportionally with the increasing sales. Whether colored peach or blue, sped up to chipmunk vocals, or lacking grit, it didn't stop several million people from wanting to own a copy over the next year. None of the stuff we disliked stopped our first album from being one of the most successful debuts ever. Sometimes I've wondered what it would be like to re-record *Beauty and the Beat* the way I would like it to sound, with thick, full tones and texture. But then I remember the ephemeral spirit infusing the recording process, the anticipation and joy of a fleeting time, and I know something else was captured that could never be reproduced.

A homecoming show at the Palladium celebrated the release of the record. The venue sold out in hours. Robert Hilburn of the *LA Times* gushed, saying our single was "a delightful mix of the sly innocence of '60s girl-pop and the snappiness of today's new-wave style." The Go-Go's had conquered Los Angeles again, to a greater extent. Friends, local musicians, and our entire record company and team swarmed the backstage, everyone drunk on our good fortune. Recklessly overjoyed, I ended up at a party in Laurel Canyon and decided it would be fun to take some LSD. Having done a fair amount of hallucinogens in Texas as a teen, I thought I knew what to expect. But the mescaline, mushrooms, and acid I had tried proved to be amateur stuff compared to this shit. It fucked me up majorly. At a peaking point, the band tracked me down at 8:00 a.m. I had forgotten about our very first in-store appearance, at Licorice Pizza Records on the Sunset Strip. A limo would be picking me up in an hour. Introducing panic into an acid trip is a really bad combination. I threw on a Go-Go's T-shirt and a pair of red patent leather stilettos and tried to freshen up my makeup from the show the night before, with clownish rouge and smudged lipstick. The car came with the band inside, everyone extremely annoyed. Belinda finally snapped at me: "I can't believe you were so stupid to do acid." It made me cry. I couldn't believe I had let down my band like that either. Crying and tripping is also a really bad combination.

At the record store Licorice Pizza, the exhilaration and delight of seeing a thousand people lined up was completely overshadowed by my freaking out. Somehow, I had to get through this. Signing records for hours should have been a dream come true, but being completely out of my mind on acid turned it into a nightmare. I would ask a fan her name, then spell it all wrong, like "Brino" for Robin. I'd pass it on to Char and she would look up at the girl and say, "Brino?" Folks kept saying "Have a nice trip" in passing as we were leaving on tour the following day. "How do they know?" I wondered, in a panic. The acid trip lasted thirty-six hours, long after the event had ended. The car dropped me off and I fell asleep, only to awaken with peaking waves of psychedelic rushes snaking around my brain. I lay perfectly still to calm down; I ran in place to move it through my system. I worried I would never come down, lost at sea forever in an LSD ocean. The last psychedelic trip of my life is one I could have done without for sure, but the story became one of our epic favorites.

As much as the Go-Go's were determined dreamers, driven to make our mark, not one of us thought the record we had made in the New York spring months could possibly end up being the number-one record in America. When we embarked on that first national tour to "Beautify America," selling 100,000 copies seemed like a lofty goal. Miles believed in breaking a band over several albums, like the Police had done, so we were in it for the long haul. Our long haul began in a white Econoline van. The five of us, our luggage, and four crew guys filled the van, while our equipment bumped along behind us in a U-Haul trailer. The crew humped and set up gear then split up to do sound, lights, and stage tech for the gig. We drove from city to city, playing clubs from San Francisco to Cleveland, from Boston to Houston. I became adept at falling asleep in contorted positions any time of day or night with the clamor of voices and music for a lullaby. Soon the van reeked of unbathed crew, food wrappers, cigarettes, and stale beer. Scrawling all over the interior with magic markers relieved our resentment for the stinky vehicle. That van, or one like it, should be in the Rock and Roll Hall of Fame Museum. There's no better symbol of determination, discomfort, and dues-paying than a band in a van. Every night brought a cheap hotel, two to a room, taking turns so a fifth girl could have her own room for a break. I didn't like having my own room. The tour checked off every slumber party and summer camp and birthday party box I had never gotten, with rock 'n' roll, booze, and some sex and drugs thrown on top. I didn't want to miss a second because of needing some time to myself. I was the girl always up in everyone's business, scared some kind of fun might slip by me.

Nonstop rock 'n' roll, playing music to a jammed club of grooving fans, is intoxicating. Enough to make me, at twenty-two, a little cocky and sharp, ready to cut open the rest of the night and let it bleed all over the place. I was willful: I could do anything I wanted. Fuck it, I could even do anything I didn't want. And on a night in Atlanta, I didn't want to go back to the hotel and crawl in bed. Right after a show, the high feels precious; it's something you own, that no one else can touch or take away, and you don't want to let it go, not yet. Connecting with my band, executing our parts, locked together, a part of a whole. Connecting with the crew, making sure everything goes smoothly. Connecting with the audience—everyone rocking out together. I had wanted this kind of connection for so long.

It was early in the tour and I was trying to live the part to the fullest. I was raring to go, looking for trouble, drunk and high on beer and blow, and someone had some quaaludes. Not used to downers, the combination left me close to incoherent. I stumbled into a party in one of our crew's rooms, where Kent, a pro at road stunts from his years working with the Runaways, had set up his video camera. The things that happened in that room would have been forgotten if not for that recording—I had no recollection of the night until I saw the tape. And what I saw the next day filled me with horror and shame.

One of our crew sits on the toilet with his pants down trying to get off, but he had taken a massive amount of 'ludes and could barely move, much less get aroused. A horrified girl who had been at the show refuses to "help" him out, despite all of us urging her to do so. As the night and the tape roll on, our poor tech passes out on the bed, where he is subjected to frat-level hazing. I participate in a zombielike daze, spraying him with shaving cream and putting matches between his toes. At one point I wander out of the room, and a drum roadie appears on-screen with a vibrator buzzing. He pulls the guy's jeans down far enough to partially stick it in. The guys are all laughing, can't wait to give their mate shit about this tomorrow. I must have returned to the room because my dress is visible in the frame. My hand gives the vibrator a tap to steady it as it slips out, and then I wander off again, at which point the tape finally ends. A few years later the video made its way to a well-known smut purveyor and became deceivingly known as the Go-Go's sex tape. There's no sex, but it's as ugly and pointless as any cruelty is. The regret I have about being there and being involved is eternal. The shame is like a tide—it recedes but always returns. Any deep reflection about how I could have participated in victimizing another person leaves me sobbing in humiliation. I'm humbled by the knowledge that moral bankruptcy existed within me that night, and regardless of drugs and alcohol, it was inexcusable behavior. Some actions are unforgivable, and the repercussions are infinite.

21

NEXT TO MERLE

The stinky van had taken us to clubs all over the country, and I'd been on tour for over six weeks. Having a musician boy-friend who understood what my life entailed was helpful; love-lorn phone calls, letters, and postcards kept the long-distance romance going. But being separated for those lengths of time added a level of angst and drama to an intoxicating rigor of shows and travel. That was all manageable, though—the real drudgery was the promotion. Interviews, radio visits, and tons of ass-kissing are all normal to push a record, but no musician realizes how draining it is until she's in the thick of it. It didn't matter if we were hungover, hungry, or hadn't slept; the Go-Go's did everything, all requests granted. It never occurred to any of us to say no. An up-and-coming guy band might have gotten perfunctory treatment or a pass from the press, but no one wanted to pass on us. They all wanted to meet us and see what we were like. The curiosity and voyeuristic element kept our schedule booked solid. Some guys I knew in bands used touring as a way to get laid night after night—that sure wasn't part of our trip. The Go-Go's didn't have time for sex.

With very few exceptions, the journalists writing about our band were men. So were the radio DJs and program directors we visited—sometimes at the crack of dawn for the high-rated "drive time" shows. We posed for pictures, glad-handed, recorded station IDs: anything to make them pay attention and play our music. There were label representatives to meet, either from IRS or the distribution label, A&M Records. More men.

On the way to an interview or radio station with our label rep, we would discuss with straight faces whose turn it was to put on the knee pads, pretending one of us would have to blow a guy for airplay. Quite a few of the label guys didn't flinch, as if that were a perfectly normal thing for women to do. With others, our warped humor earned us respect and allegiance. These more off-kilter label guys pushed harder to promote the record after seeing how hard we worked. When I'd finally get to my hotel room and collapse on the bed, the dreaded schedule would slide under the door, filled with numbers to call. The "phoners"— interviews with journalists in upcoming towns—were split between the five of us but still left me overwhelmed. I tried to sound enthused and friendly, answering the same questions as if I had never heard them before. After a full day of work followed by a sound check at the club came the show.

With such an exhausting schedule, a joke at the right time could lift any beaten-down spirits. I tried to keep everyone laughing, keep it fun. I was always on, like an amp without a standby or off switch, burning hot. It didn't take much for any of us to set each other off, and we could laugh until we were gasping for air. The joys were found in our togetherness, playing our songs at the shows, seeing throngs of new fans, and sometimes getting to a hotel with a washer and dryer and enough time to do some laundry.

People always asked if we had groupies. The answer is no. It could warrant its own gender analysis research to ask why men don't do the groupie thing. I dislike generalizations and imposing traditional roles on men or women, but it seems like guys don't want to play supplicant to strong women. To make it even more interesting, the closest thing to a groupie scenario I saw were the occasions when a woman waited at our hotel in hopes of hooking up with a Go-Go. In time, as relationships suffered with our prolonged absences and increasing success, there might be the odd fling with a support band musician or someone in our crew. It was more the result of seeing the person on a regular basis and getting to know them. We favored mini-relationships or short flings over one-night stands.

By September, after a few months of van touring, we got our first tour bus. Because we were still on a budget, the coach was hired to transport both band and crew, but it was a giant, upwardly mobile sign of success. We delighted in the new features of our sumptuous chariot, exclaiming like a bunch of kids at the rows of bunk beds, cute little kitchenette, cushy lounge with TVs and VCRs—a clubhouse on wheels. Touring already felt unreal, like the ride of my life. Now the bus made that ride a comfy luxury, and I never wanted to go home.

Except I was going home, so to speak. The Go-Go's were playing Austin for the first time. Playing your hometown isn't like any other show, no matter how experienced you are. I was nervous. In the dressing room at Club Foot, the premier Austin nightclub in 1981, my mom got to meet the band before the show. They had heard a lot about her, and she was welcomed like an old friend. I shuffled her out, hoping to get myself into a calmer head space before taking the stage. We ran out to an insane crowd. There was nothing new about that; all the gigs were sellouts. But this was different—only to me. To Belinda, it was just another show, and she was in peak form, as were all my bandmates. As we went through our songs, I felt an overwhelming pride chased with a disconcerting self-conscious shyness. Staying next to my bass rig and the drum riser in a nondescript, invisible bass player stance, I couldn't enjoy the moment. It felt like someone had tossed, and I had reached out and caught, the baggage of my past. I couldn't reconcile it with my newfound success and didn't understand why, after all this time, here and now, this weight had landed onstage with me. Meanwhile, the

With my dad at Barton Springs, ca. 1961.
Courtesy of the author.

With Mom in 1967. She was a babe.
Courtesy of the author.

Unlucky thirteen, 1972.
Courtesy of the author.

TOP: First guitar, first band with Greenbriar kids, 1974.
Courtesy of the author.

BOTTOM: The Violators at Raul's in Austin, 1978.
© *1978 Ken Hoge.*

Backstage with the Textones, 1980.
Photo by Catherine Sebastian

Whisky ad featuring my first hero, Suzi Quatro;
the X show where I met Char; and shows by
the Go-Go's that marked my joining the band.

OPPOSITE: Bathroom Posing.
Photos by Catherine Sebastian.

Go-Go's backstage with our new fan,
John Belushi, at my first show in 1980.
Photo by Janette Beckman.

Third night at Whisky with a
borrowed Mustang bass, Jan. 2, 1981.
Photo by Catherine Sebastian.

Quickie first photo session with the new bassist: me.
Photo by Janette Beckman.

So many products, so many masks;
final choice: Pond's cold cream.
Photo by George DuBose.

Bubbles and bubbly.
Photo by George DuBose.

UPSET.
Courtesy of author.

Fell in love with my teenage crush, Clem Burke.
Photo by Robert Matheu.

Hurry up and wait: behind the scenes
of the "Vacation" video shoot.
Photo by Mick Haggerty.

From the clubs of Austin to the music biz
in LA, with Stevie Ray Vaughan.
Photo by Robert Matheu.

Bandstand! This was huge;
I grew up watching this show.
Photo by Robert Matheu.

My pal is a heartthrob.
Courtesy of author.

Rockin' in Rio with Rod Stewart.
Courtesy of author.

Rockergirl.
*Photo by
Donna Santisi.*

audience barely registered that a hometown girl was on the stage with this hot new band, even when I was introduced. After the show, I said hi to a handful of acquaintances and bye to my mom, then went off to party with a bunch of strangers who had plenty of blow. Confused feelings were nothing that an all-night bender couldn't put back in their place.

If that wasn't enough personal drama, four nights later the Go-Go's opened for the Pretenders in Tulsa, Oklahoma. My dad lived in Tahlequah and made the drive. We had salvaged somewhat of a relationship and had kept in touch with occasional letters. I had kept him informed about my move to LA and progress as a musician, but I hadn't seen him in more than five years. This night, I was far more interested in meeting and hanging out with the Pretenders than hosting my dad and his wife backstage. Our time before the show was a short reunion, with me situating them in special seats and then resuming my new friendship with Pretenders guitarist James Honeyman-Scott and the Texas girl he had married, Peggy Sue. The crowd was just as enthused for our opening set as they were for the headliners. After our show, I was buzzing with excitement about the night and found my dad to bring him backstage. We had a small trailer and dressing rooms can be awkward for non-entourage people, so they didn't stay long. I walked them to their car, stopping at the security exit to hug my dad goodbye.

He held me tightly and spoke quietly, just between us: "I was wrong. You have done great for yourself." It was an unexpected admission, and I didn't realize how much I wanted to hear it. I had done everything on my own and he knew it.

"I keep your Go-Go's record right next to my Merle Haggard," he said.

High praise, even if it was an alphabetical placement. On the bus that night, I lay in my bunk with the curtains pulled shut, sequestered from the usual shenanigans, relieved that the noise of the bus stifled my sobs. For the first time in my life, I felt fully what I had missed out on—what it was like to be a daughter making her daddy's eyes shine with pride.

The Rolling Stones hit the road for *Tattoo You* and hand-picked several American bands to open for them. The Stray Cats, Iggy Pop, Prince, and many others got coveted opening slots. The Go-Go's were offered the Rockford, Illinois, concert, the smallest and only indoor venue of the tour. Nothing in my imagination could have thrilled me more. Gina and I ran in circles around the hotel room. Ginger had to put up with daily calls from me making sure nothing had gone wrong: *yes, this is real.* I invited the two biggest Stones fans I knew: my mom and Saul Davis, the Textones manager, to meet me in Rockford for the show. Neither of them had any doubts about where I was heading with the Go-Go's, but my getting to do this show blew them away. This was the Rolling Stones, the greatest band in the world.

The day before, the Go-Go's flew into the small town. The arena might have been the smallest on the Stones tour—8,400 capacity—but to me it looked massive. IRS made giant posters featuring our faces and the phrase "Going to a Go-Go with the Rolling Stones" and put them all over our dressing room. During our sound check, I got thrill-zapped seeing Keith's guitars. I kept making up excuses to wander nonchalantly around backstage in the hopes of running into a Rolling Stone. After the catered dinner, Mick Jagger appeared, especially to say hello to us. Then came Charlie, the gentleman, to wish us well. No Bill Wyman, no Ron Wood, and most lamentably, no Keith. Wondering whether the Stones would watch our set gave me a measure of stage fright—would they like us? Luckily, our show felt well received, as much as any opening band can hope for, and I ran offstage feeling triumphant whether the Stones had seen us or not. I joined my mom and Saul and watched my second Stones concert from the audience, still dazed from having just played on the same stage. "Under My Thumb" led into "When the Whip Comes Down." Song after song, I watched in near rapture, high from the wealth of my luck and the vast, unknown possibilities that might be ahead. If this could happen, anything could happen.

22

BALANCE THE BUZZ

I called the Stones date a "pinnacle of success" and gratefully acknowledged each successive event as the Go-Go's accumulated a very cool collection of pinnacles. A week after playing on the same stage as my idols, Los Angeles welcomed us back with three sold-out shows at the Greek Theatre. Santana, Cher, and Liza Minnelli did multiple nights at the Greek that fall, and now the Go-Go's were in the same ranks. This was the biggest homecoming triumph yet, but "Our Lips Are Sealed" still hadn't cracked the top forty after being on the charts for thirty weeks.

Finding a tour manager hadn't been easy. Over the past few months, our band had become a single monster body with five heads, coated in layers of protective film. There was us, then the inner circle around us, and then everyone else. Not just anyone could show up and fit in. We needed people we could be ourselves around, say whatever, act however, blow off steam, be crude, gross, goofy, nasty, and fucked up around. We needed to complain some, be babied a little, and have a tour manager who got it, who wasn't intimidated or put off. When Bruce Patron came on board, he was a perfect fit. He had been managing the Fleshtones, another IRS band, and had tour managed Blondie at their peak touring. He was like a rock 'n' roll Richard Lewis, dry as a bone and completely unflappable, which made us try even harder to make his head explode.

The band had a publicist now, sending manila envelopes to us each month stuffed with copies of all our press. *People* magazine did a big story featuring "candid" photos. Mine showed me with Danny playing guitar together. Besides the publicist, the payroll included a business manager, or accountant. Everyone graduated to getting $1,500 a month, presumably what was left after everyone else got paid. Management, business management, booking agent—they were all getting commissions. Then there were the lawyers, the touring personnel, the travel agency, and the expenses for tour buses, flights, and hotels. I had no idea how quickly a band could turn into a money-generating commodity for so many other people. After the Greek show, Danny helped me move my few belongings into a friend's apartment so I could save on rent when the tour resumed.

I had some good times with John Belushi in LA before taking off for the next leg of touring. With one phone call, John got the Guitar Center, a big music chain, to open for us in the middle of the night and let us jam on the store instruments. An employee played drums, Danny played guitar, I played bass, and John sang the blues. My Texas blues roots gave us common ground. John was passionate about blues; he had the exuberance of a true fan. We also liked to get into a little mischief. One night he cooked up a plan to get us a six-pack of beer after hours: when our limo pulled into a 7-11 store on Holloway, John said, "I'll go in and distract the clerk. You steal the six-pack." Drinking and cocaine were vices for sure, but they played a secondary role to wanting to hang out like a couple of teenagers digging music and having a couple beers.

A short tour of England broke up the Beautify America Tour. The English press, known for being snarky, had a good time being downright mean about us. With enough fans to sell out good-size venues and performances on all the major television shows, you would think some credibility would be due. But the press made us out to be overrated and not worth a bother, from "the guitars sound like they are being played through a two-watt amp" and "I've forgotten them already" to "dull and polite mediocrity." Despite having exposure and a following, something about our brand of being American didn't connect with the UK. We never broke out there with either record sales or hits.

But back in the states our rise continued, boosted with an invite to be musical guests on *Saturday Night Live.* This pinnacle of success fell from the sky and lodged in the center of my life like a meteor. It was so huge, I couldn't get my head around it. Flying from England to Manhattan, it was easy to feel like a big shot. We checked in at the hotel where *SNL* put up their guests and reveled in the luxury of the accommodations—a couple stars above our usual rooms. On the set we met the cast, including the soon-to-be breakout star Eddie Murphy and host Bernadette Peters. The atmosphere during rehearsal felt casual and relaxed as they ran sketches and camera shots.

On Saturday, an early-morning call time brought us to the NBC studios. Around lunchtime, I started having some wine backstage. A couple bottles of champagne appeared—they had to be popped open, of course—and cheers, and more cheers, and beyond cheers. The day dragged on and the drinking continued. When it seemed the drinking might be getting too much, presto, cocaine suddenly became available. I tried to "balance" the buzz. The evening rolled in, and the backstage party was going full tilt. Careless and confident, stir-crazy from being in the dressing room, high and drunk, we finally heard the stage call come. I might have managed fine, but as I walked down the hallway toward the set, someone—either Ginger or a staffer—said, "Sixty million people, girls! You're gonna play for sixty mil!" A choking, stifling reality dropped like a curtain of doom. Terror laced through my manic euphoria. I was bombed and minutes away from performing in front of the biggest audience of my life.

So stupid. With no swagger or joy or confidence, I got through our two songs, barely looking up from the neck of my bass. Like an amateur. It went by so fast that before I knew it, we were gathering our things in the dressing room. Feeling absolutely terrible, the whole band was deflated and despondent, wanting to slink out of there. Even though there were no mistakes, it had been a flat, spiritless Go-Go's on *SNL*. Everyone took it hard. I pointed out that staying there all day, all evening, and all night sure didn't help matters, but I knew that this landed solidly on us—no excuses.

And yet, in the days after the *Saturday Night Live* appearance, something unexpected happened: sales of our record spiked. Our less-than-stellar appearance still helped the band tremendously. Once again, the power of television to put us in people's living rooms shoved our career down the road. All the touring and work and promotion kept the Go-Go's incrementally moving forward, but *SNL* took us miles.

With the massive national exposure, another new tour bus arrived, one of our very own—no crew sharing it with us. With the new bus and our great tour manager, Bruce, the Go-Go's hit the road for a month of East Coast dates. In NYC Belushi invited the band to his house for brunch with his wife, Judy, *SNL* writer Michael O'Donoahugh, and Dan Aykroyd. The Blues Brothers had an unlicensed blues bar in the city, and after our show at the famed Palladium, Danny, me, and Bruce hung out at the Blues Bar, where Meat Loaf tended bar and a sloppy jam session carried on for hours. Still in the city for Thanksgiving, I spent the holiday with Danny at Richard Gottehrer's amazing apartment. It was the first time I hadn't hung out with my mom on a holiday. She had a gang of friends to hang with, and she had raised me to be on my own. I sent postcards and phoned her with breathless updates, sharing the things I could, like the

Stones concert. Fending for myself was a given, long ingrained. But the deficiencies I had grown up with weren't erased or replaced. Underneath all my autonomy and self-sufficiency was the longing to create for myself the family I hadn't gotten to have as a kid.

Finally, the Go-Go's made it happen. "Our Lips Are Sealed" landed in the number-twenty slot, a certifiable hit on the *Billboard* chart. The band had done everything imaginable (except the joked-about blow jobs!) to get program directors to add the single to their station playlists, and they had resisted. Still, we prevailed despite that reluctance. Our touring and live shows grew our fan base, and their record purchases forced the station adds, giving "Lips" its final Top 40 push. I never took for granted hearing our songs on the radio. And to this day, if I'm in a public place when a Go-Go's song comes on the sound system, I have to force myself not to exclaim to everyone within earshot, "That's me! That's my band!"

Our last big job of the year was taping a live performance at Palos Verdes High School, an upscale suburban school south of Los Angeles. The white-bread normalcy of the setting generated a wholesome excitement—they were kids after all. The show was released as *Totally Go-Go's* and sold on VHS tape. Besides being our first full-length recorded concert, it presents the first recording of the newest song in our set: my ode to summer romance, "Vacation."

Decades passed before I watched the *Saturday Night Live* performance, and I sighed in relief. It wasn't nearly as bad as I thought it had been.

23

LITTLE SCISSOR

Miles arranged for us to be the opening act for the Police, one of the most successful bands in the world. Not only did he manage them, but his brother Stewart Copeland played drums along with Andy Summers on the guitar and future superstar Sting leading the band on vocals and bass. The tour started in Europe and gave us our first major international exposure, with a new single, "We Got the Beat," to promote. Instead of being exciting and thrilling, it felt like drudgery. The winter days made the cities indistinguishable—all the character and nuance blended to a dull, gray cold, masked in snow.

The Police treated us well, and we often shared the same coach. I kept a respectful distance and didn't try to make friends, although a couple of the other girls hit it off with Stewart and Andy. Sting usually had his nose buried in a book. Being an opening band always feels like you're an interloper, horning in on someone else's deal. Used to being adored by Go-Go's fans at our sold-out shows, it was disconcerting to play to arenas of uninterested, skeptical European Police fans. Their crowd was more into expertly executed musicianship than the raw charm of the Go-Go's.

CBS Records, our international distributors, knew they only had the Go-Go's in their clutches for a short time and wanted to pack in as much promo as possible. Always being pushed to do another interview, another photo session, another meet and greet left us with no downtime. The camaraderie that normally buoyed us through pressure and demanding schedules had worn thin for the first time. I had been slaphappy with the unbelievable luck of our rising success, but now I felt inexplicably emotional and sensitive. I missed the twisted sisterhood we had created. The band had become more self-absorbed and wrapped up in our own little worldly dramas.

I turned twenty-three in Hamburg, Germany. During our performance I shrugged my shoulders up and down and kicked my feet in jerky skipping and running movements. The bigger stages begged for energy and action, and I hadn't figured out how to fill up the space. Instead of celebrating after the show, I spent my birthday alone, crying in my hotel room.

Comfort wasn't easy to come by. A common sight when overseas would be a frustrated Go-Go in the hotel lobby on a pay phone, at the mercy of a foreign operator. Calling from your room could wipe out weeks of per diems. Without cell phones or email, trying to reach a lover or family member who was time zones and thousands of miles away could drive you nuts. I couldn't reach my boyfriend, Danny, on my birthday for consolation. My relationship with him had become increasingly volatile. We loved and fought in the rare times we spent together, with my drinking putting extra gasoline on the fire. I had stayed with him for a week in New York before coming to Europe, hitting the after-hours clubs like Area and Heartbreak, and jamming again at the Blues Bar with John Belushi.

When my period didn't come, those neurotic, raw feelings I had been having started to make sense. Dread seeped into my blood like the hormones that were flooding me. A blurred memory from the month before surfaced, plunging me into despair The scene emerged, clearer now: *In the bathroom of Danny's apartment, drunk, I took my contraceptive diaphragm and filled it with the spermicide gel. Squeezing the sides to put it in, the slippery rubber disc popped from my hands and shot across the small room. Shit. Cleaning up the gel that had splattered, I tried again. Was it in right? Hard to tell, but hey, close enough for rock 'n' roll.*

As I tried to keep my anxiety hidden, fervently hoping my period would come, the tour rolled into Paris. None of us had been to Paris before, and sharing the experience lifted everyone's spirits. The label rep took us out for an extravagant meal at La Coupole, where we drank bottles of wine and tried strange French delicacies. After dinner the band crammed into a taxi, laughing together and exclaiming over the night-lit architecture and iconic images. The enduring enchantment of Paris worked its magic, causing me to reflect: I had it made, the best life imaginable; of course things couldn't be carefree rainbows all day, every day.

The happy glow didn't last long. In London, my worst fears proved to be founded after a visit to the pharmacist for a pregnancy test. Positive. Our European Police dates rolled right into an American tour, playing in big-city arenas. After leaving London, a show on Long Island waited the very next day, with twenty cities following.

I'm pretty sure most managers don't have to figure out what to do about a pregnant bass player in the midst of the band's biggest tour to date. The first day off on the itinerary put us in New York City, the day before playing Madison Square Garden. It was the only chance I would have to take care of this unwelcome development. I made myself feel nothing, just deal with it and move on, like always. Barely twenty-three, I had the maturity of a teenager. My base instinct remained one of survival. No one would ever take care of me; that much I could be sure of. The Go-Go's were my shot at being successful. Not for a minute did I consider chucking my dreams and leaving the tour, the band, the journey of a lifetime. I wasn't about to screw things up for everyone and go back to Austin to have a baby and be a drunken, broken-down mom. No thanks.

Bruce, our tour manager, and Ginger, the band manager, made the arrangements for my day off once the tour moved to America. I told the band not to worry; I had it all taken care of. My problem was my problem alone and had barely registered on the Go-Go scale of concerns.

The American shows with the Police were more effective than the European ones, boosting our rise and adding to press, airplay, and MTV rotation. The venues were massive: Boston Garden, Nassau Coliseum, the Spectrum. Tens of thousands of people saw us live every night. After the seventh concert, the bus dropped us at our Manhattan hotel. Everyone knew what I had to do the next day, but no one wanted to spend their day off in NYC accompanying me to get an abortion. I couldn't blame anyone for that. Danny knew he had gotten me pregnant, but he'd left for his own tour in England; we had practically crossed in the sky. I set the bedside alarm and asked the hotel for a wake-up call to be doubly safe I wouldn't miss the appointment. Morning came after a sleepless night. Standing outside the hotel, traffic filled the street and a winter freeze made my eyeballs hurt and nostrils sting. The cold sank into my bones, bringing all the loneliness in the world with it. It felt like my band didn't give a shit about me. No one could be counted on, ever.

Then the revolving doors spat out a slight figure in a leather jacket and pants, a scarf wrapped around her neck, over her face, and up to her tousled black hair. Ginger to the rescue. "I hated the idea of you going by yourself," she said and made a taxi pull over right away. I hadn't gotten close with Ginger, but she had been with us every step of the way. I felt a jumble of guilt and shame for the trouble I caused, mixed with gratitude and relief that she had gotten up early to step up for me.

The doctor stood at the end of the table. I winced and cried out in pain. He looked at me over his mask and told me it didn't hurt. This one didn't use anesthesia like when I had been a twelve-year-old and gone to California. He was an asshole, but I felt like one too, for being there. Overcome with misery, I lay on the table and sobbed while he did the procedure, sure that he hated me. An hour later, slumped over with cramps, completely drained, I found Ginger in the waiting room reading a magazine. Jumping up, she put her arm around me and took me back to the hotel. It was our secret: the tough little rock 'n' roller who had joined the Go-Go's a year before was really a pitiful little girl.

For the next twenty-four hours, I stayed in bed. Each hour that passed with no one checking on me snipped away like a little scissor, reshaping the way I viewed my band. I believed that no one judged or disapproved of me. But as always, it was my job and mine alone to look out for myself. Looking back at the arc of our time together, a pattern emerged. The Go-Go's knew how it felt to be asked the same questions over and over; we'd give a nudge in the side or a certain look at each other: *Yeah, here it is again.* Everyone in the band felt the electricity generated when the lights went down, currents that caused us to bounce and jump in the wings before running out on stage to thousands of people. Together, we were elevated when the lights went up and the roar of an arena surrounded us as we launched into a song. We were experts at making each other laugh, compadres who knew how it felt to be hungover and tired from lack of sleep. We knew how to bullshit an industry guy, how to arrange ourselves for a photo. We could deal with just about any part of this new life, together, a girl gang, exclusive to the max. Bring it on, world, anything goes. Except for actual feelings. Those were left to each other to manage privately.

The very next day, I played a sold-out nineteen-thousand capacity Madison Square Garden. The show must go on. I so badly wished I could enjoy the feeling of being on the stage of the famed arena. Instead, I felt sore and depleted inside and couldn't wait to crawl into bed.

24
PRIVATE JET

At the Omni, a sports arena in Atlanta, I picked at our deli tray in a dressing room lined with lockers and team changing cubicles. The wardrobe cases could be arranged to make a private area, and I sometimes laid towels on the floor to try to nap. The faint sounds of the Police sound checking drifted down to the exterior rooms, Stewart's syncopated rhythms lost in the guitar effects and Sting's vocal, "We are spirits in the material world . . ." I knew nearly every word and phrase. After they finished, our sound check would get squeezed in before meal time, when everyone—crew, truck drivers, production, staff, and band members—loaded up plates and picked a seat. The Omni went silent, but this time, instead of Bruce coming to get us, Sting burst through the doors.

"Time for a celebration," he said, a bottle of Moët in each hand.

We were surprised and happy to see Sting, who never came bounding into our dressing room. Bearing bottles of the good stuff, no less.

What on Earth?

"Congratulations, ladies! You've passed us on the charts!" Sting said, and then, realizing that we still didn't get it, "Your album! It's passed ours!"

Oh! Their record, *Ghost in the Machine*, had slipped downward, and *Beauty and the Beat* was going up, and higher than . . . *oh, my.*

A stunned moment passed while it sank in. The Police were huge. Both bands were touring in support of our albums, yet *ours had overtaken theirs*. Sting popped the champagne open, and as the news bubbled and rolled over our collective disbelief, everyone toasted and whooped and hollered. I didn't watch sports, didn't know what a team felt like when it won a championship, but I knew what it felt like to be on this team: like a massive shot of vitamin FuckEveryLastOneWhoToldUsNo. Too bad there was no one to gloat at—everyone around us had been believers. It was the industry, the gatekeepers, who had tried to block us.

The Go-Go's went onstage that night with an unruly confidence and rapport. After our set, the Police gave us big shout-outs, confirming once again that most of the time, the men who truly celebrated women musicians were also musicians. Their acclaim encouraged the crowd to follow suit and cheer for us again as we stood at the side of the stage. This roller coaster was creaking and straining to the top of an eight-month incline.

The Police graciously offered to let us join them on a private plane after a concert in Denver to the next city, Tempe, Arizona. An unsettling premonition crept into my heart. I couldn't shake it. All through the set, I worried and tried to rationalize away the bad feeling. Our crew packed the equipment; they wanted to get started on the thirteen-hour drive. While the rest of my band watched the Police, I made a decision to ride with the crew and left. Better safe than in a plane crash, I thought, as if Patsy Cline and Buddy Holly were sitting on my shoulders wagging their fingers at my imagination. The idea of something bad happening and the last thought of my life being *I knew I shouldn't have flown* had gripped me. Riding on the crew bus was a drag, with me sleepless and wedged into the luggage bunk. *At least I'll be alive*, I thought, trying to conjure up a small, smug comfort. Rolling in at noon and seeing Bruce in the lobby, I knew immediately that everyone had arrived alive and well. They had made the trip in two-hour-food-and-drinks-luxe-private-jet style. On the way to sound check, the band made sure I heard every detail of what I had missed. "Yeah, yeah, I'm an idiot," I said, annoyed with the stupid hunch that had kept me off a freaking private plane with the Police.

Things were moving too fast to dwell on false premonitions. Tempe marked the last show with the Police. Plenty of last-night-of-the-tour hijinks, a rock 'n' roll tradition, made it more than business as usual. Even Miles Copeland got in on the fun, singing their huge hit into a microphone offstage that went into Sting's monitor. The audience heard Sting singing, but Sting heard an off-key and ridiculous Miles bellowing "Rooooooooxxxxxannnnne." Sting cracked up and the song shambled to a stop, with the audience not really knowing what was going on but picking up on the lightness and levity of the night as prank after prank was played on the band.

Everyone was in a great mood, and the Police invited us on their plane again to fly to Los Angeles. Home in an hour instead of the nine-hour drive and a second chance to fly on the private jet—*hell, ya*! Carousing and talking, both bands rode together to the private airstrip. I wished it had been like this the whole time, relaxed and hanging out. The group settled into the plane, no waiting, no lines. *Normal flying sucks*, I thought. We rolled down the runway, picking up speed.

"Fire!" Sting yelled. "There's a fire on the wing!"

Sure enough, out the window, flames whipped in the wind. Panic ensued. The plane rolled to a stop and the door opened.

Belinda went into full-on survival mode and shoved everyone out of the way, trampling over Go-Go's and Police like furniture to be the first one off the plane. For decades it made us laugh when recalling the story. And I lamented my sense of intuition and premonition, which obviously had a broken timer.

Beauty and the Beat rose on the charts along with our latest single, "We Got the Beat." The Go-Go's had a Grammy nomination for Best New Artist of 1981. Everyone bought fancy thrift-store dresses; I chose one in red lace with a red slip. Danny came out to be my date, dressed like a dandy in a tux with a pink carnation. Charlotte brought her boyfriend, my old friend Peter Case of the Plimsouls. Of course, I scored some cocaine. If this wasn't a night for partying, I couldn't tell you what was. We giggled and smirked our way down our first red carpet, feeling a little bit like the outcast relatives you're obligated to invite to the wedding. Pat Benatar, Rick Springfield, Quincy Jones, Tina Turner, Yoko Ono, Kim Carnes, George Carlin, James Brown— the league of standard bearers was there.

The organization seated us close to the stage, proof that our rise had definitely put us in the upper tier, regardless of how it might feel sometimes. My heart raced with the thought of walking on that stage at the Shrine Auditorium. The Best New Artist category came early, the second Grammy they handed out. But instead of hearing our name, we heard Sheena Easton, a singer from Scotland, get the nod. During the following commercial break, the Go-Go's decided it would be a complete bore to sit there for the rest of the show. Leaving the building and an empty row of seats, off we went in search of the party. Later, I heard the Grammy people were pissed. They scrambled to get seat fillers and thought the Go-Go's were very disrespectful. We weren't trying to be; it's just that the Grammys were about as hip as your grandparents were. In a prior year, the Best New

Artist Grammy had gone to A Taste of Honey over Elvis Costello and the Cars. Even the Pretenders hadn't scored a Grammy. If nothing else, I felt proud to have joined the ranks of overlooked but deserving bands.

Out in the parking lot, five twenty-somethings in vintage dresses and high heels looked aghast at the sea of limos, stretching all the way to the horizon. Where was ours? *Fuck, this is a bummer.* Splitting up, everyone went down aisle after aisle yelling "Go-Go's looking for driver!" Chauffeurs leaned against cars, having a smoke and talking shit about their passengers. Finally, we converged on our driver and demanded to be whisked off to the A&M Records party at Chasen's. Even newcomers like us knew the best part of the Grammys was the after-parties, where labels and organizations hosted lavish free-for-alls and the stars got loosey-goosey and mingled with each other. We busted through the doors of Chasen's and kicked the party into high gear, by ourselves. The Go-Go's had arrived.

25

DON'T LEAVE

A movie producer had a huge, star-studded party in a gorgeous mansion. I spotted John Belushi and threw my arms around him in a big hug. I thought of him as a friend by that point, someone I had shared some good times with: jamming together, seeing Iggy Pop, going clubbing, and a few long, deep talks. Uncharacteristically, he backed off and introduced me to a woman standing at his side. I hadn't noticed her until then. He made a point of telling her, "Kathy is friends with Judy too." I thought, *How odd to mention his wife during the introduction. Why did he want her to know that?* An affair didn't seem possible; John worshipped his wife, and he never appeared to be looking for sex. The woman had a bad haircut and unstylish attire. She acted possessive and unfriendly and pulled him away. No prob. I didn't want to deal with their weird vibe.

Less than a week later, she became notorious as the woman who overloaded Belushi with speedballs and left him to die at the Chateau Marmont. As soon as the news broke of John's death and her face turned up on television, I gasped with recognition.

His struggle with drugs had been well known to everyone who knew him, and though I wasn't part of the innermost circle, I had witnessed it firsthand. When I got high, it felt crazy and fun. Being high made me busy, wanting to write songs all night long, go places, do things, or have wild, wanton conversations and feel connected with people. The downside came after, not during—with burning out or being too wired to get sleep or feeling like shit the next day. A few of my friends got high more intensely, without joy. Like they just had to do it, no choice in the matter. Sometimes it felt like that with John. He wasn't a drag by a long shot, but he was a lot more fun when he wasn't high, and he knew it. One night in New York, Belinda and I had run out of steam partying with John, only to find out that after dropping us at the hotel he had gotten the taxi driver to drive him to Florida, where they'd binged for a few days. I disliked the idea of him being with a stranger on a bender then, and now he was gone.

John was the first person I had ever known as a friend, someone I'd hung out and gotten high with, to die shockingly and suddenly. I didn't see him as John Belushi the comedian and actor, or the Blues Brother, but as a sweetly enthusiastic and complicated guy who opened himself up to nearly anyone. Sometimes the wrong people. I read in an interview that the last thing John said to Cathy Smith, the drug dispenser, was "Don't leave me alone," which she promptly did. It troubled me to think how he might have lived if she had just done what he asked. At a band meeting, I made everyone promise to never, ever leave each other in bad shape. None of us seemed heavily into drug use or in danger of overdosing, but we all agreed to watch out for each other.

The ride I had gotten on had clearly been designed by a madman. In a whiplash of extremes, within a couple of days of John's death, our album went to number one. *Beauty and the Beat* remained the top-selling album in the country for six weeks, with our single "We Got the Beat" at number two. Never before, or since, as of this writing, had a record written and performed by an all-female band gone to the number-one position. The Go-Go's had made music history. Suddenly we were everywhere: *Life* magazine, the *New Yorker*, *Newsweek*, *Teen*, *Circus*, *Hit Parade*, *Vogue*, the *New York Times*, and newspapers from cities across the country. In addition to MTV interviews, the Go-Go's appeared on mainstream shows such as *American Bandstand* and *Solid Gold*. Sales hit two million. Girls and guys did our songs at school talent contests, with face masks and towels turbaned on their heads. Even better, they were inspired to start their own bands. Every story mentioned how the Go-Go's could barely play when they started, and look at them now. It gave every writer a ready-made story hook, the fairytale fable. Gina and I weren't thrilled with being lumped into the incompetent part of the myth, but it did give budding young musicians a lot of inspiration. In an interview around this time, I kept it real, though: "I get hangovers, have no car, and I'm broke."

Somehow, after picking up a guitar seven years before, I had ended up crossing a bridge that connected a devout and fervent desire to rock 'n' roll with some cool gals to a shadowy dream of making music my life. Not only did I revel in where I had ended up, I thought with absolute certainty it would never end. No one could be stupid enough to fuck this up. Holding on to it became my driving passion now that I had made it.

IRS Records hosted a party at Francis Ford Coppola's Zoetrope Studios, presenting each of us with a platinum record commemorating sales in excess of a million units. The black-and-white photos show us beaming with our prizes and posing with celebrities such as Martin Sheen, Tatum O'Neal, Rick James, and Timothy Hutton. Out of all the accolades, recognition, articles, and celebrations, my favorite blessing came in a telegram from the Ramones: "Congratulations Go-Go's," it said. "We are so proud of you," signed Johnny, Joey, Dee Dee, and Marky.

Our team at IRS had shown the big labels they were players and shared in our unlikely ragamuffin long shot heroine success. Everyone loves when the underdog wins. On top of the world, the view is 360, and I'd never seen anything like it.

And then, money changed everything.

It had been decided somewhere along the way that the songwriters in the Go-Go's would share 8 percent of their publishing share with the other band members. In the simplest terms, that means, say, if I wrote a song by myself and made a dollar, I would keep half, my writers' share. Out of the other half, or what is called the publishing share (fifty cents of the theoretical dollar), I would give four cents each to the other four Go-Go's. A song publisher might take a percentage, too, depending on the deal I had made. If I gave the band nothing, I would make more, so it's definitely a difference to the writer—a loss.

We divided the money equally in every other activity, that is, shows and merchandise. Record sales pay a royalty to both the composers/publishers and the performers, or the band. Basically, the songwriters, with the publishing income, which includes all radio airplay, and the other royalties, make substantially more than the non-songwriters.

With a couple million records sold and being on the road for eight months straight, a significant payday was long overdue. At our accounting firm I sat on the edge of my chair in an office waiting for my check to be issued. Looking at it, I swooned. I had made over $300,000, almost $800,000 in present value. It was more money than I knew what to do with (of course, the accountants had ideas for that). My head reeled. I'll buy a car! Definitely get a cool place to live. Almost out the accountant's door, I turned back, suddenly curious. "Hey, what did everyone else get?" Surely it couldn't be a secret. Everyone had busted ass to make the record sell. The numbers came: Charlotte, with most of the songwriting and the biggest hit, got a huge check. Next came Jane, just under Charlotte's. My amount came next. Our lead singer, the star with the charisma and voice, made less than me, and Gina, the hardworking drummer who had turned the band into contenders, made the least. I had to let it swish around in the wash cycle of my brain for a while: this didn't bode well for the band. The first real money had been paid, and there were some awfully big gaps.

It didn't take long before I got the call. Gina had asked too. Our little drummer was a stick of dynamite, her fuse always lit and ready to explode. Most of the time that meant just playing with all her heart and soul, like a machine, making every ounce of her energy pour into her limbs and onto her drum kit. Other times it meant being a manic, loudmouthed ballbuster, yelling out truths most people would rather not hear. Gina had a straightforward worldview: hard work pays off; be loyal and fair; honor your family and friends. The discrepancy in our earnings violated her sense of justice, and I couldn't blame her. It gave me a big problem because everyone had to be happy and it had to be fun, or else all would be lost. My number-one priority had become keeping the band intact. I was living the experience of a lifetime and I wanted it to last.

Some issues aren't clear-cut, black and white, one way is right and one way is wrong. I've had a lot of years to think about songwriting and income issues in bands and have my thoughts and opinions about it, but that's all they are. There's no law or manual. In the case of the Go-Go's, the money issue became like the sixth unwanted member, always in the room. For my part, I had made a tidy pile of dough when the whole thing reared its ugly head, and I would only be contributing more songs. If things could have been more equal, with more songwriting money going to our singer and drummer, it would probably have been best for the band. But I couldn't make anyone do something against her beliefs, and I understood the other point of view: this is my song, I wrote it. The argument can get very circular: a writer can say, "Without my song, the Go-Go's wouldn't have a hit," and someone else can always counter, "Without the Go-Go's, your song wouldn't be a hit."

Ultimately, I believe if a band has a working chemistry and the members are all working equally to make the band succeed, why not value everyone equally, whether they wrote a song or not. Some bands, U2 for example, do it this way—no matter who writes the song, the cut is equal. I think their longevity speaks to the efficacy of this approach. It has to be done willingly, though, with the unfettered acknowledgment that you have a star to sing your song and a band willing to slog around the country for months to sell your song. If the band can't agree, it's just a lose-lose situation and someone is going to feel cheated. If our primary songwriters, Jane and Charlotte, felt taken advantage of, it would be terrible for the band. That was obvious, and it would lead to a bad outcome too. But still, I thought Gina and Belinda were getting a raw deal. I tried to be neutral. Then I tried to fix things. Belinda and Gina should write more songs so the next record wouldn't be such a buzzkill on payday. I didn't see why not—Belinda had strong opinions about lyrics and melody, and she had worked on tunes before, including writing the words to one of my favorites, "Skidmarks on My Heart." And Gina had more encyclopedic knowledge about bands and music than anyone I knew. She came with a soundtrack playing, took her cassettes everywhere, always had her Walkman headphones on, listening to music.

The song publishing income situation grew like a cancer. It went into remission sometimes, but then it always came back. It wouldn't kill us by itself, and plenty of good times and success lay ahead. But in time, it metastasized and poisoned other areas. Everyone got more paranoid and self-protective. The band became like a microcosm of a failing society.

Each band member got a stake in real estate, and that helped. It took up enough space and energy to redirect money grumblings. Everyone got homes in LA, from Studio City to Malibu to Los Feliz. Houses and furniture were purchased, everyone stepping up into a new level of living. I did things a little differently and rented a one-bedroom in a Hollywood high-rise for myself and bought a condo for my mom in Austin. I was positioning myself deeper as the caretaker in our relationship. I wasn't conscious of this. At the time it just felt good to be able to provide things for her that she couldn't get for herself. When I visited her I would buy the things I thought she needed, like a parent visiting her kid in college.

More money, more problems. Margot, the original bass player, got a lawyer and sued the Go-Go's, saying her time in the band had contributed to our success and she wanted a share of the payoff. The band had a chance to make a settlement when they replaced her with me, but they didn't, and now it came back to bite us. Ginger, our manager, was becoming another brewing problem. She relied a lot on our lawyer for guidance because things had gotten so big and she didn't want to screw anything up. The band loved Ginger, but as great as she might be, she let us make stupid decisions. Maybe with more experience she could have stopped some of our really bad ones.

The one that may have been most shortsighted and dumb came shortly after hitting the top.

IRS wanted to release a third single from *Beauty and the Beat*. They were absolutely right to want to do so. But we wanted to make our next record instead.

"They want to bleed us while we're hot," I said.

"No more touring playing those songs; time for new songs," someone said.

"We need to show everyone our band isn't a fluke," we said.

And so on. Jay and Miles, our IRS bosses, couldn't sway us. It wasn't uncommon to have multiple singles from an album at the time: Blondie, the Cars, and Hall and Oates all released four singles from records that came out around the same time. Singles give the record more life and more sales, which solidifies a band's stature. *Beauty and the Beat* could have easily dropped a few more hits, and going deeper probably could have broken our band better in England and Europe. The smartest, most career-building plan would have been for us to take the exposure from opening for the Police along with the momentum of a hit album and play more shows as headliners. The songs for the second record hadn't even been written, making the decision to record right then even more of a pointless move. But the Go-Go's got our way, feeling good about how we called the shots—no masterminds pulling strings or telling us what to do! And what could have been became something else entirely.

26

TUTUS AND TIARAS

Frazzled and frayed from work, a little less shiny and happy after the money issues, and haunted by the phantom "sophomore slump," the Go-Go's set out to reproduce the carefree exuberance of our debut. My song "Vacation" had been in our repertoire for months. I had played Charlotte the Textones' version before the Beautify America Tour. Thinking the existing song needed more of a chorus, we got our guitars and notebooks out and wrote a new section to the song and then showed it to the band. Being the newest original, it made a perfect start for the next record. Miles hired producer Richard Gottehrer again. He had been vindicated for the recording of our first album, an easy grudge to let go of after it became a hit. A few rejects from *Beauty and the Beat* made it to the short list of songs, and the band got busy writing. I brought in "We Don't Get Along," and it made the cut. Charlotte, Jane, and I wrote a song in Detroit during a blizzard called "The Way You Dance." It was one of the only times we wrote together on the road. Belinda and Gina both cowrote songs, ensuring they had more credits this time around. Jane and I contributed a ballad, "Worlds Away," thinking it would showcase Belinda's voice in a way she hadn't been heard before. Jane and Charlotte brought in a couple of strong songs with "Get Up and Go" and "This Old Feeling." I thought both had the spirit of the Go-Go's, and I began to feel optimistic about the new record.

Richard came to us this time, choosing the rustic and vibey Indigo Ranch in Malibu, a studio on top of a remote hillside. It couldn't have been any further away from the NYC recording of *Beauty and the Beat*. Isolated and secluded in nature, surrounded by orchards and vegetation, with rock formations and trails giving way to views of the canyon and ocean, the place was steeped in history. Neil Young, Bob Dylan, Van Morrison, and now the Go-Go's had recorded here. Richard and Thom Panunzio, our new engineer, were a dream team to work with, and our sisterhood was intact. But the pressure was tangible, and even Richard's enthusiasm was a little forced. Everyone was uncertain how to follow up our huge success.

Within the first weeks, Ginger, who had a strong art and design background, suggested that "Vacation" be the name of the album. Having the title track was a big bonus, and I was fairly certain it would be the first single as well. After recording the instrumental tracks for the song, Belinda went to the vocal booth. I turned to Jane, suddenly overwhelmed with insecurity about the biggest songwriting contribution I had made to the band. "I'm not sure about the first line," I said. It went: "I've thought a lot of things about you." Jane said, off the top of her head, "Can't seem to get my mind off of you." I liked it.

The songwriting designations had gotten very arduous since the publishing debacle, with writers claiming exacting percentages for their contributions to any given song. It was tiresome, and I took things in an overly generous direction, splitting the song evenly with Charlotte rather than trying to mete out what bits of the new chorus she had come up with and which chords or word I'd suggested. I siphoned off another chunk for Jane's first line. Looking back, it probably wasn't the best business move, but the song has earned me a good living for decades now, so I can't find much to complain about. More interesting was how I would often say in interviews that the two of them wrote the new chorus, for many years after it was a hit. The fabrication revealed a monster of self-doubt lurking in my shadows. I was terrified by the idea of having my song compared to the hits Jane and Charlotte had written for the band.

Richard and Thom ran off a cassette of "Vacation" for everyone to take home and listen to. When we reconvened a couple days later, they brought up the mix on the board. For the life of them, they couldn't get it to sound as good as the cassette. No matter where the faders got pushed or how those EQ knobs got turned, something about the cassette sounded better. In an unheard-of solution, when it came time to release the song "Vacation," they mastered the single off the cassette tape. Fittingly, it also became the first ever "cassingle" issued as a format for the public.

Some of the album sounded like filler, but I thought about half of it might be strong enough to keep the Go-Go's on track with our career. The production moved to a couple of other studios for overdubs. At Sunset Sound, we spied on Prince shooting hoops in high heels in the courtyard. At A&M I befriended a good-looking young guy whom I would sit outside and smoke cigarettes and talk with. He struggled because record companies resisted signing a black guy doing rock 'n' roll. He didn't like how they were trying to pigeonhole him into being an R&B or soul artist. I told him how no one wanted to sign us either. Seven years later a fantastic record came out launching the career of Lenny Kravitz, making me happy he had stuck with it.

Ginger had the idea for the waterskiing cover, inspired by a Florida postcard featuring synchronized water skiers. The kookiness of the concept, along with not having our clothes and hair date the record sold us. Art director Mick Haggerty analog-edited our heads onto the Cypress Garden skiers' bodies. On a soundstage at the A&M records lot, the music video continued the waterski theme with cheesy back projection and drunk Go-Go's having a go at acting in tutus and tiaras. Our team and the band had some much-needed fun with the photos and videos. Mick and Ginger went on to receive Grammy nominations for their artwork.

Vacation came out in June 1982 to mostly good reviews. It did its job well enough. The band had already started an over-due tour of Japan and Australia. I loved getting back on the road and seeing exotic, faraway places. Tokyo blew my mind. Every normal, daily activity, from eating breakfast to buying a razor or taking a walk, was infused with a foreign unfamiliar-ity. Even getting sushi was unrecognizable—a couple of times Gina and I ate at a Shakey's Pizza Parlor just to be sure of what we were getting. Jane and Belinda connected with Japan more than any of us. They both loved the fashions and nightclubs. Jane learned a bunch of Japanese phrases, making the band look good with her efforts to communicate with our hosts and the press. In Harajuku Park, they met a bunch of Japanese rockabilly guys called the Black Cats and promised them some American tour dates with us. Our Japanese fans showed up in droves, going wild at the concerts and bringing us amazing gifts. Charlotte started calling the hotel lobby the "mobby" because of how long it took to get through, past the polite but insistent fans with gifts, poster boards, and shiny gold markers to get autographs exactly how they wanted them to be.

Before going on stage in Nagoya, I learned of the accidental drug death of the Pretenders' James Honeyman-Scott. Unable to stop crying, I had to play with my back to the audience. It was a rare instance of my not being able to shed the world and stop time while performing. Both Jimmy and his wife, Peggy, had remained friends with me after we played together in Okla-homa. In LA, we had seen our hero Chuck Berry together, the first time for either of us. One of my favorite memories was sharing our disappointment with his lackluster and soulless performance, yet being thrilled to meet him anyway. Jimmy struck me as an occasional drug user—not out of control. I wondered briefly if the same thing could happen to me, then decided maybe his constitution was weakened and it was just too much at the wrong time. *Carry on.*

The press was waiting for us on the runway when we landed in Australia. To our horror, the next edition of a tabloid pictured us on the front page, two photos side by side. One was a nice band publicity shot with the caption "This is how the Go-Go's publicity machine would have you think they look." Next to it was a shot from the runway arrival, with us looking raggedly jet-lagged, un-made up, and quite dressed down. "This is how they really look!" was printed under that photo. I wondered if Duran Duran got the same treatment.

Australia felt familiar to me—it had a rough, wild west element but looked British—like Texas done up in English wrapping paper. CBS Records, our international distributor, kept us happy in between promotional appearances and interviews with harbor cruises, extravagant dinners, and visits to wildlife refuges. Charlotte and I spent an entire day off at a vineyard and returned with a case of wine each, determined to drink every bottle before leaving the country. It was rare for just the two of us to hang out on the road. In the year and a half since I'd joined the band, Charlotte had gotten a bit more withdrawn. I didn't worry—her personality, a disarming combination of modest self-efficacy and laser-focused acumen—had stayed intact. She still had a sharp wit, usually let loose in pointed little zingers, and never had a shortage of musical ideas. Not everyone reacted to the constant activity and stimulus the same way, and it didn't seem strange that she would want time alone.

It had been damn near impossible to score drugs in Japan and Australia, so when the band landed in Hawaii for a couple of shows and days off, I went completely out of control. No beaches or luaus or ocean sunsets for me—I spent my time in paradise holed up in a hotel suite drinking champagne and snorting cocaine. Success at last.

The Go-Go's knew how to have a good time. Illicit consumptions kept us united part of the time—maybe not in the healthiest way, but still, a bond is a bond, and blowing off steam together was fun. Everyone laughed together and laughed a lot—more than any of us had done with anyone else. No one ever felt left out or was made the butt of jokes. After a show, while we piled onto the tour bus, a series of invented entertainments with names like disco bus, wise old curtain woman, or love canal kept everyone amused. Being a gang of gals who had seen and done a lot together still had a powerful pull.

27

BASH AND CRASH

A deep disconnect between the way we saw ourselves and the way we were presented to the public began to develop. As the band grew, the media began to characterize us in a way that didn't feel right. Our music sounded like the adjectives they used—the Go-Go's actually were danceable, energetic, fun, and exuberant. In hundreds of show and album reviews, "bouncy" in particular was a favorite descriptor. Also, our story had an easy hook: the incompetent, unlikely former punk band played Cinderella to the public's Prince Charming embrace. But soon the stories took on a condescending and demeaning tone. Guy bands were never described as perky and chirpy or adorable and cute. Increasingly, I read about us being frothy girl-pop and the band described as cheerleader-fun.

Our culture has long made it natural to form-fit straitjackets to all manner of women—successful women in particular. The Go-Go's had infiltrated the most male of domains: rock 'n' roll. One could call us a pop band with commercial, catchy songs, not unlike male bands from the Raspberries to our contemporaries the Knack or the Cars. But it was all rock 'n' roll, and we had made it to the top. Our popularity couldn't be contained, but they could wrap us up in a lady-box. Thus, the Go-Go's were anointed as America's pop sweethearts. The girls next door. The most benign of all lady-boxes.

I hated the cutesy label. The Go-Go's were as potent and lusty as men, and I'm not talking about sexuality. We came to every show ready to bury everyone there with a bash and crash attitude. Fans knew a different band than what the simplistic media described. We were smart, hip, and liberated. But that portrayal didn't find its way into very many writeups. Not one Go-Go was remotely like the girl next door (whatever that means in the first place). If "pop sweethearts" did acid at Graceland, threw up on the floor at fancy restaurants, cheated on their boyfriends, took nasty Polaroids, made out with girls, watched fringe porn, and stayed up all night writing songs and playing guitars, well, maybe their stupid label might fit.

Among the worst offenders were stylists and photographers. I don't think male bands get dressed up like dolls or get handed lollipops and balloons to pose with. Sometimes, we let them: *Whatever! Let's just get it over with; who cares.* Other times our strong objections and griping branded us as . . . wait for it . . . bitches. Bet you didn't see that coming.

All of us were thrilled and waited anxiously in a Manhattan loft studio for a session with the famous photographer Annie Leibovitz. Her assistants buzzed around testing lights and setting up backdrops. Being shot for the cover of *Rolling Stone* is beyond a pinnacle of success. It's more like an obelisk of success. Annie had the presence of a rock star herself, imposing and weighty but not self-important in the least. We had brought our own clothes for the shoot, with plenty of options. Whether a show, television performance, or photo shoot, each band member always turned up in whatever she wanted. Dressed in our outfits, all made up, we had the feeling that Annie was stalling. An associate came in with bags of stuff and dumped them in front of us.

"Hey," said Annie. "I thought you all could wear this stuff."

Spread on the floor was a dozen or more packages of Hanes underclothes. T-shirts, tanks, underwear, and bras, all of it white cotton. It was seriously appalling. *No way. We don't wanna wear that.* Annie looked equal parts disappointed and determined. I think she had gone through this before. Quite a few back-and-forth exchanges commenced: "just try it" and "no, we won't do that." Then, like some swift, real-life edit, there were the five Go-Go's posing in the white underwear, Annie happily clicking away. In the end I thought, *Well, at least it's not sexy underwear, lacy and garter belts and all that.* I still don't know what it was about the Hanes stuff that Annie wanted to capture—going along with the wholesome image, or making a statement on it, or mocking it maybe. She had something in mind for sure but didn't feel any need to share her vision for the photograph. She just aimed to get us to serve her creative vision. In the end, we put our trust in Annie's artistry and were OK with the photo session.

But when our *Rolling Stone* issue hit the stands, a headline of big, pink block letters proclaimed "Go-Go's Put Out" alongside the underwear shot. I was so confused. It was a dream come true to be on the cover of *Rolling Stone*, but why had they gone out of their way to make a joke out of our cover? Sure, we "put out"—I got it—we put out records, we put out energy, we put out fun. But the pun most certainly carried an ambiguous put-down with its "put out" message. I never knew what exactly the nudge, nudge, wink, wink point might be. These women are harmless fun, even without their clothes on? Was it a reverse de-balling, sexualizing us without being sexy? The worst part was having no say, no control, and no advance notice. This pinnacle had a bitter aftertaste, but ultimately, I loved being on the cover and what it represented in terms of how far the Go-Go's had come. Still, I couldn't help but remember how we had been good girls and done as we were told—and ended up hating how they represented us.

Within two weeks of its release, our second album reached the top-ten-selling releases in the country, and "Vacation," our single, peaked at number eight, staying on the charts for over three months. The Go-Go's hit the road again, this time bigger than ever. "Don't Bother Me, I'm on Vacation," our merch t-shirts said. I kept a pair of roller skates on the bus and zipped around in the aisles of empty venues while waiting to soundcheck, or in the parking lots of truck stops in the middle of the night. In hotel restaurants and lobbies, people came up asking for autographs, even if they had no idea who we were. That was weird. The band could tell if the person wasn't a fan, and sometimes it was fun to make them squirm a little: "Do you have tickets to the show or any records?"

"Uh, no."

"Why do you want an autograph?"

"Because you're famous," they would say. We'd always shrug and give them the scribble, but it shows how strangely enamored with celebrity people in the United States were, even back then.

The tour took us to over sixty cities, headlining arenas, concert halls, civic centers, and the summer circuit of outdoor sheds and fairgrounds. The more money we made, the more we had to spend. Touring personnel had grown to over twenty-five people, including a wardrobe person to clean and press stage clothes. True to our word, we had the Japanese rockabilly band the Black Cats open some shows. They confused the hell out of our fans, speaking no English, wearing all black, and sticking to a set of Gene Vincent and Johnny Burnette renditions in which they got the words all wrong.

I thought things would never end. When you go from playing clubs to headlining the Hollywood Bowl in less than sixteen months, it's hard to imagine ever going backward. The upcoming LA show had Charlotte beside herself. The world-famous venue held a special significance for her: she had seen the Beatles perform there. Our old friends the Blasters played as support, keeping it all in the family. I walked out on the iconic shell stage, a stunning view surrounding the hillside venue. Looking out at the thousands of people who had come to see us play very nearly caused me drop to my knees in disbelief.

Nearly two months later, I would want to fall to my knees in disbelief once again. As proof the patron saint of second chances looked out for me, the Go-Go's returned to Madison Square Garden—this time as headliners. Midshow, the lighting director illuminated the arena. Time went underwater, a formless and liquid moment as I took everything in, astonished at the sight before me, to the side of me, behind me. From the floor to the last nosebleed seats at the far round edges, every seat a placeholder, twenty thousand fans, each on their feet, spilling into the aisles and dancing with a collective, delirious abandon. Going nuts to our music, to our songs, to our singing and playing. I took a mental video and snapshot; it has remained the most vivid and tangible memory of my entire Go-Go's career.

28

GIANT BABY

A week after the triumph of Madison Square Garden, Charlotte, Jane, and Belinda were in a hot tub at the Sonesta Hotel in Amsterdam. We'd had some days off, trying to be as decadent as the city invited visitors to be. Finding the sex shows depressing, uncomfortable with the red-light district strolls, done with the novelty of buying legal hash, the band had settled into more sedate pursuits like shopping and eating. Until those girls met a middle-aged, balding European man in the hot tub.

I got a phone call to meet them in the guy's suite. For twelve hours straight, we hung out in the man's room. Later, we named him Jeff Jet-Set because for hours on end he name-dropped alt high-society icons such as Andy (Warhol), Bianca (Jagger), Halston (designer dude), and Liza (Minnelli). Who knew the incessant name-dropping was seduction foreplay? We sure didn't.

Even bringing out a bag of sex toys he had collected and invented failed to alert us. Instead, we looked at each one with clinical curiosity, patient little Go-Go engineering students: *Wait, that goes where? What happens then? Oh! It does that? Wow. Can you chop out more lines, please?*

Only as the time slid way past midnight did his wishful intent become apparent to us. Charlotte wandered into a bathroom and found a huge bubble-bath-filled tub, the room flickering in the light of a dozen candles that Jeff Jet-Set had painstakingly lit. She blew them out and drained the tub.

"Ewwww!" we said when she told us what she had found. "No way."

Jeff Jet-Set wasn't easily deterred. He set up the room again, and another Go-Go drained it. This time he asked us straight out if we wanted to get naked in the tub and "relax." *Nope.* We want to keep getting high, we told him.

"American women are such prudes," he said.

Then the guy actually left us in his suite and went off to replenish his cocaine supply—which we had depleted. He must have assumed he would come back and wear us down. Instead, he came back to find the room empty. We had waited for a while, decided we should eat, ordered three carts of room service filled with everything that sounded palatable after a night of drink and drugs, and finally worn ourselves out.

Jeff Jet-Set became one of our favorite stories to rehash and tell friends. Instead of questioning our judgment or asking, *What were we thinking?!* we only wondered, *What was he thinking? How dare he!*

In another hotel, in another city, the Go-Go's were in the bar having a good time, just the five of us. A businessman and his drinking buddy smirked and looked down upon us a few too many times. When the buddy left, the businessman settled back in his chair and had a couple more.

"You guys, look. That asshole passed out," Gina said.

"He has a wedding ring on," Belinda said.

"Let's teach him a lesson," I said.

Gina ran up to her room and got her trusty Polaroid camera. In the morning we hoped he, or better yet, his wife, would find the photos we took right there in the bar and slipped into his jacket pockets. Each was a staged masterpiece: the back of one of us very close to his crotch, looking like he was getting a blow job with his head back and his eyes closed. Or a trio of girls draped carefully around and in front of him, as if he were about to have the best night of his life.

I had a blast in Europe. It was a great change of pace after being on the road for months in the United States. Touring was the best part of being in a band, I thought. Like being a giant baby with a bunch of babysitters. Someone's arranging everything: telling you where to be and when to go, getting you there. Dinner is here at this time. Be in the lobby at 10:00. Have your luggage packed and ready to be picked up at 9:30. Many mornings I was too hungover to pack and made Bruce come do it for me. I would have toured year-round, just for the rhythm and structure. Touring enabled me to live in an adolescent bubble. No need to grow up for this job. When a tour ended, I couldn't make the shift smoothly. Staying away or going somewhere else helped. After our dates in Europe ended with a performance on the hit UK TV show *The Tube* and a sold-out Lyceum Theatre gig, I moved from the band hotel over to my friend Carlene Carter's home, where she lived with her husband, Nick Lowe, and their daughter, Tiffany.

These friends were the coolest couple of the era. Nick, both solo and in his band Rockpile, was one of my favorite artists. He made it easy to transition from fan familiarity to an actual friendship. Nick could charm a cobra with lyrics and a melody. He had a disheveled elegance and sharp wit, and everyone loved Carlene. Daughter of June Carter, heir to the Carter family legacy, stepdaughter of Johnny Cash—she wore her Americana pedigree like some old shirt she had tossed on. She was a walking lens flare of good nature, and a like-minded troublemaker. We stayed up writing songs till daylight gloomed its way through the window, using our last ounce of burned-out zeal to show the results to Nick for approval before stumbling off to sleep until afternoon. Most songs stayed unfinished, but one, inspired by a guitar hook Danny had given me, had promise. Titled "I'm the Only One," it sounded too classic rock 'n' roll to be a Go-Go's song, but I hoped Carlene might cut it.

After I returned home to LA, the band and a load of friends celebrated my twenty-fourth birthday at a Beverly Hills restaurant. I wasn't unaware how far I'd come in the two years since I'd joined the band at the age of twenty-two. Now, Go-Go birthday dinners had become competitive bacchanalian feasts, each one trying to rack up the highest bill that the accountant would pay out of our band account. These dinners were one of my favorite things the band did. Not only for getting a "free" over-the-top meal at a high-profile, fancy restaurant, but because whoever's party it was got to invite all her friends, and it was rare that band members got a chance to hang out with each other's best pals. The dinners were a way to get to know each other a little more deeply and in a different way than being in a band together.

Our hit records and sold-out arena tour obliged the music industry establishment to make room for the Go-Go's. Presenting the Best R&B Soul award to Marvin Gaye for "Sexual Healing" at the American Music Awards thrust us into a surreal setting of the major stars of our time. It seemed like most of the old guard didn't really get us. Maybe it was my imagination, but I sensed they thought of us as temporaries more than contemporaries, bits of fluff blowing by eternal monuments. All the award winners were artists who had been around my whole life, with decades of success behind them. A year later, poor Marvin Gaye would be tragically gone, and the Go-Go's would still be going.

The January cover of the *New York Times* Sunday news supplement proclaimed, somewhat prophetically, "It's Not Easy Being Rock's Sweethearts." The business behind the Go-Go's had gotten turbulent. IRS Records owed the band a million dollars and couldn't pay. The problem centered on the original contract calling for an advance and payment for the second record being determined by the sales of the first. No one expected millions of records to sell, and pipeline money—money stuck in the process from distribution to various sales outlets—takes a while to reconcile. Suspicious and uncertain whom to trust, the band found a new level of solidarity in our paranoia. In one meeting, we arranged separate talks with our lawyer, manager, and record execs, recording the conversations to "catch the liar" with a very un-spylike cassette recorder in a bag. The bumbling subterfuge and incompetence cracked us up so much I don't think the recording was even heard—too boring. The fun was in the plan and execution. It felt like our representation was just as inept. The lawyer threatened to have the band leave IRS; in turn, each band member was served with a lawsuit. It was an unnecessary and frightening way to handle our affairs.

Legalities and lawsuits ceased to be a problem when IRS presented the band with a check for one million smackers. Everyone passed it around to hold, kiss, rub on various body parts, and so on, but the relationship and trust with our label and team had suffered.

The Go-Go's had gained, along with our success, considerable financial, contractual, and legal interests, and the IRS contract fiasco wasn't the only trouble. With the advantage of hindsight, I can say that several of our business judgments were questionable. The first big mistake, when we refused to further exploit *Beauty and the Beat*, had been the band's choice—but we weren't stupid and probably could have been advised to change our minds. Rushing *Vacation* hadn't ended up a disaster, but I always wondered what kind of album it might have been with more time and writing put into it. Other missed opportunities added to my concerns. The Go-Go's, when offered a corporate sponsorship with Panasonic, complete with stock options, decided not to "sell out." I thought the deal provided visibility and lifelong income but got outvoted. A second sponsorship proposal came from Honda for a new scooter in its line; we rejected it for the same "selling out" reason. Within a year, artists from Lou Reed and Devo to Grace Jones and Miles Davis were all shilling for the cute little motorbikes. So much for righteous, dumb integrity. The next offer, for Suzuki Jeep, got a quick green light. At the photo session in Japan, stylists arranged us for posters and commercials dressed in an array of bright-colored new wave stripes and polka dots.

Yep, things had gotten bigger than anyone could have expected. After several discussions between ourselves, we asked Ginger to join up with an experienced managerial firm. Finding a big-time partner for Ginger became our primary focus. Gina and I became friendly with some guys from a New York firm, Champion, headed by Tommy Mottola. Champion managed John Cougar and Hall and Oates. While Ginger held meetings and suggested different managers, Tommy treated us like pals, inviting us to dinners where actors including Christopher Walken, Joe Pesci, or Robert De Niro casually sat at the table shooting the shit. I wanted him to be our manager and was steeped in frustration along with Gina when the rest of the group voted for Front Line Management, a company headed by industry mogul Irving Azoff.

Front Line made me uncomfortable. Walking through the office, the sun streaming through the windows of offices and cubicles, I felt like a curiosity. Champion headquarters had floor-to-ceiling dark wood and comfy leather sofas. The guys acted boisterous and fun, like big brothers. Tommy and Champion were as New York as it gets; Irving and Front Line were as LA as it gets. On paper it sounds good to go with the LA powers, but Champion had a street feel and edge far more suited to the Go-Go's than the slick LA offices of Front Line.

Ginger stayed only a month before just disappearing—*poof*. At first it wasn't noticeable. There were a lot of people on board by then: new handlers at Front Line, Ginger's assistant, and Bruce, our trusty tour manager, were never far away, even when we weren't on the road. It took a long time before anyone realized she had just stepped away. No one ever talked about it, a typical Go-Go's reaction to things no one was ready to deal with.

Soon after Ginger disappeared, Irving left to be the president of MCA Records. He left an accountant with gray hair and a suit in charge of his management clients and brought in another barrel-bellied guy in a tan suit to help. That guy also happened to be our lawyer's boss, the head of her firm. I squawked about it to the band nonstop. We had gotten screwed. With no Ginger looking out for us anymore, and now our industry veteran heavyweight Irving gone, we had somehow gotten stuck with an accountant and a lawyer running things. What did they know or care about us? All they cared about was if the band was making dough for them! How could our lawyer ever advocate for us and also be under the thumb of her boss, our manager? It made no sense, and again, I stewed in righteous impotence.

No one starts playing in a band thinking about business. There's nothing cool and rocking about that crap, but dealing with those issues was pretty much the only thing going on—for way too long.

29

DIVERSIONS

I tried to enjoy our time off. Instead of feeling carefree, I was aimless and lost. Not playing together, touring, or writing songs was unsettling and fear inducing. I didn't want to lose any piece of what I had managed to get. I tried to enjoy my big paychecks and push the fear away with good times: buying rounds, picking up tabs at dinners, getting pricey gifts for my friends.

Jane and Belinda fared better; they were making new trails. Jane worked with Sparks, a band she had always loved. The collaboration produced a hit song, "Cool Places," and a video, and led to her appearing with Sparks at some of their concerts. I went by myself to see her perform with them in Hawaii, wanting to show support and keep a connection. We didn't get much time together when our band had time off, mainly because she was super into her guitar-player boyfriend and home life. I don't think Jane had the same fears as I did. She seemed fine closing the door on the Go-Go's if we didn't have work scheduled. Maybe because it was her first band, or maybe because she commanded a lot of attention between being one of the main writers and a primary focal point on stage. She was the quickest and most articulate with answers in interviews and the most comfortable with stage banter between songs. She never, ever seemed unsure or unconfident, and I was pretty much in awe of her.

Belinda, the bandmate I had shared the most fun and crazy times with on the road, started a high-profile romance with one of the stars of the LA Dodgers. By May she had gotten a part in a movie, *Swing Shift*, and starred in a live theatrical production of *Grease*. I went with Gina to see her performance as Sandy Dumbrowski, both of us cheering wildly from the audience every time she walked onstage. Gina and I were kindred spirits, locked together not just musically but in our desire to make the band be the best it could be. She seemed happy to relax for a while and had a close network of longtime friends from way before the Go-Go's hit it big. I admired how normal and centered she stayed, squarely focused on family, friends, home, and pets.

Having time off bolstered Charlotte's increasing inclination to isolate herself. She and her boyfriend, Peter Case, split up, and she lived alone in a beautiful 1920s home up in the hills. Not so long before, she and Pete had double dated with Danny and me on New Year's Eve. We had spent a lot of time together in the past, and I thought of her as my anchor in the band: it was Char who had gone out of her way to approach me, to ask me to be a permanent member, and to advocate for my song on the first record. Now, it seemed like my anchor was floating away. Her distance and indifference to our friendship and bond added to my overall sense of unease.

It wasn't just the band taking a break that pushed my abandonment button. Danny and I broke up. He'd been a good sport and boyfriend during a dizzying time. I'd been a crappy girlfriend and couldn't blame him when he found a normal, non-musician chick in New York. Living in two different cities and spending months apart, along with the fights, my drinking, and wild all-nighters, had worn us both out.

Miles Copeland got everyone together in July to discuss the third record. *Finally!* Six long months had gone by since our last concert in the UK. Aside from the few TV appearances on Dick Clark's *American Bandstand*, the *American Music Awards*, and *Solid Gold*, we had done nothing as a band. I would have thrown my arms around Miles if he hadn't been so darn aloof.

Ready for a change of producers and wanting badly to show some real progress on the third LP, we set to writing. This was more like it. Charlotte played me a song, sitting at the piano. It rocked like mad, and she played with an ease and comfort that sometimes still eluded her on the guitar. Not only was I relieved to see her being her normal, creative self, I loved the song. The hooks matched perfectly with several notebook pages of lyrics I had been messing about with, and "Head Over Heels" became a collaboration. I was sure it could be a hit and pointed the way to the band's evolution. What the hell, I thought, and played the gals a demo of "I'm the Only One," the song I'd written with Carlene Carter and Danny. To my surprise they liked it, and the rocker was added to our growing list of new songs. I exalted in the new charge in the air, the revving up of the machine.

And then everything came to a screeching, grinding stop. Charlotte revealed that her left hand had been numb and tingling for some time. Reluctant and afraid, she had waited months before seeing a doctor. I'd never heard of the diagnosis, carpal tunnel syndrome, and didn't understand it. Immature and lacking a fully developed sense of empathy, I panicked at what this meant for the Go-Go's. Maybe it was psychosomatic, a problem brought on by stress, somehow brought on herself. Waiting for the outcome, I spun out frantic scenarios. Did this mean the end of the band? Maybe someone else could play—maybe Char would write songs and then not perform with us? Being a Go-Go had become more than a career, more than fulfilling a dream. Being a Go-Go was my entire identity. Being a Go-Go enabled me to do everything that I valued. I could take care of myself; I was sending money to my mom too. Without even a thought, I had stepped right into the reverse role of a daughter caring for a mother.

Once again in a holding pattern, I sought distractions from the fears and worries. I went to Hollywood parties and met cool people. Eddie Murphy threw a big birthday bash, where I met and befriended Rob Lowe. We clicked right away, probably because I was enamored more by his grounded sincerity than his looks. Through Rob I met Jodie Foster, and another easy friendship began. When Rob's on-and-off romance with his actress girlfriend faltered, we went on casual dates to Dodger games or concerts. Being single for the first time since my success, I found crushes and romps with cute guys as good a way to pass the time as any.

A new band named Chequered Past played the Roxy. The band featured Nigel and Clem from Blondie, along with Steve Jones from the Sex Pistols, Tony Sales, and bon vivant Michael Des Barres. I had heard that they covered "Vacation" and couldn't wait to hear the take on my song. Plus, I'd had a thing for Clem since my teen years. I had only met him once before, when he introduced me to Andy Warhol at an NYC party in honor of the Go-Go's.

Clem Burke doesn't just play; he performs on drums—and not as a gimmick. He's a volatile balance of frenzied freedom and perfectionist control. All his cylinders fire with a combustion and power impossible to look away from. It says a lot about Debbie Harry's self-assurance that she had let a showman like Clem rave behind her in Blondie. I was attracted to both his rock-star persona and his shy charm. Clem had a consummate charisma and innate class beneath a mop top of black hair and Ray-Bans. He was a sophisticate drawn with a philistine pen, a rocker in a mod suit, certain of nothing more than what in pop culture should be revered and what should be ignored. At the Chequered Past gig, I rethought my single status.

Chasing Clem, flirting with cute actors, hanging out in Hollywood clubs, and scoring invites to cool parties proved to be nothing but diversions compared to the next score. The real deal—the absolute random insanity and perfection of fortune—found me again. The Go-Go's were asked to open for David Bowie. Squealing like schoolgirls on steroids and reeling like fevered dervishes, any concerns about Char's wrist were quickly shoved aside. If she hadn't healed, her ex Peter Case, or Jane's boyfriend, Tim Scott, could learn the songs and fill in. Nothing was going to stop us from sharing a stage with Bowie, a deity to everyone in the band. The Serious Moonlight Tour would be his first since his *Low* and *Heroes* albums. The combination made sense; MTV brought crossover audiences to countless bands, and the Go-Go's added a contemporary freshness to the bill. And Bowie's endorsement gave us the gravitas we had craved.

Two solid years of touring and recording, then nine months of stop-and-start bullshit, and now: the biggest gig of our lives at Anaheim Stadium with David Bowie. Our booking agency put together a string of shows to warm up, starting in Austin. We named it the Serious Bar-B-Que Tour, riffing off Bowie's Serious Moonlight tour name. The Bowie people weren't amused, but no one stopped us. Backstage in Austin, I had an awkwardly weird reunion with a cross-section of old friends, including my high school mate James, who'd had an affair with my mom, and my old drug dealer boyfriend, Charlie.

I had left home less than five years ago. Since then, I'd written a hit song, sold millions of records, and toured ten countries, and now I could play the biggest place in my hometown. Not bad for a fucked-up wild child. All that stuff from the past was far away, and I didn't like being reminded of it.

The crews kept an industrious backdrop, setting up tuning stations, pushing road cases out of the way, and adjusting lighting rigs. The warm-up shows served us well, Charlotte playing all of them with no hand problems. The band sounded great during the sound check, our music blasting from vertical lines of speakers into the stadium of empty seats. Gina's pounding drums and the melodic rumble of my bass laid a solid foundation for the jangling crunch of Jane's and Charlotte's guitars. Belinda's voice, now one of the more distinctive ones in pop, had gotten stronger and sassier. Our harmonies and unison singing weren't perfect, but the girl gang choruses came from a place no other band could lay claim to.

I could relax again. The band had gotten through all our problems and even come out further ahead. David Bowie had chosen us to play this huge show. I couldn't wait to meet him. I had encountered or befriended plenty of famous people but few of my rock 'n' roll idols. There's a photo in one of his tour books with Gina and me talking to him backstage. I'm gazing at Bowie, awestruck and dumbfounded. Gina did the talking while I grinned and nodded.

Thousands of people streamed into the stadium as the band got ready backstage, all nerves and anticipation. Then we hit the stage.

"This town is our town," our voices sang, unaccompanied and in unison. The declaration hung in the air, bold and brash, exuberantly youthful. The crowd roared. A pause for several seconds before continuing with a stylized, four-part harmonized a cappella repetition. Just two words, repeated: "this town." Chugging guitar and staccato drums came in, followed by a reverb-drenched guitar line anchored by sub-heavy low bass notes. Our set launched flawlessly and set the pace for one of the most electrified performances the band had played. We had risen to the occasion. We were still the Go-Go's.

30

HELICOPTER

Energized by the success of the Anaheim Bowie show and knowing a third record was imminent, I intensified my songwriting efforts. I partnered with Jane and Gina much more than in the past. Miles Copeland suggested Martin Rushent, another perfect producer choice. The Go-Go's were the first American band he had agreed to work with. Martin had earned a British Producer of the Year award and had made records with the Stranglers, Buzzcocks, and the Human League, including their massive hit "Don't You Want Me." I worried Martin might make it heavy on synthesizers, and Gina didn't want him to dominate the record using drum machines. A phone call convinced me that Martin could be trusted to elevate our sound. Everyone loved the idea of recording at Genetic Studios in England. He had built it as part of a compound where he lived in Goring, a small village in the countryside on the River Thames.

Late in the fall the Go-Go's arrived in the UK with our songs written and our instruments. Our tour manager, Bruce, settled us into the Swan at Streatley, a rustic country hotel minutes from Genetic. It seemed a mismatched choice for a hard-partying rock band but added to the breathless adventure of making a new record in a different country. Miles Copeland had done a splendid matchmaking job with Martin and us. Martin would have made a lovable pirate or Viking, with his broad, ruddy face and uproarious laugh, holding court with a goblet of mead. His unruly hair and beard, along with a bawdy humor, were all kept in check by the smallest measure of obligatory English restraint. Right away, the chemistry ignited, fueled with jokes, irreverence, and mutual respect.

As a prankster, Martin had me well beat. Breaking for dinner one evening several weeks into the record, I had spied his pack of smokes and spiked one with a cigarette load. These little charges usually did nothing but startle a smoker—a harmless, old-school joke. The band left the studio, giggling at the idea of Martin coming in and lighting up. I returned from dinner having completely forgotten the prank—until Martin looked up from the mixing board in the control room, a bandage patch on his eye. A whoosh of horror saturated my blood. Confessing didn't make me feel any better. Martin said the load had shot right into his eye and burned it. He would be seeing a doctor in the morning.

I was terrified his eyesight might be permanently damaged on my account. Martin occasionally tried to console my guilt-ridden ass with a sad, resigned demeanor, making me feel worse. The rest of the band slunk around like bad dogs, shame-faced but relieved it hadn't been one of them who had inflicted this injury on innocent Martin. After a sleepless night, I ordered flowers the next morning, delivered with a handwritten groveling apology.

The session started after lunch the next day. He was masterful to the end. Despondent and worried, when I entered the studio, I saw him sitting behind the console, his back to the door. He thanked me for the flowers, swiveling around and ripping the patch off his eye, his deep, gleeful laugh multiplying until he nearly collapsed. All the while, I went from slack-jawed disbelief to flooded relief that he'd made up the injury in a massive prank retaliation. A big bear hug and all was forgiven, but never forgotten. Later, in my hotel room, a bouquet of flowers from Martin waited for me with a card. They were the same flowers I had sent him. Nice touch, bastard!

The Go-Go's were lucky to work with producers who weren't music snobs and who understood our strengths. Gina impressed Martin so much with her timing and consistency as a drummer that he bypassed his beloved drum machines and had her play every drum part. He was pleasantly surprised to find us to be far better musicians than he had realized. The songs came to life as he expertly added modern touches that gave the record a new finesse, getting great vocals out of Belinda and the most ambitious backup vocals we had ever pulled off. I thought the teamwork and commitment seemed to be making the band stronger, and the self-imposed pressure to prove ourselves yet again brought out our best efforts.

For a producer into synths, Martin sure knew how to get a great guitar sound. In a big departure, the band let me provide some different guitar skills for several solos and parts. The sessions were moving at a good pace, and Charlotte was under a lot of pressure to deliver. Timing, inspiration, physical setbacks— I wasn't sure of the factors making it difficult for her. I just wanted to contribute anything I could to keep the record and the band thriving, and knew I could bring some good playing to the table. But I had also developed some diplomacy skills and didn't want Char to feel displaced or inadequate. After a day of recording, I would take a cassette of backing tracks to my room at the Swan and play along for hours to write a solo for the next day. Neither of us were improvisers, and our structured songs didn't need long, noodling solos, just a melodic and memorable lead that could be part of the song. In the studio, I would show her what I had come up with, get it approved by Martin and whatever band members had shown up, and continue on to record it. I ended up playing any needed guitar solos on side one of the album and a B-side single track. It thrilled me to both play them and hear how they worked in the songs. I hadn't gotten to do that on guitar in a few years, and never on a major record release. Charlotte could learn them later to play on tour.

I also got to contribute more writing on this third record, with six cowritten songs. After successfully finishing "Head Over Heels," I had shown Charlotte an acoustic descending guitar riff, and it developed into the ballad "Mercenary" with Jane's lyrics. Gina and I wrote two songs for the record, both almost unrecognizable as Go-Go's songs: "Good for Gone" and "You Thought." The former, a kind of rockabilly-pop hybrid, backed a single, and the latter worked well as a synth-pop album track once Belinda sang it. I gave Jane a cassette of a song with just a chord progression and a melody. She came up with the title "Beneath the Blue Sky," and we wrote the lyrics to perhaps our most political song. Jane delivered complete lyrics on three other songs, cowriting or writing seven songs for us. Charlotte revealed she had struggled with writer's block, but what she did contribute made the record shine brightly and happened to be the first two singles. Belinda had been too busy to join in the writing, but her voice made every song a Go-Go's song. The band had come up with great arrangements working collaboratively, no matter who wrote what. I loved my bass parts, and I loved my guitar solos. I had grown as a musician and had room to shine with melodic runs and hooks.

Still, I fantasized what the band would sound like if things could get switched up a little sometimes. Char had played bass in her previous band and could tear it up on piano. Her keyboards slayed in "Head Over Heels" and added great effect on "Forget That Day," a song I'd played lead guitar on. What would it hurt if we moved around a little? It might make the band more dynamic, I reasoned—only to myself, certain no one would go for the idea.

Apparently, I wasn't the only one fantasizing about loosening up the format of the band. Except Jane didn't keep it to herself.

She asked to sing "Forget That Day," a track that had turned out to be an epic favorite of all of ours. It was personal to her: her song, about her life. The four of us gathered to discuss Jane's request and shot it down immediately. *How the hell would that work? What if it became a single—wouldn't it be confusing? What if everyone wanted to sing a song? And what would Belinda do while Jane sang her song?* It was decided. Everyone had their role, and Belinda sang.

Jane didn't take the rejection well. The rigidity of the band angered her. Without telling any of us, she left—just got on a plane and left the record, left the country. Aghast at this affront to our uniform goal, I thought her ego had gotten out of control. In my view, letting one person have the power to decide something as major as singing a song didn't seem democratic. I couldn't see that right under my feet, in front of my nose, the band I wanted so badly to keep together had splintered to a degree that would prove to be beyond repair.

Only the wisdom of maturity would allow me to reflect and wonder what the big fucking deal was—why not give Jane what she needed to feel fulfilled in the Go-Go's? I've wondered many times how it would have been if part of the whole deal had been to keep everyone happy. If we had written songs together in rehearsals and made sure everyone contributed. Treated Belinda more like the diva she had rightfully become instead of making her feel guilty for being the breakout star. Recognized the sadness and pain engulfing Charlotte and carried her through it. Let me play the damned guitar I loved so much on a cover song. We could have supported each other and granted space for each of us to grow instead of confining ourselves to a formula with a limited shelf life.

Until the drama with Jane, the recording of our third record, *Talk Show*, had been business and pleasure as usual. Belinda and I went on regular shopping trips into London, I had my

English family and friends to visit with, and we enjoyed band dinners where some of us got elegantly wasted. I had acquired a taste for expensive wines and cognac, becoming more of a high-brow drunk than before. Rob Lowe came to film a movie, *Oxford Blues*, and I found time to meet up and hang out. When Johnny Cash played the Hammersmith Odeon, I got tickets and took Rob and Belinda. The three of us hadn't hung out before and it seemed like it would be fun, especially seeing the two of them being spotted like crazy. The fun stopped when Rob and Belinda disappeared, slipping away and leaving me backstage after the show. Realizing I had been ditched and feeling like a fool, I couldn't keep myself from crying in Johnny Cash's greenroom. June Carter Cash, ever a mother and caring human, pulled me close and hugged me tightly while I sobbed my tale of woe.

"You listen," she whispered in my ear. "Any man going to leave you like that just ain't worth cryin' over." Being comforted by June Carter Cash was worth getting dumped. My sniffles stopped and, shrugging it off, I treated myself to a nice hotel for the night. It's not like we were a couple, after all. Better to keep being pals and not get my ego battered again. The next day in the studio, Belinda apologized and it became a running joke—no one wants to fight with her best mate over a guy she's not even in love with.

I had a new guy pal to flirt with, anyway. I had met Dave Stewart from the Eurythmics. He lived in London and we became good pals. I was enamored by his talent but quickly found his character to be endearing. Dave moved about in the world with a generosity of spirit I hadn't encountered before. He wanted everyone around him to be reveling and enjoying the full potential of his or her gifts—and if he could help make it happen, that's what he did. I learned a few life lessons hanging out with Dave. He had retained a childlike enthusiasm and wonder about the world. His nature brought out my own sense of innocent curiosity and softened me. I thought he seemed most cool when he wasn't being cool, when we were goofing off. After a Eurythmics show I attended, I watched how he and Annie Lennox stayed to sign autographs and meet fans afterward, treating each one with kindness and respect.

Belinda had her vocal coach fly over to help with the tracking of her singing. The rest of us couldn't stand him. I had once taken a "lesson" from the same coach. It consisted of doing vocal exercises on all fours, with him always positioned behind me for some reason. I thought it a complete waste of money to have him there. He made eye contact at the breast level, he wore pleated khakis, and he hovered around all our conversations trying to listen in, earning the nickname "Helicopter." He just generally annoyed the hell out of me. But I could still have some fun with him there. One day in the studio, everyone waited to do backup vocals while Belinda worked on her part.

"It's weird, but Helicopter seems to always be around where I am," Charlotte said to me. "He's always rushing to open doors for me or sitting next to me and making conversation."

I tried to keep a straight face and not snicker. Impossible—my shoulders shook, my cheeks and mouth pursed to keep the howling in, my eyes teared up, and my face turned red.

"God damn it, Kathy. What did you do? What the fuck did you do?"

I could barely speak. "I told him you were into him. That you liked him." I was nearly rolling on the floor.

We laughed about this for decades. "You bitch," she would always say, but Charlotte knew it was the best part of having to put up with the Helicopter.

31

CONVERTIBLES

Recording with Martin had been fantastic. We made great music, made each other laugh, and made great memories, but still: a fuzzy frame of darkness stayed around the edges. It was like trying to keep smoke behind a door; it just kept finding a way in. The obvious culprit would be drugs and alcohol, the cliché vices of artists through the ages. Everyone drank; everyone was amenable to getting high or low or whatever suited the occasion. For me, working with the band again had put some control and balance back into my life. I'd had my share of binges and hangovers but had no real regrets other than the video fiasco in Atlanta on our first tour. I assumed everyone could handle their recreational drinking and drugs, and I thought no out-of-control problems existed. The deaths of my friends John Belushi and James Honeyman-Scott from overdoses didn't portend any similar tragic endings for a Go-Go—we were your standard, boilerplate '80s-era party gals. Sometimes I wondered if Charlotte seemed to be in a little deep, but then things would normalize, the good times would roll, and concerns would dissipate into the wisps of smoke that seeped through.

Right before we broke for Christmas, Clem Burke called me at the hotel in England. He had broken up with his girlfriend and wanted to know if I would be his date in New York for the first MTV New Year's Eve party. *Fuck yeah, I wanna do that!* At twenty-five years old, I felt like a teenager when he asked.

I bought my mom a ticket to England to spend the Christmas holiday with our family there. She had no trouble getting time off because she didn't really have a job anymore. She partly owned a hair salon after I gave her money to invest, but it promptly failed. Then she started managing a musician friend. She did what she wanted to do for as long as she wanted, and I picked up any financial slack. We weren't nearly as close as we both liked to think. Our bond came from partying together and from me taking care of her needs. The abnormalities of our mother-daughter relationship just kept mutating—it would be impossible to rewind and untangle the dysfunction. The only thing normal about us was that I loved her and she loved me. Sometimes love comes with just the basics, no bells and whistles.

Spending New Year's with Clem in New York cemented us as a couple. He was successful and handsome, a rock 'n' roll gentleman with style and elegance—just as comfortable having high tea with the queen at Claridge's as he would be at a drag queen show in a dive bar in Berlin. I wasn't just getting the teen crush I'd had for a decade. Clem made me feel like I had a solid and loyal supporter from our first real date. He was attentive and respectful, and he totally got the whole deal of being in a hit band—the work, the creativity, the strong personality dynamics.

The Go-Go's reconvened in the UK to wrap up the record and listen to mixes. The time apart for the holidays had buffed out the troubles before taking a break. Jane had been gone longer because of her abrupt departure after the singing issue, but as usual, the incident was ignored. She kept a professional but frosty veneer that I felt sure would blow over and melt with time. I didn't have a care in the world: I played in a great band, we had made a record in England that I felt extremely proud of, and I had a new boyfriend whom I was crazy about.

On the first two record covers, our appearance didn't date the music. We probably should have kept the kitschy outfit idea and left the bad hairdos and wardrobe off *Talk Show*, but everything had to be different this time. "Head Over Heels" came out as the first single. In the video, filmed on sets awash in shifting palettes of color, each Go-Go featured equally, with little cameo moments and close-ups. I played a custom-made bass made with a Thunderbird-type body and heart-shaped tuning pegs. Today, the bass hangs on the wall of some far-flung Hard Rock Café. The video captured us well. Belinda looked glamorous without trying, Charlotte came across as the serious musician, I shyly rocked and rolled, Jane did her best innocent sultry, and Gina looked gorgeous while kicking ass.

Gina always looked cool and in command behind the drum kit. As a Go-Go, she arguably had more influence than any of us in inspiring young girls to pick up an instrument. Gals that could play drums like Gina were rare, and she took her playing very seriously. I could see her listening to a new song, deciding in her head how she wanted to try it before picking up the sticks. Gina didn't want to just keep time and power a tune along; she wanted it to have parts, crafted and fitted to give the song something special, hooks only she could supply. Once she found the perfect parts, she executed her drumming flawlessly every time. I could probably count on one hand how many mistakes she made.

Gina took care of herself in her own unique way too. If her nose got stopped up, she would see the sinus doctor. If she got a tummy ache, she got medicine. Antibiotics, antihistamines, antacids—the cure was in the pill. Recently, she had asked for oxygen at gigs and complained of dizziness. I teased her about being a hypochondriac, and the band gave each other plenty of eye rolls. Then she came to rehearsal one day with a recording device taped to her chest. I thought she might be taking things a bit far, but the lines tracking her forehead and the hollow fear in her eyes gave me pause. I shrugged it off. Surely it was an overreaction, the doctor appeasing her nerves.

The next day at practice the band lounged on sofas in the biggest, lushest room the rehearsal place offered. We had an expensive "lockout," our equipment always set up and ready. The couches got used much more than the gear did. In the hallway on a pay phone, Gina spoke with her doctor. Pushing the heavy door open, she entered, trembling. The pink had drained from her skin. The doc wanted to see her. Not next week, not tomorrow—he wanted her to come immediately.

Without hesitation, Charlotte said, "We will go with you," as the rest of us chimed in our support. The five of us charged into the doctor's office and waited in a row of seats in the reception area until Gina's turn. In the consult room, a light box displayed an X-ray of her chest. The results of the tests and exams had revealed a congenital hole causing abnormalities in blood flow and oxygen levels. Gina needed major, all-out, breastbone-cutting, rib-cage-shifting, organ-moving open-heart surgery. It was staggering, frightening news for anyone, especially a bunch of twenty-somethings.

Time rushed, whooshing like a whirlpool of disorder. The surgery was scheduled for the following week. The thought hit me: the only way through the next few dreaded days was to whisk Gina away, take her mind off the operation, have a blast. *We are all in this together.*

"Let's rent a couple of fancy cars and do a road trip," I said.

The next day, the band split into a Cadillac and a Jaguar, both convertibles with the tops down. Speeding down the I-10 freeway, whooping and waving, overtaking each other in turns, the Go-Go's were at our offstage best, united in purpose and intent. As we passed mountains and dinosaurs and wind turbines, the landscape blurred from industrial parks to low, flat commercial centers and finally morphed into the desert. Three suites awaited at the Two Bunch Palms, a well-known resort in Desert Hot

Springs. Our mission was to help Gina relax and forget about her surgery. She watched, Zen-like and bemused, as her bandmates "helped" her by carrying on like madwomen, instigating wild antics in hot tubs, laying hungover at the pool, indulging in spa treatments, and keeping the room service staff busy. At one point, Gina lay on her back, arms crossed over her chest like a corpse, while everyone gave spontaneous eulogies. All our antics were documented in typical pre-phone camera way, with Polaroids. When the getaway weekend ended, the bedraggled Go-Go's piled into the two luxury cars and took our patient back to have her heart mended. The surgery took half a day and the recovery would take months, but it saved Gina's life.

By the time "Head Over Heels" peaked at number eleven at the end of May, preparations to hit the road again were underway. IRS sent a double-sided test record out to radio stations in LA, with "Turn to You" and "I'm the Only One" for feedback in choosing a second single. The two biggest rock stations chose "I'm the Only One," but IRS went with "Turn to You" anyway. I took their choice as a slight, certain Miles and Jay didn't respect my songs or contributions to the band.

I got over it quickly when plans for our next video took shape. Director Mary Lambert, who had made some Madonna videos, had signed on. Mary turned in a clever script for "Turn to You." The story line set us in the '60s at a fancy party in a mansion. We would play dual parts, in drag as a guy band with a girl drummer, and as female party guests dancing to our guy band selves. Seeing a part for a male lead, I suggested Rob Lowe. His heartthrob star was shining bright, and our friendship had endured. Short-haired wigs and terrible suits didn't quite do the drag transformation justice, so everyone tried to outdo each other in body language manliness. In one segment, the Rob

Lowe character ditches my character for the Belinda one. The three of us laughed at the absurdity, even though Mary had no idea she had written an art-imitates-life scene.

INXS joined us on tour, making an outstanding bill. The Prime Time Tour turned out to be the most sober and healthy one I had given myself. I missed Clem and went back to my hotel room after shows to talk on the phone. Jane had a boyfriend, too, so she and I were in the same headspace and hung out more, even starting a jogging routine. Being more of an observer than a participant, I saw a patina of reckless wretchedness to the tour. It's not like I became a Goody Two-shoes all of a sudden, but being somewhat well behaved highlighted the contrast between feral and wild. For the girls who were single, the INXS boys could be tons of fun, awfully good-looking, and happy to indulge the night away.

The Go-Go's got along, laughing and entertaining ourselves as always. We were a little slick with wear, conceding the lightest of isolations, avoiding factions. The friendships in the band overlapped, rising and falling like tides, with no real issues in terms of personal difficulties. Resentments, jealousies, and insecurities had their own undercurrent, but these, too, came and went without real damage. I had no desire to sing lead or be the star—growing up a Stones fan had imprinted me with their format as the ultimate band template: I was fine with there always being a "Mick Jagger." Would I have rather been the Keith? Absolutely. But the unmitigated blessing of getting to do what I loved overrode my preferences. To actually make a living playing music to cheering crowds on giant stages in more cities and countries than I had ever dreamed of going to could override about anything.

And yet . . . I had really expected Char to step it up on the guitar after *Talk Show*. I badgered her to practice more. The guys in INXS were dynamic and fantastic musicians. I thought they highlighted our limitations, and the question whispered in my mind: How much further could the band go if we were better musicians? It was the raven sitting on the amp head and became an inner conflict and an outer division—a negligible divide with the girl who had gotten me in the band, had helped me get "Can't Stop the World" on the first record, and had always been willing to write songs with me. Charlotte had been my ally. Now my insecurities about our band being taken seriously worked to undermine the friendship. I didn't take into account that she'd had a lot to deal with between carpal tunnel syndrome and writers block for our third album. And unbeknownst to me, she had an even bigger problem: a very secret and serious drug problem.

32

SHRINKING, SINKING

After we had toured for months, "Turn to You" didn't crack the top thirty. I hated feeling like a flop. A second *Rolling Stone* cover and story came out—the Go-Go's had landed the *Rolling Stone* cover twice in less than three years. At least this shot featured us looking fierce and empowered. Most of the reviews were generous, and a lot of exposure came from appearances on the biggest television shows on all the networks, as well as a deal for a live concert video. Still, the usual hot momentum evaded *Talk Show*.

The very first MTV Video Music Awards took place in NYC at Radio City Music Hall. Viewers got an extravagant array of music stars and actors, and a new idea of a nontraditional awards spectacle where anything could happen. This was the show where Madonna writhed on the floor in a corset and wedding dress, flashing her underwear while performing "Like a Virgin." The audience of stars watched uncomfortably, smirking and giving each other side-eye glances to gauge reactions. It turned her into an icon for life.

Belinda and I flew in on a day off from the tour to represent the Go-Go's. Dan Aykroyd announced us in a word-of-God-type speech, saying, "First there was the beat, and it was good." Shy and nervous, Belinda and I approached the podium and took turns reading from the teleprompter to announce David Bowie's win for "China Girl." Later, we weren't so shy, staying up most of the night at after-parties with everyone from Iggy Pop to Roger Daltrey.

IRS anointed a third single, Jane's "Yes or No." I wanted another song, maybe her "Capture the Light," or a second shot for my tune, "I'm the Only One." Something rocking. Jane's lyrics were usually quite good; she inspired me to up my game and work much harder on my own writing. "Yes or No" might be catchy, but for my taste, it was too lightweight. Gina agreed—she and I fumed over our powerlessness. The video had a low-budget, homemade look, with nothing going on but the Go-Go's meandering and goofing off poolside. The single barely made the top one hundred.

If *Talk Show* had been our first record, selling the several hundred thousand records it did, we would have considered it a huge success. But instead, the sales made the Go-Go's look like we might be on the decline. *Vacation* sold less than our *Beauty and the Beat* debut, but the touring for it had been our peak. Now there were slower sales and smaller venues. Everything was shrinking. A string of college and university shows brought the Prime Time Tour to the final dates in Texas. For the first time, the Go-Go's played Lubbock. I hadn't been there in years, since my summer visits as a child. In what may have been a rock 'n' roll first, a few of my aunts and cousins worked at the Convention Center concession stand during our concert, proudly wearing their backstage passes as they served sodas and popcorn. Back in my hometown of Austin, at the major venue, the Frank Erwin Center, a black curtain obscured a large section of seats to accommodate our reduced ticket sales. Last time, it had sold out. Disappointment had taken a toll on all of us, the excitement harder to muster up after going from headlining arenas to convention centers.

I didn't see the ship as sinking, but Jane did. She told us prior to the last week of shows that they would be her last. (Jane's memory is that she told us before the tour began that she was

quitting the band, but I am writing this book from my own recollections.)

I wondered how long she had pondered her decision: if it
had begun in England after her request to sing had been shot
down, or if she got disillusioned at a point on the tour. Between
our songwriting and the travels, I had spent more time with her
than ever before, but she'd kept her feelings to herself. The rest
of the band were just as surprised as I was. Next to Belinda,
Jane had the highest profile and was very popular with the guys.
I had little concern about such things and never rated any of us
in terms of sexiness or attractiveness. My main thoughts about
appearance concerned having a good haircut in an unnatural
shade of red. Jane changed her image often, always dressing
flamboyantly. Currently, she liked wearing her hair slicked back,
shiny and tight against her head, tucked behind her ears. It
added a hardness she could get away with because of the girl-
ishness of her voice. Jane's voice gave her a distinctive character.
It could have been cartoonish except she used it with a swift
decisiveness, always to the point and never frivolously. On the
road, she didn't stay out as late or indulge as frequently as my
other bandmates, so that form of bonding had its limits. Off the
road she always had a boyfriend and kept to herself. We weren't
the closest, but she had something I recognized and knew well:
a gritty determination driven by a need to produce and accom-
plish. She was integral to the band.

I knew it, she knew it, everyone knew it.

Jane quitting triggered a fight-or-flight response deep in my
psyche. If I felt this blindsided, her decision had to be devas-
tating to the others. This could destroy everything. Charlotte
thought of her as her main writing partner. Belinda and Jane
started the band together; they were the OG Go-Go's. Gina
and Jane loved each other. This sudden turn made me very
afraid. Hugging and crying, each of us in our own way asked

her to please reconsider. I knew she wouldn't. Jane doesn't un-make up her mind. Playing the final shows, going through the motions, forcing smiles and bouncing around the stage as though things were normal was the most artificial week we had ever spent together. Jane wiped tears away throughout the last concert. Seeing her sadness confused me. This couldn't be the right thing to do. We had history, love, and a sisterhood.

In the dressing room, everyone was drinking together one last time.

"You know we're going to get a replacement for you, don't you?" I asked her.

No one had talked about it, but I needed to voice it. I said it before anyone could utter the unthinkable: that the band couldn't go on without Jane.

"Of course," she answered, unsurprised.

I dealt with Jane's leaving by looking straight ahead. *D&C the loss; suppress any feelings getting in the way of survival.* I created a narrative and it became my hope: the Go-Go's had suffered a run of bad luck. The reduced sales had battered our morale; the level of drinking and drugs and touring had exhausted us. Maybe, I thought, the band needed this—new blood. If Jane wanted to abandon us and be a solo artist, we would learn to carry on without her—maybe even be bigger than ever before.

The five Go-Go's who had made a little slice of music history together were gone, leaving four of us uncertain and stunned. Before parting ways, I suggested moving me to guitar so the band could look for a new bassist. Female bass players were more plentiful, easier to find. Everyone agreed. Management got the word out right away.

Clem met me in Austin to depart for our first vacation together. On a cliff in Jamaica looking over the Caribbean, the happy warmth of the sunshine and locals melted the past months away.

I felt elevated by this new and wonderful present, making lifetime memories unconnected to the Go-Go's. Each glorious day had a variant on the same theme: ocean swimming, exploring walks, reading, getting high smoking giant spliffs. Every evening, a chef brought meals of fresh fish, curries, and plantains. I loved the simple luxury of sitting on rickety chairs outside our thatched hut, painted in pastels, the doors and windows opening to the sea. Without electricity, the only modern convenience was a battery-powered radio playing dub and reggae music while the sunset horizon gave up its color to a pitch black, stars shooting across the sky. After Jamaica, I felt recharged, invigorated, healthy, and absolutely ready to jump into my new role in the band.

Everything was going to be OK. Everything had to be OK.

33

LET'S HAVE A PARTY

The Go-Go's lived for fun. It was built into our band. Our rise had come from perseverance and talent, but plenty of bands have those qualities. Not all bands get the timing and luck. Nor were all bands able to conjure joy. The genuine exuberance of our music gave people an escape and a respite from the meanness and greed defining the era. The country had been changing radically under Reagan, who had just been elected for a second term. Beneath the guise of the "bright new morning" he heralded, dark forces were shaping the country. Thousands upon thousands were suffering and dying of AIDS while the government, under Reagan's lead, looked the other way. From the Moral Majority to the rise of morality-free capitalism, wealth and excess trumped everything, while the poor became the pariahs who deserved what they got.

The Go-Go's didn't write protest songs or make political statements in our music. Reporters never asked our opinions on anything of substance. There were no conversations about sexism or feminism. The most common question remained "What's it like to be in an all-girl band?" My rants about politics and social issues happened at three in the morning after copious amounts of blow and booze. But the against-all-odds story of a bunch of young women who started a band and took it all the way to the top had a nice echo to it. Maybe it was a reminder that this is exactly the sort of thing that's supposed to happen in America.

In order to believe that the band had any hope of moving forward, everyone had to know it could still be fun. The crucial element to the success of the Go-Go's couldn't be thought out or planned: it was chemistry. Ours was potent as hell, but without Jane, it would certainly be different. Finding our new Go-Go proved to be both bonding and entertaining, and a lot more work than any of us anticipated.

Convening in a conference room at Front Line Management, we saw a stack of videos and demos waiting—hundreds of them. Right away, the audio auditions were shoved aside. A search for chemistry needs more elements than listening to someone play "We Got the Beat" on a tape. The first vetting left us with several days of viewing, listening, and reading letters and credits until ten women remained in the running to be the new Go-Go.

Within days, they descended on LA and were given time slots to come play with us. Imagine walking in and having to play with a band that's been together for years, knowing you have four women scrutinizing everything about you: how you're dressed, how you style your hair, how you carry yourself, whether you're comfortable or nervous, aloof or overly familiar.

Out of the ten nervous wrecks who auditioned, only three were left standing at the end. Could there be a spark of chemistry? It was too soon to tell, but it sounded and felt good with each of them. A vote went around, and Paula Jean Brown became our new bass player. We were unanimous. Like me, she also played guitar; perhaps why she sounded familiar on bass. Paula's sweetness was nearly confounding—ours had splattered on the road years before. She didn't seem concerned or uncomfortable with the bond between the four of us. Paula kept focused on the music and the enormous opportunity before her. She had a couple inches on Belinda, making her the tallest in the band, and moony, liquid brown eyes and a large, full mouth. She wore her hair in a blunt bob with bangs and moved with an uncommon blend of awkwardness and grace. She had little to no coolness factor but was steady and observant and played everything right. We had made a good choice with Paula Jean. In December the press announcement came, along with our annual holiday photo session and greeting card.

The new lineup of the Go-Go's had our first dates booked, jumping straight into the biggest shows the band had ever played at the Rock in Rio festival in Rio De Janeiro, Brazil. Moving to guitar energized me, kicked my ambition into overdrive. I had lost weight in Jamaica on my vacation with Clem and looked fit and healthy. I had never felt more like a complete, fully realized rock star, my Strat set up and ready to take the band to the next level. The turmoil of the last year had been surmounted, and the biggest stuff felt yet to come.

It sure looked like we were on top of our game. A van drove us past an epic landscape of lush mountains, cascading to the sprawl of Rio along the South Atlantic. *Who gets to do this?* I thought, still in awe that I had the best job in the entire universe. Soon after checking in to the hotel, which was crawling with musicians, managers, and music-biz types, I went looking for the action. Rock in Rio featured a couple dozen big-name bands. Around the hotel pool, a motley array of rockers had arranged themselves, like a record store with no filing system. AC/DC guys lounged next to the B-52's, Iron Maiden's Bruce Dickinson chatted with James Taylor, and the Go-Go's scattered among the Scorpions, Ozzy, and members of Yes. Being in Rio for the concerts brought all the bands together in a temporary camaraderie. Each would perform twice at the festival, with the Go-Go's scheduled as openers for Rod Stewart the third night and Queen on the seventh night.

That left a lot of time to get into trouble.

It took barely a day to find great shopping, backstage parties, plenty of expensive wine, and cheap cocaine. Having a wild, two-person party in my room the second evening, Belinda and I went out on the balcony to find the source of nonstop Chuck

Berry music blaring from outside. Across the pool, on another balcony, sat a shirtless, tanned guy with blond hair and a choppy, spiked haircut. Rod Stewart sat in a chair, his feet up on the rail, Chuck Berry practically blowing the curtains out of his room. I waved. He shouted a greeting, his North London accent carried over by the chorus of "Maybelline." In moments we were in his suite, soon joined by members of his band. Hanging out with Rod felt as natural as meeting any other cool musician guy despite his music being some of my mainstay favorite songs of all time. We shared proximate Capricorn birthdays; he had just celebrated his fortieth a couple days before on the tenth, I had my twenty-sixth on the seventh. Drunk and high, overcome with warmth toward my new friend, I ran back to my room and rummaged through my stuff for a gift. Settling on a pair of binoculars, I returned, holding them behind my back. Rod seemed pleased enough, and the night wore on until daybreak. We finally called it quits after making plans for a double band dinner date.

The next evening, all the Go-Go's and our small entourage joined the Rod Stewart band and crew for dinner at Maxim's, the fanciest place in the area. The bands were well matched for pranks and goofiness. At one point, Rod insisted his band members follow his lead and push their trousers down to their ankles, unbeknownst to the proper waiters who brought out bottle after bottle of Cristal champagne, wine, and platters of pricey entrees.

On day three, our tour manager, Bruce, ushered the new Go-Go's from a van to a waiting helicopter. Rock in Rio was so large and spread out, the promoter needed to fly bands into the backstage area. The festival crowd numbered over 300,000, a swarming mass of people. After four years of touring, I felt like a pro, but nothing came close to this show. Running onstage, I couldn't remember feeling more electrified. My old Strat felt good in my hands, familiar and beloved. All the fear, upheaval, and problems of the past had disintegrated. I bounded around the stage smiling and thrilled, determined to make our new lineup work. Rod Stewart, an iconic classic rock star, now a pal, watched from the side of the stage.

On the last song, "Let's Have a Party," Charlotte did a keyboard solo, and for the first time on stage with the Go-Go's, in front of a quarter million people, I played the guitar solo—and it rocked. Paula, our new bassist, played perfectly and sang on every song—her very first show as a Go-Go, with no breaking in or warming up before the huge concert. Gina took care of business like always. Charlotte seemed to be having some issues, and Belinda tried her best but didn't look happy. Without Jane our chemistry had been altered, but no one could have convinced me it didn't work. Thrilled the band had survived together, being in the company of rock legends like Rod Stewart, I reveled in my new position, oblivious to anyone else's discomfort or struggle.

Denial came easy in Rio, where the band occupied a chaos bubble hovering over a suspended reality. Charlotte got thrown out of Ozzy Osbourne's dressing room for being over-the-top messed up. It was a badge of honor and made us proud. Helicopter rides took us careening on a swinging, tipsy flight past Christ the Redeemer and Sugarloaf Mountain. At press conferences and interviews, everyone looked wild and beautiful, joking around, singing "The Girl from Ipanema" to the reporters. Everything was happening in every direction: We saw a Carnival show with the B-52's, along with Chris Frantz and Tina Weymouth. We walked along Copacabana Beach in the afternoon. We spent late nights on streets lined with homeless street kids sleeping in tangled groups, the musicians sticking money into the kids' clothing. Gina fell in love with a Brazilian drummer. Belinda and I rode around in a taxi in the middle of the night, asking the driver, "Coca, coca?" trying to score. One night after ending up at a scary dealer's house, his giant girlfriend acting as translator and a gun on the table, we purchased much more cocaine than either of us wanted. Who was going to argue with them?

Rod had worked himself into a state, horrified to go perform his second headlining show. He had been up with us all night and day. I couldn't believe he had never, in his entire career, stayed up on a binge before having to play. "Hey," I told him. "We'll stand on the stage the entire time. Every time you start to feel terrible, look over at me and Belinda and know that as bad as you feel, we are worse!" We had been up two and a half days to his one, and this was my way of being a helpful, supportive friend.

Looking out at the crowd, being at the concert without having to work, I couldn't wait to get another chance to play guitar on that stage.

A few nights later the Go-Go's had a slot before the B-52's and Queen. I bounded exuberantly around the stage again, all smiles. The band did much better this time, with more energy and confidence. Doubling up on the microphone for some vocals, me and Char, me and Belinda, our faces inches from each other, we traded big grins. I lived for the song I would get to play the lead on, knowing this was just the start. The band had persevered through Jane quitting and new member tryouts. A month of rehearsals, interviews, photo shoots, and travel, and the two biggest shows of our lives offered the proof I needed: the Go-Go's were still the Go-Go's.

I had rocked in Rio all right, and I was sated from the experience. In our dressing room, the band waited to be shuttled back to our helicopter. Except for Charlotte—no one knew where she had gone. Paula took the opportunity to say something no one had said before.

"What is the band going to do about Charlotte?" she asked.

We looked at her with dumb, blank expressions. What's the new chick talking about?

34

FALSITY

Paula's entire purpose in the Go-Go's may have been to save Charlotte's life. She had returned our confused looks with an expression of disbelief—how could anyone not see that Charlotte needed help, that she was a heroin addict? *Well, shit,* I thought. I didn't know what was wrong, but yeah, this made sense. I didn't know because secrecy on the addict's part, and denial on everyone's part, keeps the game going.

Paula told us about her sister, who had needed an intervention and rehab to get sober, and how she thought rehab could help Char. It was decided that Paula should be the one to talk to her, partly because none of us had any idea what rehab and sobriety meant and partly because why would anyone listen to someone who liked to drink and drug themselves? I didn't see myself as having a problem, especially in the context of comparing drug uses. *C'mon.* Heroin is a league of its own, far removed from snorting coke and drinking pricey bottles of wine and cognac.

Leaving Rio behind, on the long flight to LA, the first-class lounge was filled with bands. Having played guitar at Rock in Rio not once but twice, I held an illusion of a secure future that nothing could pierce. Even though Charlotte had insisted on staying behind, I felt sure she would get back and go into rehab, and the band would write a batch of new songs, make a new record. Maybe I would even get to play some lead guitar, part of a new era, a new sound, new heights.

The first of my new heights perched at the top of Sunset Plaza Drive in the Hollywood Hills. After returning from Brazil, I finally bought myself a house—on the same street I had lived on with Catherine Sebastian when I'd learned the Go-Go's songs from a rehearsal tape.

My house was less than nine hundred square feet. From the street, the front door led into a kitchen and living room, with windows along the entire length of the south-facing wall. In the daylight, the city spread out in both directions from downtown to the ocean in a mottled design of indistinguishable textures, the imprint of hills and fauna, buildings and streets, homes and cars. At night the view pulsed and twinkled with life, a blanket of sparkles shook out by a giant hand. The top of the hill made me eye level with the fog that rolled in from the sea, swallowing my view in steady gulps, moving past Westwood and Beverly Hills, and coming after us in the hills until I became part of it, my windows just useless sheets of glass separating me from the outside.

The walls were white as an art gallery, built in a cubist modern design. I moved into the last house on Sunset Plaza, before the street curved around and moved into other neighborhoods. Since I had so little room in the house, I set up a four-track TEAC recorder in the garage to make home demos.

Buying my first house in LA was an act of faith in the future. Paula was good; Charlotte would be fixed by rehab. I did not for one second consider that my band was in a precarious place.

On a family-and-friends-visit day, Gina and I drove out together to visit Charlotte at her rehab facility. On the way we smoked a joint, obnoxious and unaware what a slap in the face it was to show up stoned. Waiting in a room where the chairs were arranged in a group session circle, I elbowed Gina when the head counselor came in. Looking at each other, our eyes begged the other not to bust out giggling. When Charlotte came in, everyone hugged and sat together listening and talking about their progress and program. I felt good for supporting her but was glad to get the hell out of there.

While we waited for Charlotte to return to the band, I was asked to play guitar in the house band for a benefit concert called Trouble in Paradise for the Los Angeles homeless. It was an all-star band with the Doors' Ray Manzarek and Fleetwood Mac's Christine McVie and Mick Fleetwood. Working in this new context, backing up an array of singers from Brian Wilson to Jackson Browne, along with my old friend Carla Olson, I felt like my star might rise a little further than ever before. The Go-Go's just needed to have a great record and comeback.

Charlotte got out of rehab in early spring. Eager to rev up the band right away, I fully expected her to be a new, improved version of herself, a revitalized band member ready to relaunch the new, improved Go-Go's. If she seemed a little quieter, a bit more distant, maybe it should be expected. If she gravitated to Belinda and Paula more, maybe that was okay too. Shrugging off the lack of electricity when the band got together, thinking it needed more time to settle, I leaned in close with Gina, who I knew wanted to keep things together as much as I did.

One of the guys at Front Line Management, Andy Slater, had taken on a bigger role in our management team. He arranged for the Go-Go's to record a song for a soundtrack in New York. Recording something one of us hadn't written didn't seem like the best idea, but he said being featured on the title song of a movie would generate a lot of buzz.

It was a disaster. The song, supposed to sound like slick, modern pop like "Eye of the Tiger" or something, didn't suit us. The producer, Reggie Lucas, didn't know what to do with us. When I was given the chance to play the lead solo, he wanted me to improvise something rockin' on the spot, which I tried and failed to nail in the intimidating, short time given. It was a terrible squander of time and money. I hated the blow to how things needed to be, how imperative it was for us to feel like a functioning band again. Maybe returning to songwriting, our strongest foundation, would bring some normalcy back. I tried to stake a claim with Char, to bridge the forming factions. All that our sessions yielded were a couple of crappy songs, each line and note sounding forced. I don't think a hundred songs would have made Char confident in our ability to be providers— she missed writing with Jane. Thankfully, Paula brought in a couple of good songs: "Mad About You" and "A Shot in the Dark."

An extraordinary twist of luck power-blasted any lingering concerns. Mike Chapman agreed to produce the next Go-Go's record. Mike Chapman had produced tons of hits for Blondie and my first heroine, Suzi Quatro. I knew he would understand exactly what the Go-Go's needed to become bigger than ever. For several weeks I continued to write songs with Paula and Charlotte and came to band practices trying to raise the level of excitement to match my own.

Chapman came to listen, exuding rakish Australian charisma, charm, and confidence. After playing our song ideas, Mike assured us he would help us make the biggest hit record of our career. I noticed that Belinda and Charlotte didn't seem nearly as thrilled about this whole prospect as Gina and I did. Sometimes they looked at each other in that way people do when they've had conversations you weren't privy to. When I saw them, it felt like an unstoppable gloom invading the room, like the fog that came from the sea to my house.

The pretense I insisted on living in contributed to the falsity that enveloped us. For Gina and me, the Go-Go's held our future. But for Charlotte and Belinda, the fun had stopped.

On May 9, 1985, I got a call. Front Line wanted a meeting. Immediately, I got in touch with Gina. "Something is wrong," I said. Picking me up in her Corvette, Gina's face was clouded with worry. We rode over together, using the winding drive down Sunset Plaza to float theories. For months we had been left out of discussions I wasn't even sure were actually happening. It had been like suspecting your spouse or mate had a lover but not wanting to know the truth—so you keep talking about your future, making dates, and reminiscing about all the good times you've shared. Gina and I had both left our hometowns and families, moved to LA in search of identical rock 'n' roll fantasies like so many other musicians. Our destinies had intertwined, and neither of us could imagine them unraveling. It was unfathomable that anyone, ever, would destroy something as rare as our band. Maybe one of them wanted to quit. I wondered how we would get through it. It would be bad, but surely the Go-Go's could go on.

When we walked into the corporate office, Belinda, Charlotte, and some Front Line Management people had already assembled. No Paula. It felt like an ambush. No preamble, no setup, just a cold sucker punch of a statement: "We've decided to break up the band."

The sentence exploded so swiftly and destructively, I don't even know who said it. Looking at the managers, at Charlotte, I saw no emotion. Belinda wouldn't make eye contact. Beside me, Gina nodded her head slowly. Did she feel like I did? Grief and shock, disbelief and anger, all thrumming like the wings of locusts, my nervous system and adrenaline in full panic. Infuriated by their smug authority, I tried to stay calm.

"One in a million bands gets to be where we are, do what we do. That's crazy." I barely got it out. My words were swatted away, annoyances.

"We've made up our minds," Belinda said.

"But Mike Chapman is going to produce us," I said, trying again. "I just bought a house."

To each of my arguments, Charlotte repeated, "I'm sorry you feel that way." Like a robot, or like Valmont in the film *Dangerous Liaisons* saying "It is beyond my control" again and again as he shattered and betrayed Madame de Tourvel. It was as if sobriety had turned her into some cold automaton.

Andy, the proxy-manager, perched on a desk corner, looking self-important and haughty. They probably already had Belinda's solo deal in place.

Gina spoke up: "It's our band too; you can't just decide it's over." Belinda looked Gina dead in the eye and told her, "Yes, we can."

Suddenly, Charlotte proclaimed, "I write the hits and she is the voice." It enraged me. How dare she? After everything, after the tours and radio visits and shows and interviews that gave us our careers, all of it done together, Miss Hits and Miss Voice were tossing us aside with less emotion than getting rid of old clothes. Furious and helpless, I turned to Charlotte. "I hope you go back on drugs and OD," I said.

"I'm sorry you feel that way," said Robot-Char. I felt horrible and took it back.

"I'm so sorry, I didn't mean it. Don't break up the band," I begged. "Please. Take a break, make a solo record, make movies. Take time off. Just don't break up the band."

But the meeting was already over. Everything I had worked for was gone in an instant: Four years and three albums worth of songwriting and playing music together. A chaotic connection formed over hours upon hours on bus rides, in dressing rooms, at airports and hotels, and during all those epic shows. My family was gone. In its place were strangers.

Gina dropped me off after a silent, stunned drive punctuated with outbursts of impotent fury. The phone rang as I came into the house; I answered to hear Andy from the management office. My hope soared—maybe they had changed their mind? But he plunged the knife in deeper.

"The *LA Times* are gonna phone in thirty minutes to get your comment about the breakup," he informed me.

God, I hated him.

"Are you fucking kidding me? Why now? Less than an hour later? What is wrong with you?" I hung up, shaking.

For hours I made phone calls: to Saul, to Bruce, to my friends, to my mom. I paced, smoked, and tried to make sense of what had happened. The Go-Go's had been the vehicle to all my dreams and had taken me on the journey of my wildest hopes. When the tires fell off, the transmission broke, the motor fell out—I was the stubborn mule trying to push the broken-down wreck of a band further along the road. It all meant so much to me, more than a band or a career. My self-esteem, my identity, my family, my purpose were all encased in Go-Go's wrapping, tied up in band life. The pain felt greater than any loss I had endured.

35

CAMOUFLAGE

The only person in the world besides Gina who knew how I felt was Clem. He had found massive success doing what he loved in Blondie, also at a young age like me, only to see the band fall apart a few years earlier. Fortunately, he was in LA. If we'd had cell phones and texting back then, his phone would have exploded. Instead, he walked in the house to find me in hysterics. Incredulous, he called Andy at Front Line and berated him and the company for fucking up a great band. My champion. Drained from the despair, we decided to go to the movies. And there, on the worst afternoon imaginable, as I careened through the shock of losing the band, I found a thread back to myself in front of the big screen. Watching the understated comic genius of Albert Brooks and Julie Hagerty in *Lost in America* unfold, my laughter—and the wonder and joy that I could laugh at anything—reeled me back to solid ground. It was just enough to get me through the rest of the day.

In the weeks following the breakup, I tried, along with Gina, to find some semblance of control or power. Taking action seemed imperative, and maybe there were legal rights. What about using the band's name and putting new members in place? Neither of us really wanted to do that, but still, something had to be done. We got an injection of excitement finding a great singer, Holly Beth Vincent, and tried to start a new power trio, but it was short lived.

Clem suggested a holiday in Greece. The submersion into a different world gave me a respite. I liked traveling with Clem.

He had an East Coast intensity and focus that made it more of a gift when he was laid back and dispensing with easy smiles. During those weeks on the island of Crete, the music business felt far away. Neither of us had driven stick-shift cars, so we lurched and gear-grinded our way through villages along the coast until finally our driving smoothed out and my nerves were calmed by the rugged, rocky landscapes and crystalline sea. The food and wine didn't hurt either.

Returning stateside, Clem had to go back to his home in New York. My home in LA was now where dreams had become nightmares, but I owned a house and had to try and plot a next move I had no idea how to make. The thought of going back became much more appealing when my friend Carlene Carter asked if she could come stay with me. Carlene could cheer up a zombie, and I sorely wanted some fun. The girls were gonna go wild.

But Carlene wasn't her usual upbeat self. Her marriage to Nick Lowe had broken down. Now me and my friend were both in the dumps. One night I invited some people over to cheer us up, including my Austin friend Charlie Sexton, who was in LA to record. Besides being a fantastic musician, Charlie had the pure and genuine sweetness of a puppy dog. When he spoke, his voice was gentle, and his humor and warmth made you feel good; he listened and paid attention. Besides these personality attributes, he was stylish and drop-dead gorgeous—like if you took Natalie Wood and Audrey Hepburn, Rudolph Valentino and James Dean, mashed them all together, and molded a porcelain-skinned, black-haired, full-lipped young dude out of them. Carlene and Charlie hit it off, and I reveled in my matchmaking skill even though it made me a third wheel. None of us minded—we stayed up till daybreak chatting, laughing, getting high, messing around with guitars and song ideas. We were an inseparable trio and my spirits lifted, surrounded by the talent and beauty of my friends.

The high heat of August and no air conditioning in my house caused Carlene to open the French doors in the guest room as she and Charlie slept late one morning. In my bed, I heard voices. I slowly swam to the surface from a deep, submerged sleep. I had only packed it in a few hours before. Leaning on my elbow and rubbing my eyes, I saw the door open and a large man enter, holding Carlene in front of him, his arm around her neck.

"It's ok, he's the gardener," Carlene said. She seemed frantic. The man, wild-eyed and sweating, didn't act like a gardener. Confused, I thought, *I don't have a gardener.* I did have a gardening shed outside, and he had been in there, evidenced by the trowel I now saw digging into Carlene's neck. My mind came alive along with a surge of adrenaline, kicking my hangover's ass.

He ordered me to get up. "Do what he says, Kathy," said Carlene. "He doesn't want to hurt us." I did as I was told. He wanted us all in the other bedroom. We stumbled from one room to the next, and in a whoosh of horror, I thought, *We are going to die.* Charlie lay on the bed, facedown, spread-eagle like a beached starfish. *Why had he stayed there so inactively?* I wondered, then recalled how the man had held the garden trowel to Carlene's neck. I tried to pay attention to what the intruder said, which was difficult because of how facts, assumptions, reasonings, and questions churned in my mind.

"I have people outside. We have guns. We are going to burn this house down. Lay down: You here. You here. Now I must secure you." He had no emotion, no panic.

He took a sheet, then a bedspread and covered us all and tucked it in tight under the mattress, like a tightly made bed in a hotel. "Now I must camouflage you," he said. He began picking up items of clothes, pillows, and towels, whatever he could find, and piling them on us.

All the while, amid his nonstop statements I had my own questions running through my mind. *Why is he using a trowel if he has a gun? I don't believe he has a gun. I don't believe anyone is outside.* The room went silent. I hissed, "We need to escape."

"Kathy, don't. Do what he says," Carlene said.

"We can take him," I said.

"No, no we have to stay," they said.

The conflict between terror, self-preservation, survival, and indecision puts them all at war and can leave you paralyzed. We're trained from earliest childhood that if we do as we're told, we will be rewarded. Disobeying brings punishment. You don't realize how ingrained the belief system is until you're in a situation with a human predator.

Our intruder came back, continuing to load stuff on top of us. I shook items off my head so my face could be visible. I had decided he wanted to kill us and was covering us up because it would be easier to kill a pile of fabric than an actual person. I wanted him to see me as a person. I talked to him.

"You need to go," I said. "People are coming over here soon. For a barbecue," I told him. "Take whatever you want. My band just broke up. All I want is to play in a band. Please don't take my Stratocaster but anything else."

The man told me to shut the fuck up. He walked around.

"Where is the money? Where are the drugs?" he asked, frustrated and angry. I told him that we did them all and he came too late. *Keep showing him my humanity*, I thought.

Time stopped; there was no order to anything. Statements, talk, action, events—they happened without gravity, floating in the air all at once, next to each other, passing each other. He stepped out of the room, and I pushed off the stuff piled on me and jumped up. Immediately I saw, at the foot of the bed, three butcher knives. They were mine, from my own kitchen.

Each one was placed at our feet, one for each of us. He barged back into the room, and I grabbed a knife and lunged at him. Carlene sobbed, Charlie lay silent. The intruder had no fear of knife-wielding me, and with reflexes like a soldier he grabbed my wrist and twisted it until I dropped the knife. "I'm sorry! I didn't want to hurt you; I'm just so fucking scared," I cried.

"You're going to get it for that little stunt!" he yelled and then pushed me on the bed, shoving my face into the pillow and yelling, "Shut up, shut up, shut up."

An electric sizzle and shorting-out sound made Carlene scream. "Shut the fuck up," he said. He tied us up, first Carlene, then Charlie. My turn came, and I felt a cord being wrapped around my wrists. I thought, *Once I am tied, all of us will be captive and he will have won.* I had read something—maybe in a Robert Ludlum book—about holding your wrists a tiny space apart when being tied up. Any space, any give, could make the knot come loose. I tried it, and it worked. I got my hands free of the cord but kept them behind my back as though they were still tied together. He thought we were all tied up, but I was free. Now I felt certain that there were no others, no guns, only one psycho terrorizing us. We could have overpowered him if we had stood against him, all of us together, but not now. There was only me, pretending to be bound.

"I hate to be the one to waste Kathy Valentine," he announced.

I tried humor again, trying to connect in a human way. "Don't be the one. I have an appointment to get wasted next week," I said. Carlene let out a fake, terrified laugh.

"I may have to take you with me," he said. It dawned on me: he must have seen my gold records hanging in the bathroom with my name on them. He thinks I'm some rich, important person living in the hills, someone he could kidnap and ransom. The other option, just as terrible, was that this would end like the Manson murders.

"You need to hurry. Take my car. The keys are in my purse. Take anything. I have very little but it's yours. I have insurance," I said, babbling now. As I slowed down, I noticed the room had gone silent. He had walked out again. *Now.* I jumped out of the bed. *Was there time to untie Carlene and Charlie before he came back?* If he returned and found me out, I knew he would kill us. *Escape and get help.* I flew through the French doors, ran down the rugged hillside and up again, scrambling, barefoot, heaving. I sidled up to my neighbor's house, rang the bell, and buried myself behind bushes. When I heard the door open, I jumped out and begged him for help.

My neighbor called the police and went back with me to free Charlie and Carlene. The guy had left. The evidence of the intruder littered the house. He had cut the cords off the fan, hair dryer, and a cassette player for binding us, the ruined electrical items like little victims lying around. The knives were on the floor. Clothes, towels, and bedding were scattered and piled around the bed where we'd been made to lay face down. He had taken Carlene's jewelry, including an heirloom diamond necklace from her mother, her rings, and a watch. He knew his stuff—he had thrown my cheap silver on the floor in my room. Drawers were pulled out, ransacked; my telescope was gone. It occurred to me to look at the time: two in the afternoon. The man had been there for over three hours. I went outside and saw that he had taken note of my suggestion and stolen my car.

The police came and offered some sobering insight. An officer told me that many murders occur just like this. What starts as a robbery escalates when the intruder gets in too deep, fears being recognized and caught. "You did everything right if you're alive," he told me.

I never stayed in my house again. It couldn't be my home, not after what happened. After getting the locks changed, we checked into the Sunset Marquis. The three of us piled into a king-size bed in a suite and wallowed in PTSD. The next day I went to the house with a friend and found my keys on the ground by the door. The intruder had come back and tried to get in. Afraid and freaked out, I rushed back to my fellow sufferers in our little sanctuary. My car showed up abandoned on a street in the Hollywood Hills, but I didn't want it anymore. Everything reminded me of the trauma. The police called and asked one of us to come give a description to the police artist to make a perpetrator sketch. Since I'd had the most interaction with the man, the job fell to me. For two weeks I stayed in the hotel with Carlene and Charlie, ordering room service and booze. Someone brought some drugs over and chopped out lines on the coffee table. I did my share and fell asleep, aghast to find out it had been heroin when I came to. Terrified at having done heroin, panic-stricken at having a house and a mortgage but nowhere to live, hyperventilating when I saw large men, it felt like only Charlie and Carlene understood. When some people suggested we needed to put it behind us and move on, we hunkered down and isolated more.

The band breakup, the home break-in—now I was broken.

My friends Saul and Carla knew someone hoping to sublet their apartment. I took it. Moving out of the Sunset Marquis, I gave no thought to the enormous bill I had helped rack up for the weeks I'd hung out in the king-size bed of the suite with Carlene and Charlie. June and Johnny picked up the tab.

I woke up to the late-morning sun coming through a musty bedroom window with floral drapes and matching bedspread. In front of where I lay, a table was piled high with sewing accessories, and shelves of tchotchkes lined the walls. My life felt as unfamiliar and cluttered as the stranger's home I had moved into.

36

THE SAME UNION

I missed Clem and needed some time with him. Being his girl-friend felt like the only vestige of my former life. He wanted me to meet his dad, a Polish widower with sad, sweet eyes and a gentle demeanor. We had a mutual understanding of what it meant to be an only child with one parent, and we both felt the weight of responsibility and duty augmented with guilt and worry. He had legitimate worries about his dad's health; mine were centered on my mom's well-being and happiness. Clem showed me the Jersey shore, desolate in the winter. The amuse-ment rides all had German names, like they had been hand-me-downs from a carny thrift shop. I met friends he had grown up with and helped him sort through dozens of drum kits in the basement. One night, he drove us into Manhattan and left the car in a stacked garage. An Arctic-level, record-setting, brutal cold had swept into the city. A homeless man tended to a fire of busted-up crates and cardboard inside a metal drum barrel. Hanging out with Clem, I experienced a different way of being in the city. He had been there for everything, the halcyon days—CBGB, Mudd Club, Max's, all of it—and he had the know-it-all, seen-it-all entitlement of downtown royalty.

I ran into Holly Vincent at a bar we stopped in. She was the singer Gina and I had tried to start a band with. The night was still young at 2:00 a.m., so when Clem suggested, "Hey, let's go to the studio where the Stones are recording," Holly and I were game. I thought maybe I would get to see the tracking room or some equipment set up. Thirty minutes later, walking down

an upholstered corridor, I passed Mick Jagger in the hall. In a
large lounge, Keith sat at a table surrounded with chairs. Clem
had stayed in the front reception area, talking to his friend who
worked there. Letting me have this moment, keeping a low profile and out of the way, showed pure class and coolness. Holly
and I did our best to look comfortable and like we belonged
there. Under my breath, quiet and nonchalant, I asked Holly,
"What should we do? Dare we sit at the table with Keith?"

Mick emerged, and the air bristled with the tension between
him and Keith, who kept referring to him derisively as "Brenda."
He didn't care who heard, but I tried to look like I hadn't been
listening to every word, in case Mick got mad that we were
there, hearing Keith talk so disrespectfully. While I was rack-
ing my brain to think of something to say to Keith, he lit a cigarette. *That's it. Just wait for the door to open and then walk on
through.* The very first thing I said to my idol was "Can I have
a smoke?" I hadn't smoked in over a year; Jane and I had quit
together before the *Talk Show* tour. Keith gave me a smoke. I
knew not to gush or act like a fan. *Be cool.* I told him I had written his name in a will to get my guitar if I died, and he wanted
to know about my '62 Stratocaster. I remember every single
word he said. He joked about wanting the record to sell a lot,
because he needed some new boots. I only briefly mentioned the
Go-Go's—only to tell him about opening for them in Rockford
in 1981. He remembered. After a while, I asked if we could go
in the control room, because, uh, Jimmy Page just happened to
be overdubbing a solo.

"Eh, why not? We're all in the same union," replied my hero.

Keith walked us in and situated us on a sofa in front of the
console. The producer, Steve Lillywhite, had met with the Go-
Go's before; he smiled and gave me a nod. Behind us, Jimmy
Page sat on a chair and did his thing on the song "One Hit to
the Body."

The night couldn't have been more perfect. Leaving at four in the morning, I said goodbye to Keith and thanked him.

"I hope I see you again before I see that guitar of yours," he said.

He knows he's going to outlive us all.

Celebrating my twenty-seventh birthday without the usual big band blowout dinner drove home the loss of the Go-Go's. Outwardly, I ragged on my former bandmates Charlotte and Belinda. Inwardly, I grieved the loss of the band. I wrote pages in notebooks detailing the hurt dragging me through the weeks. I didn't manage being alone well at all. With my house on Sunset Plaza rented out and the short-term rental coming to an end, I leased an apartment in a nondescript complex on Riverside in the Valley.

The home invasion still haunted me. Even with the security door and garage of my apartment complex, I felt unsafe. I would never lose the new compulsive habit of checking and rechecking locks on my doors and windows. My apartment had a loft space, and I set up my four-track recorder. Writing songs had gotten me through the lonely days when I first moved to LA. The songs I wrote and recorded here had no magic, but the act of doing it kept me from sinking.

The first positive career thing to happen since the band split came like a rope being thrown over the edge. A management team wanted to work with me.

"I can get you on *Fame* next week," the guy said. *Fame* was a popular network TV show. Both flattered and horrified, I protested: "I don't know how to act." But the manager, who later went on to be president of a big film studio, believed in me. They sent me off to the *Pretty in Pink* film premiere to get my face out there on the red carpet. Some of the nicer paparazzi knew me and yelled my name for photos. I thought maybe I should do what my managers suggested. I did a photo session trying to look the part and agreed to take acting classes. The lessons were a welcome focus, and the teacher moved me quickly through the levels.

An agent friend thought I would be perfect for the lead role as a rocker chick in a new Paul Schrader film, *Light of Day*, and my hopes revved up. She got me the script and set up a reading with writer/director Schrader himself. I desperately wanted the part. It combined something new with what I knew how to do—there could be no better way to give acting a shot. I memorized and practiced with the same intensity I had put into learning the bass for my first Go-Go's gig. I felt prepared and confident the evening before my meeting. Then came the phone call: my reading was canceled. Schrader had just cast Joan Jett.

The likelihood of there ever being another film so custommade for me was a big, fat zero. The brief interlude of prospects and promise had lifted me and then dumped me back on the lost treadmill of my life. Who was I kidding, anyway? I didn't want to be an actress and I didn't want to be a solo artist. I wanted to play in a band.

Things were blowing up in the world. Literally. Man-made disasters like we had never witnessed: the Space Shuttle *Challenger* disintegrated in a plume of fire and smoke, hurtling all on board toward the sea; a nuclear reactor at Chernobyl exploded radiation over miles and miles of people, air, land, and water. The magnitude of failure could go deep. In my life, no one knew how hopeless I felt. Drinking had become less of a lifestyle choice and more of a necessity, a crutch.

And then, suddenly, Belinda was blowing up too.

She emerged as a new streamlined, glamorous version of herself. All the rough edges had been polished and buffed, shaped and molded into a wholesome pop confection. I couldn't see her being the girlfriend who had been my wacky coconspirator for nearly five years. The first single off Belinda's album was the song Paula Jean Brown had brought into the Go-Go's. "Mad About You" became a huge hit, impossible to escape. Charlotte had played a big part in making Belinda's solo album. They had brought Jane into the fold, with both of them singing on the single. Now the whole breakup felt like a personal rejection.

My thoughts churned in an obsessive taunt, imagining what could have been, what we might have accomplished. "Mad About You" was supposed to be our song, and Mike Chapman had been ready to produce what surely would have been our biggest hit record. Now another all-female band, the Bangles, had taken our place. Our success enabled them to get a major Columbia Records deal. They had corporate budgets and Prince on their side. I wanted to love them. I'd always wanted to see women in the charts, running with the guys, making memorable music for our generation. But I wanted to be along for the ride, not watching from the sidelines.

Clem had been recording the new Eurythmics record, *Revenge*, in Paris, and he invited me to come join him. I would have done anything to get away from LA, where I felt like a has-been. Each morning after he took off for the studio, I grabbed a map from the hotel lobby in Montparnasse and set out with no plan. All day I walked, wandering the streets of Paris with nowhere to go, nowhere to be—and yet I still felt less adrift than I did in LA. Sometimes Clem and I socialized over dinners with the Eurythmics, a crack team of seasoned musicians. All of them were wonderful, welcoming, and interesting. In the middle of enjoying myself, forgetting, everything would come rushing back. I ached to be doing what they were doing. To be in a band again.

Dave Stewart wanted to help. He suggested I play bass with a singer he had worked with, inviting Clem and me to stay at his house in London after the sessions wrapped. The gig didn't happen, but he matched me up with his engineer, a songwriter and musician named Jon, a skinny Scottish dude who had worked on all the Eurythmics records. Jon was super smart and way ahead on the tech curve—the first person I knew who had email. I hit it off with Jon as a music collaborator, and hope grew some tiny little wings. Jon had some great songs, much better than what I had been writing. Things were looking up.

Jon joined me back in LA and found an eight-track recorder. We worked on songwriting and finding a studio to record in; I could put a band together after I got a deal. I approached Tommy Mottola, revved up and confident, selling myself. He still had a fondness for the Go-Go who had advocated for Champion and offered to finance everything. My little hope wings grew. Maybe I would be flying before too long. Everyone I asked to play on my demos readily agreed: Eurythmics keyboardist Pat Seymour, Clem on drums, Jon on bass, and Earl Slick, who had played guitar with John Lennon and David Bowie, including on the tour with the Anaheim show the Go-Go's had done. With all this help and an amazing group of musicians, I could see a future. The only sign something was amiss was the drugs. I thought an event as momentous as making my first solo recordings would definitely be enhanced with plenty of cocaine.

I had been an undeveloped writer, musician, and person before the success of the Go-Go's, letting the band define me, making my talent form-fit the shape of where I'd landed. I'd forgotten about the music I loved growing up, the Austin scene: guitar players and bands that had inspired me to play. Insecure about my writing, I demurred to Jon's input on everything. After identifying as a musician for over a decade, I didn't even play an instrument on the demos. We had these great, cocaine-fueled overproduced tracks, and I had only one job: sing. Me, who had never wanted to be a singer or a solo artist, had managed to get to the point of spending thousands dollars of someone else's money and putting together a top-notch team to give

me a leg up in the business I didn't know how to belong in anymore.

I tried. I really tried. I sang the songs over and over. Then I
went back and did it all again. Jon tried, too, with all his tricks
and knowledge, to make the vocals work. He cobbled together
the best vocal tracks he could. My singing didn't sound bad—it
just didn't sound good enough. Dozens of friends would have
attested to me having plenty of personality in the field. But in
the studio, on the microphone, no character emerged. After I
had spent my recording budget and the musicians moved onto
their real gigs, I had to face the results. Either I wasn't a match
for the material, or I simply didn't have what it took.

"Weak," said Tommy Mottola.

"I'll pay you back," I said.

"Great tracks," said Dave. We both knew what that meant:
everything is there except the voice. I knew I would never be
an Annie Lennox, but accepting that I had put nothing of value
into the work we'd done sent me into a sorrowful spiral. I'd
gotten people to back me and give me a great opportunity, and
I didn't deliver. They knew music and thought I could do something good. For a minute, I believed them. Then I proved us all
wrong and it knocked me flat.

37

QUEEN BEES

Clem and I were a rock 'n' roll couple; there wasn't a cooler pair than the handsome drummer and the shaggy-haired ex-Go-Go. My drinking and drugging got on his nerves but only when I overdid it. We enjoyed plenty of nights in front of the TV or hanging out with friends. Going out for dinner and seeing a band could be a perfectly normal experience—but if I had enough to drink and someone offered me some blow, I would never turn it down. Then off I'd be on a hell-bent, nonstop all-nighter. Clem didn't understand why this kept happening without warning. One minute everything would be fine, then I might go to the bathroom and come back with a whole new intention: figuring out how to stay high, even if it meant ditching my boyfriend. Despite these common episodes, which inevitably led to terrible arguing, we loved and supported each other. When he left for a long, worldwide Eurythmics tour, I was thrilled for him. But I was also happy to drink and drug and do what I wanted without getting hassled.

I had been on my own for nearly four months when my pal Holly Knight invited me to her birthday party at producer Mike Chapman's house. They had written a bunch of hits together for Tina Turner and Pat Benatar. He was the one that got away, the one I had been so excited to work with when the Go-Go's broke up. I pulled into the grounds of his hidden estate in Beverly Hills. The September temperature had dropped enough to wear tights and a hot pink sweater knitted in a pattern with holes all over it. I teamed it with a black miniskirt and big hoop earrings, my wild red hair in lockdown under a black hat. Somehow, I ended up staying there all night. Waking up alone, I looked around his elegant room, the bed a jumble of imported Italian linens. I remembered nothing of the night. I had seduced him as a blackout drunk. On cue, a housekeeper brought in a tray of toast and orange juice. I chugged the OJ down, wishing it would make me disappear.

Slinking out of the house, I escorted my hangover over the canyon, back to the Valley, up the elevator to my apartment, and into bed, where I hung on to a pillow, sobbing. Whatever had gone on after a certain point at the party, whatever had happened in Mike Chapman's bed, it was all nothing but vanished hours. I had shamefully cheated on Clem, and I'd humiliated myself with a man who I practically worshipped. I had probably embarrassed Holly. Trying to make myself as small as I felt, I hunkered down into the pillow, now wet with tears. The phone rang for a long time. Finally, I answered with the tiniest hello ever.

"Hello, sweetheart." Mike wanted to have dinner with me.

With my boyfriend on tour, my ambition in tatters, and my confidence wrecked, this handsome Australian man wanted to spend time with me. This guy who had written and produced songs I'd loved since my teenage years.

The affair with Mike grew quickly. His talent, credits, humor, and confidence were irresistible. I distanced myself from my relationship with Clem, rationalizing that his career had been increasingly thriving while mine lay dormant. Recalling how we fought over my drinking, I reined in the party-girl monster with Mike, passing off the blackout as an aberration.

One night I told Chapman about the bad demos I had made. A little buzzed on fine wine, I sang one of the songs I'd written with Jon. He reclined on a down-stuffed sofa, chin in his hands, checking me out with a professional eye. I stopped abruptly, insecure.

"You're great," he said. "I'm going to produce you. You'll be like Suzi."

Suzi! As in Quatro. *Well, now.* My emotional range had no middle. It was a bungee cord, a ricochet tearaway from one low to another high. The clouds parted with his few words of promise, making everything clear now: I needed to break up with Clem and date Mike. We would record an album, relaunch my career, and ride around in his Rolls-Royce to dinners at Le Dome and Mr. Chow. Take that everyone; check me out. My mind spinning like car wheels, finally getting enough traction to get out of the mud, I had formulated my new destiny. There were a few obstacles: Mike says I'll need a band and some more songs, and there's the business of telling my boyfriend, "Uh, I have a new boyfriend." Yeah. I needed to meet up with the Eurythmics tour somewhere so I could tell Clem in person.

Holly Knight went with me to Europe, and we had a blast at first. I got a room in a trendy hotel in London with black furniture, walls, and fixtures—black everything. *All the better to see lines of coke,* I thought, laughing, feeling like a decadent rock star. In clubs and at concerts, I hung out with happening English musicians. I hadn't felt this hopeful since being in the Go-Go's. Then it was time. I flew to Milan and saw the Eurythmics concert at a huge arena. Back in Clem's hotel, I told him the truth: in his absence, I'd fallen for Mike and wanted to work on a record with him. I thought it rather lucky this all happened in the context of Clem doing what he loved more than anything—playing drums with a wildly successful band. He hadn't ridden this high since Blondie. In my mind, he understood how a musician has to do what she has to do. In truth, I didn't allow myself to see how he took the breakup, shuttered my mind to the idea that I had hurt him. Figuring my drinking and our arguments had worn him down, I thought maybe he would be glad to move on.

In most careers, there's a path, starting at the bottom and working up to the top. You show initiative or leadership skills. You might hit a glass ceiling or get stuck in a dead-end job, but the limits are eventually tangible, observable. Not so much when your life's work is an artistic pursuit. A creative person gets used to subsisting on unequal parts of passion, delusion, and relentless hope. No matter what happens, as long as I keep doing it, I'm still in the game, there's still a shot. It's like playing the lottery, thinking you can't win, even on the minuscule odd chance you might, if there's no ticket in hand. Maybe it's worse after achieving success like I did, knowing it really can happen. I might as well have been chasing a spark. How could I create the same chemistry that had organically come to fruition when I joined the Go-Go's?

The band Girlschool had made their mark in the hard rock and metal world, especially in the UK and Europe. They had toured, made records and videos, and earned the fandom of a male-oriented, hard-to-convince audience. I'd kept up with them after playing in their early incarnation nine years before, and I'd seen a few concerts in London. When I heard that Kelly Johnson, the lead guitarist, had left Girlschool to launch a solo career in LA, I set my sights on her and found her living with Vicki Blue, the Runaways bassist I'd befriended in Austin. All the teenage female musicians I'd met in the '70s seemed to drift apart and resurface in Hollywood. I knew as surely as if lightning had split open a tree in front of my eyes that I had found my next partner in Kelly. It made so much sense: the rocker chick from the pop band and the guitar slinger with pop leanings from the metal band. What a combo! We would be queen bees, helping each other through the uncertain territory of starting over.

No more all-girl stuff, though. I handpicked three guys, each with talent, experience, looks, vibe, and great chops. Kelly loved them. Jesse Sublett, my old friend who had known me when I first started playing, moved to LA with his wife, Lois. He brought some tall, Texas straight-shooter talent. My old friend had kept his movie-star handsome good looks and understated defiance. Taking a sideman role or back seat to Kelly and me didn't come naturally to Jesse, who had spent the past decade leading his own bands. Jebin Bruni, a brilliant multi-instrumentalist keyboard player with a cool vibe, joined—a huge score. He's the type of musician you never have to make suggestions to—anything you can think of won't be nearly as good as what he will come up with. He wore his hair long, with the type of granny glasses John Lennon made famous, and often took moments to gather his words, his hand held near his mouth as if it could help form them as he spoke. His slender frame and slight stoop, probably from leaning over keyboards since boyhood, were offset by a boyish charm and a dash of flamboyance. I also snagged drummer Craig Aaronson, a Keith Moon look-alike with Ringoesque technique. He was like the kid in the back seat along for the ride, and he took some relentless teasing and kidding with a laid-back, good-natured shrug. Craig's youthful energy lowered the average age of our band, and his mod look rounded out our image.

This band had it all: star power. Every single one of us thought we had everything it took to make it, and we ought to know: none of us were beginners. I'd put together the perfect coed rock 'n' roll gang, still young in our twenties. And we had Mike Chapman, with his own RCA-distributed record label, Dreamland. We would be sure to have a deal.

I will so fucking show them all, I thought.

38

THE RIGHT WAY

In my new band, my drinking went completely unchecked. In the Go-Go's, I had learned to pace myself to cope with touring schedules and had even tried kicking around some health bouts. These days, just the sun going down was an excuse to get blasted.

Kelly moved in with me. We could match each other pint for pint, smoke for smoke, snort for snort. I had the sturdy resilience of European peasant stock, and Kelly was an Amazon. She had long fingers, forearms, femurs, tibias—as if all the bones between her joints had been given an extra stretch for good measure. Returning from a night out, arms around each other's shoulders and holding each other up, we would crash into my apartment, collapsing on the floor or sofa. Kelly possessed an androgynous, effortless sexuality. She would look at you with sleepy eyes, screened by long swooshes of bangs, and a feline indifference, making her even more appealing. One plastered night, we lunged at each other and made out until the laughing made us stop. I figured if I couldn't ditch my hetero preferences to have wild, drunken sex with Kelly Johnson, I probably should stick with guys.

Onstage, fronting the band, Kelly and I were just as well matched, pros with years of gigs and touring between us. She played her tiger-striped Ibanez and a half Marshall stack; I played my baby, the '62 Strat. Our band was good and propped up my battered confidence. I knew what a band should feel like, and this felt right on, with all the elements: the camaraderie, the chops, the wisecracking. I sang lead more than Kelly, but the vocals got spread around. It gave me a chance to get used to singing without having to carry the whole band on every song. Our set comprised a mix of material: a few songs from my work with Jon Bavin, the catchiest being "Careless Lies." Kelly had some solo songs we worked up: crunchy, guitar-driven tunes with good melodies and structures. Jesse was a song factory. He wrote with a tough irony and hard-boiled literary flair. When we began writing together, songs like "I'm Kicking You Out" and "Nails in My Heart," I learned as much about writing songs from him as I had from anyone else, including Jane and Charlotte.

No one in the band got paid to be a member, but I footed the bill for all our expenses—mainly because I had been spoiled and didn't want to go back to rehearsing in the seedy Hollywood dumps where I'd already paid my dues. I paid for a locker to store equipment so I didn't have to haul it back and forth to the top-notch rehearsal room I'd rented. Soon, I would be paying to rent vans and for hotel rooms. I figured these were temporary outlays; our success felt inevitable. I stayed positive that we would get a record deal. I had gone from floundering dismay to cocksure certainty.

I wanted to do everything the "right" way, walk the same line as the Go-Go's. Play, get popular, get a record deal, make the record, make history. Boom. The band name was chosen: World's Cutest Killers. Someone saw it on a tabloid headline about female assassins. Our band had tons of cuteness and we were badass, so the name worked. But *World's Cutest Killers* didn't roll off the tongue—even an abbreviated *WCK* was a mouthful. And the name never looked good on a sign outside a club. I should have known right then the band would go nowhere.

There are an awful lot of pit stops on the road to nowhere. Musicians who move to the big city to play in a band just don't imagine nowhere as a destination. I had been in a band that made it, so I thought it was just a matter of time before it happened again. WCK posed for band photos, and I wrote our bio. A booking agent got us a bunch of Northern California club gigs. I didn't mind piling into a van with our equipment in the back; that's basic stuff for starting out. But I paid for a crew guy and soundman.

After months of upscale rehearsals and song arranging, WCK was ready. It was our time.

I didn't realize that once I had found fame and fortune in the Go-Go's, I would never be able to just be a member of a band, and every band I played in would be known as having Kathy Valentine from the Go-Go's. Every single ad announced this fact, often above our long name. Occasionally ads mentioned Kelly Johnson from Girlschool, but mainly it was just my name. Those tactics dilute the power of the band and diminish the present, putting the past into a context with no relevance. And no matter how much a club owner or promoter says it will pull in a percentage of the former band's fans, the payoff is miniscule, tiny compared to the price paid by relying on one person's legacy.

Our first gigs were exercises in humiliation. The agency booked us into clubs with a five- to six-hundred capacity, but the band barely drew a hundred people. It made the whole "featuring" business even worse. It had been a while since I'd played live, and the harsh reality of where I'd landed gave me a jolt. My expectations had been much higher, and not just mine—the whole band thought we would be able to fill a club. Still, as soon as we hit the stage, I found joy.

When I pick up my instrument and play music, I stop thinking about anything else. That's the way it has always been: as a Go-Go or as a regular working musician. Playing music is the one thing that puts me squarely in the present moment; it's as Zen as I'll ever be. Once I'm focusing on what I'm doing and what my bandmates are doing, I'm gone. Packed shows are awesome—I wish every musician got to experience people singing along to every song, reaching their adoring arms up in the air in total acceptance, having the time of their lives. The money, traveling, success, fame, validation—it's all splash and flash. But most musicians will play without any of these gifts and do it again and again for years and lifetimes. We lug our amps and drums out of the garage and pack them in the trunk of our car. We unload the gear at the gig and look for a place to park. Often, we get disrespected by club managers and bookers. And we might play for little money or for free, to audiences that may or may not care that we're up there. Still, there's nothing like plugging in and playing together. Making music.

I loved playing as I always had, but I was also supremely intent on rubbing the genie lamp and trying to make some kind of cosmic power come out and give me a career like the Go-Go's had. Our club shows in San Francisco and up north weren't packed, but the press showed up, and the reviews started coming: all great write-ups. It's that carrot-and-stick incentive that keeps the donkey moving forward. The writers raved about us, although they gave our band name some grief. Encouraged, Kelly and I went through our paces. Onstage, we leaned into each other, masses of hair and leather, boots and chains and belts flashing in the lights. She shredded like I had dreamed of doing back when I first started to play, and now, I vicariously and proudly showed off the best guitar slinger chick I'd ever seen or heard. The guys in our band looked good; they each had a stage presence that would have been plenty in a standard-issue band, but because they were teamed with two female rock stars, the band really stood out.

The World's Cutest Killers debuted in Los Angeles at a Rock Against AIDS concert featuring a mix of LA bands. The next day, the front page of the coveted Calendar, the music section of the *LA Times*, had a huge picture of me, fist in the air, in full rocking glory. The first sentence read: "Former Go-Go Kathy Valentine might have a goldmine in the new band she unveiled Sunday at the Variety Arts Center."

I didn't mind the "former Go-Go" business one bit in the context of an *LA Times* headline. It had been two years since my band had broken up, and finally it seemed like things were going to be OK. The high far surpassed my increasingly commonplace blow and booze binges.

39

GOLD AND PLATINUM

Soon after the Go-Go's broke up, the business managers—the people who helped band members buy stuff, pay bills, and take care of all the band expenses—sent a delivery to my door. A guy unloaded a dolly with stacks of boxes containing all my financial files and expenses. Panicked, I called them to ask why. The accountant in charge said I was no longer a client—I didn't generate enough money to warrant representation. Royalties ran dry in the years after the band broke up. No radio airplay or record sales, no touring, no merchandise or endorsement deals meant no income. I went through the boxes determined to figure out how to get statements and bills sent to me, to learn how to live like an adult. Without any experience with finance or family to guide me, I had no skills managing money. I also shouldered financial burdens I'd never had before: two mortgages, rent, living expenses, and bankrolling a band. I argued with my mom constantly about the condo I had bought for her. "Get a job," I would say. "Get a housemate. Help me." I needed her to take care of business and not rely on me. I felt taken advantage of and resentful. I was the caretaker and I didn't like it.

I wished fervently for songs I had written to be used in commercials: "Head Over Heels" in a shampoo ad, "Vacation" for an airline. That shit never happens when you're desperate. In my new circumstances, it wasn't just ambition driving me to succeed again. Real life was knocking down the door. By the time the World's Cutest Killers got in the studio, I was feeling the squeeze. This had to lead somewhere. I sure didn't want to count on Mike Chapman, but he had a soft spot for earthy, wild girls who knew what they wanted. No promises were made, but I hoped he would both get attached to me and help the band land a deal with him at the helm of our demos. That's a lot of wishing, and I knew enough to play it cool.

Once the songs were chosen, our sessions began. After only a couple days of tracking, Mike called to say he couldn't be there. "But don't worry," he said, "my engineer will take care of you." That was the end of him producing WCK. He'd gotten a gig making the next Divinyls record and bailed on us. Let down and disappointed, I couldn't blame Mike for choosing the Divinyls. After all, he had already produced one hit for them in 1985, the song "Pleasure and Pain." They were on a major label, they shared his Australian roots, and they had a killer female rock star singer. I couldn't wait to meet Chrissy Amphlett.

Chrissy and I hit it off. She was completely fearless and absolute in her sense of self and did not give one fuck what anyone thought. As a performer she came across as explosive as hydrogen, smoky and rich. A siren. Her voice revealed every contrast and nuance that made up her nature: raw, vulnerable, dirty, and very feminine. But I knew her as a friend. Being her friend gave me the luxury of discovering that she had the ability of a true empath to sense when her friends needed something she could help with. Knowing I needed building up, she made sure I got it. Chrissy came to our gigs, raved about us, and offered to take my band on tour in Australia. I loved her.

I had a great new friend, but my band had been passed off by the producer I'd hung my hopes on. Chapman got our finished tape. He listened to the first song, "Careless Lies." Being an expert at saying exactly what he thought, he laid it out: "You're not a lead singer." I knew the tune didn't have the delivery it needed but wondered what might have been different if he had recorded the song instead. If I could stand in his living room, sing it to his face, and have him get all excited and call me the next Suzi Quatro, what the hell had happened? None of the other tracks made him excited either. He had been completely absorbed by making one of the best records of the Divinyls' career.

"Does this mean you don't want to sign us to Dreamland?" I asked.

"No, sweetheart," he said. Then he passionately kissed me, his tanned, muscled arms holding me tight. Rejection and desire collided, crushing me in between.

I dealt with the failure by pushing it away and trying to escape. Chrissy and her music partner and longtime lover, Marc McAntee, were rock 'n' roll versions of Honeymooners Ralph and Alice. "Maaahk," she would scream in her broad Australian accent from across the house they'd rented. "Whaaaat," he would yell back. Together, the three of us could whip up all kinds of trouble. An ordinary dinner turned into a four-day trip to Mexico when I mentioned a hotel in Rosarito Beach I liked.

Arriving in Tijuana at dawn, all of us blotto, we watched the sun rise with a cheery taunt while the locals started setting up their market stalls and getting ready for the day. We crashed until late in the afternoon and rose to margaritas and beers in the bar. On the way back to LA, we drove past the Hotel Del Coronado, a massive, century-old beach resort near San Diego. It was too beautiful to pass by; I blew a small fortune, checking into a suite, ordering room service, and documenting the lost weekend with Polaroids. The phantom of failure was deferred for another day with the only way I could cope.

Chapman took me out to dinner, a miserable date to tell me that he had met the girl he wanted to marry. Our affair had lasted barely six months. I tossed the pieces in a bag—a sad collection of broken heart and battered ego—and took off for Austin. This escape had me holed up in a room at the Omni Hotel with a cute musician ten years younger than me and a bunch of blow. I'd run out of ideas and optimism, but a few days later, I picked myself up and went back to LA to keep trying to make it with the World's Cutest Killers. What else was I gonna do?

Feeling stupid for breaking up with Clem, a guy who actually loved me, for a fantasy life with a guy who didn't, I tried to make things right and begged him to take me back. It was a free pass and a huge relief when he did. We had our problems, but we had accrued some history, and history carries some weight—even if it's baggage weight.

"Why don't I book us a vacation?" I suggested. Our trips made good memories; we traveled together well. And running away from LA kept my demons in check. Belinda had returned to the spotlight with a new single, the massive hit "Heaven Is a Place on Earth." The song, the video, the press, and her overwhelming success were everywhere. The Bangles were everywhere, too, on tour, on the MTV awards, on the cover of *Rolling Stone*. I read the cover story, incensed about how they gave no credit to the Go-Go's for kicking the fucking door down and making it easier to convince a big label to sign an all-female band. The conflict between being proud and protective of our legacy and yet so bitter and depressed over losing it magnified my frustration and unhappiness. When Clem agreed to the vacation, I got busy and focused on the perfect holiday. After choosing a high-rise hotel in Cancun, I waited for him to return from tour, in the meantime playing gigs in LA with WCK. The scene had some good clubs: Club Lingerie, Club 88, the Coconut Teaszer—rock 'n' roll had surged back to the strip with an onslaught of hard rock and metal bands.

After Clem and I got back together, we were the same couple: we argued about my hotel choice, and my choice of Cancun, the entire plane ride, then had a blast. Back in LA, we fought more. We fought about my clutter, whether to go to the beach or not. We argued about what movie to see, what band to see, whether to go backstage at a show. I sobbed and screamed; he stomped and seethed. We fought about stupid, pointless stuff, but mainly we fought about my problem.

"Please don't get drunk tonight," he'd ask.

"Don't tell me what to do," I'd say.

"Kath, please."

We bickered and quarreled some more. Then we decided to move in together. Despite the constant turmoil, we loved each other. Clem was generous and demonstrative. I had fought with my first boyfriend all the time, too, and probably thought that's what couples did. We had the bonds to keep us together and felt our contentment would bypass the conflict if we were together more. For a lifelong New York East Coaster, moving to an LA suburb was radical, but Clem bought a house in Studio City for us to live in. The commitment to us and our future wasn't lost on me, and I had immense gratitude that he had let go of the affair I'd had with Mike.

In August 1987, Dave Stewart invited Clem and me to attend his wedding at a chateau in France. He had found happiness with Siobhan Fahey from Bananarama. I wore a black Yohji Yamamoto suit and giant hair. Clem wore a crème linen Agnes B suit with sneakers and a red tie, his hair slicked back, black and shining in the summer sun. The chateau looked like a monument, centered on grounds of paths, shaped shrubberies, fountains, and statues. It had to be the fanciest, most extravagant wedding I'd ever been to, and it lasted all day and most of the night. Dave excluded no one: Siobhan's and his family mingled with assistants and housekeepers; studio techs and drivers stood in groups with friends and managers, musicians and band members. Annie Lennox, Bob Geldof, and Paula Yates were among the smattering of big names, and we all crowded outside, oohing and aahing together at the fireworks display signaling the end of the long celebration. It had been a joyful, comfortably drawn-out affair. On the drive back to Paris, Clem and I got in an argument. As soon as we reached the city, the driver pulled over and kicked us out of the car onto the Boulevard Montparnasse, where disbelief and surprise made us stop, mid-gripe, and laugh at ourselves.

Back in LA, we moved my furniture into the house and bought a few extra things. We put Clem's Blondie gold and platinum records and my Go-Go's gold and platinum records all over the den. It looked like a room at Graceland with the gaudy framed metallic discs everywhere. We set up his drums and my eight-track recorder, and a couple of amps. We set out to be happy together.

40

CHEERLEADER

I couldn't stop comparing myself to the other Go-Go's. The way I saw it, they were my only true peers. Nearly three years after the band broke up, their rockets seemed to be soaring while mine was a dud firecracker. Belinda had continued her solo explosion of chart hits. Charlotte had firmly positioned herself as part of the Belinda solo team, earning a steady supply of songwriting credits on albums selling in the millions. Jane had the hit "Rush Hour" on her second solo record for EMI. And Gina had gotten both a publishing deal as a songwriter and a major-label deal on Capitol Records for her band, House of Schock.

None of them were writing, singing, or making rock 'n' roll records. I felt completely out of step with my old bandmates and sometimes wondered how they had moved so far away from the music we'd made together. I couldn't have written or played any of the songs giving my contemporaries such success. Recognizing this was a sorry consolation prize. I still just wanted one thing: to play in a band, one that fucking rocked.

Except being in a band that rocked didn't pay my bills. Or at least the one I'd put together didn't. The World's Cutest Killers had built a small following, enough to get bookings but not much else. My financial problems increased, and I cashed out the retirement fund the accountants had set up when we first made big bucks. Mom had never helped with the burden of her condo payments in Austin, leaving me with no choice but to sell it. The decision caused more turmoil for me than it did her. I had wanted to set things up so she would have a nice place of her own, some security. I didn't get that she was content to take what she got, without a lot of fuss. If she wanted more, she didn't have enough of the go-for-it gene. I fixated on giving her what I thought she needed to be happy. It took a really long time to realize that my plans for other people rarely worked out.

I hadn't figured on the housing market collapse and recession. The value of her condo had plummeted to less than half of what I had paid. I chose to foreclose and dump the place on the mortgage company. I wasn't alone—people all over Texas were doing the same thing. Mom got an apartment, taking the furniture I had bought her. I was amazed to see she had held on to the Kraft Korner box from my childhood. Foreclosing took debt away and trashed my credit, but it didn't infuse me with any cash. I refinanced the Sunset Plaza house, taking equity loans to live on. Foolish money management and no strategy for how to survive financially caused me to waste the assets I had.

Asking my dad for help never occurred to me. I had been on my own too long, taking care of myself, taking care of my mom. The only time I had turned to him, over a decade before, when I asked to buy some music equipment, he'd rejected me. I didn't want it to happen again. Still, I longed to have something between us. My dad knew nothing about me, only the cheerful, proud musician I fronted to him. He had come to visit us in LA a few times, and I'd gone to Tahlequah. He had met and liked Clem, he knew I'd done well in the Go-Go's, and he thought I was doing fine. He had his "real" family to think about, which didn't include me. The sadness I had about him had been buried so deeply, I'm surprised it didn't just suffocate away.

My mom visited several times after Clem got a house for us. At some point, we would end up snorting coke and talking throughout the night, always with other friends, never just the two of us. We had been smoking pot and palling around since my early teens. It seemed like we used drugs as a basis for a relationship, but the role-reversed dysfunction needed buffer people to prop it up.

One night I saw Charlotte at a Neil Young concert. I had imagined a confrontation, how I'd let her have it, give her a good smackdown insult or two. We were talking to friends, separated by only a few groups of people, and our eyes locked. In one moment, the toughness I had constructed around my anguish collapsed. Overcome with grief, I moved away to the edge of the room, afraid I would break down right there in front of everyone. I missed her: our friendship, our songs, our band. No matter how hard I tried or what musicians I found to play with, nothing came close to the Go-Go's. But I couldn't accept that, couldn't let it be a fact.

I felt like a cheerleader, lifting myself up on the hands and shoulders of whatever good I could collect in my treasure bounty. After all, I had moved out of my apartment and lived in a house again, where it felt safe. I had great friends who stuck with me no matter what my status was. I played guitar in a bad-ass band. I had gotten to do what loads of people only dreamed of. And I had the coolest boyfriend in the world.

Clem had been bouncing around playing some super gigs, including with Pete Townsend in London, and jamming a bunch with Bob Dylan. Dave Stewart had moved to the Valley, not far from us, and invited us to his gatherings and parties. I saw what would become the Traveling Wilburys get seeded right before my eyes over at Dave's house. Roy Orbison wasn't there—he would get recruited soon—but sparks were flying between George Harrison, Dylan, Tom Petty, and Jeff Lynne. Covertly, I eavesdropped and hovered close enough to try and get a sense of George Harrison's personality. On this day, he seemed like a playful and fun guy who nodded and complimented my outfit. An hour later, I sat with a small group on the tennis court while he and Tom played "Taxman" on acoustic guitars. I might have been the big loser in the former Go-Go lottery, and for sure drinking and drugging too regularly for my own good, but I was no fool. I was acutely aware this moment would be one to remember for a lifetime, and my heart still knew how to soar.

At another Dave party I met Bob Dylan. He was very down-to-earth and friendly for an icon. Groveling and genuflecting doesn't get you much conversation, so instead I asked him about a cassette I had heard of him jamming with Clem and Dave. Once he identified the music, I asked if he intended to do anything with the song. I really liked it. "No," he said. "You can have it."

"Really?" I asked him. "I can put some lyrics to it?"

Bob said, "Sure. It's all yours." Then he chatted with me a little about the Go-Go's. I let him know I still played and that I had nothing to do with what any of the others were doing. He seemed interested, then said with laser-like perception: "It must be kind of hard for you, losing your band and then seeing that other band be so successful now, the Bangles."

"Yeah," I said, looking right in his eyes, wondering how the fuck he knew. Meeting me for the first time, Dylan nailed in one second an insight no one I knew had ever picked up on. "Yeah," I said again. "It was stupid to break up."

I never encountered him again, but I liked our short inter-action. He saw inside me for a second and gave me permission to cowrite a song with him. Oh, and our song? I wrote some words, called it "Clean Up This Mess," and then lost the cassette tape with the music.

Playing in a band remained my salvation. Leaning into the local club scene, I saw bands that were playing music I liked. The Broken Homes were my faves: a classic, guitar-driven band that had gotten a record deal fairly quickly. *Maybe I'm on the right track after all*, I thought. *It's just taking longer for us.* When their guitar player, Craig Ross, needed a place to live, I suggested that he move into one of our spare bedrooms. I disliked being alone in the house with Clem gone so much. Craig had a shy, serious way about him, kabuki white skin, and black curly hair, and he moved with the grace of a dancer—one with bony knees and elbows. After seeing the ample space in the house, the music room, the big retro kitchen with black-and-white tiles and red booth, Craig moved in right away.

Like just about anyone raised in Austin, I knew enough about guitar players to recognize a standout. Craig was the real deal; he had the soul, the style, and the passion. He played in his room for hours, every night, every day. He played along to records, the best way to learn. I regaled him with my story of meeting Keith Richards, of knowing Stevie and Jimmie Vaughan, of seeing all the blues guys when I had been a teenager. Craig's dedication and influences should have been a reminder of where I came from, of the musician I had been before the Go-Go's. But I was stuck. They still had a hold over me. I longed to have my past get out of the way and believed the only way to move on would be for my band to break. If I could just figure out what that would take.

When our drummer decided to move on, I thought the change and chemistry magic would happen with a new ingredient. The wrong history was repeating itself. Craig Aaronson was smart to leave—he ended up being a huge success as a record company president. We got a kid who happened to be the drummer in the band featured in *Light of Day*, the Paul Schrader movie I had wanted to be in. Not long after that, I met a young bass player and decided to replace Jesse. Jesse was one of my oldest friends. Telling him we wanted someone else had to be the worst conversation I had ever initiated. He and his wife, Lois, had moved from Austin for this band. They loved LA, but feeling betrayed and insulted by a friend is hard to take. I couldn't explain to him how desperate I was to push the band forward and yet how lost I felt at the same time. With Jesse's songs dominating the set and the way we split the singing up, we had become like my first LA band, the Textones—each writer and singer doing their thing, with no cohesive direction. I couldn't find my bearings and needed to cut down some of the input and stimulus. Maybe in what was left, I would see myself more clearly. Kelly and I gave our new lineup a new name: the Renegades. We were still game. I couldn't imagine doing anything else in life.

41

FRIED AND RAW

When I first got to know Clem, he was part of the all-star band Chequered Past. The singer, Michael Des Barres, and I were acquaintances. Talking at a Hollywood party one evening, he told me about his sobriety. He thought I should try it. I knew AA wasn't for me, but I also knew I drank too much. A life without drinking didn't seem possible. I had to control my problem. The solution seemed obvious, if I could just stick with it this time: I had to be stronger. I thought making it into a contest or game might help, but the rules were continuous, shifting as needed. Each broken rule was replaced with a new one.

"I will only have one glass of wine with dinner, and that's it."

"I will not drink for two weeks, and then I can have a margarita."

"I will only drink on the weekends."

The "controlling" method meant drinking was always on my mind, whether I did it or not. Control took a lot of mental energy, and invariably there would be the blowout where I stayed up drinking, doing coke, and reveling in the excess. I was up for anything once I was drunk. Sex, more drugs, hanging out at any club, anywhere, any time. Finding people to get high with was easy—who didn't want to hang out with a party girl, reckless and rockin', laughing and talking? No one avoided me, no one saw me as a falling-down, melodramatic sad sack. As long as I kept the fun dialed up, the denial methodology that keeps an alcoholic drinking stayed intact. I could always point to someone worse, way worse, than me. How bad could I be if I was so much fun?

Fun was the phantom that had shaded my entire adult life. But increasingly, I would wake up in a hungover hellhole with specters of shame slinking through the fog in my brain. An all-nighter might end up as a one-night stand once there was nothing left to say or do. I lived in a cycle, trying to find relief from myself but only intensifying and compounding the problem of being me. When I found myself hanging out in a Studio City park until sunrise after taking ecstasy all night with a guy I barely knew, I decided to clean up my act before completely sabotaging my relationship with Clem. Running away, my default response, seemed like it might be just the thing.

There was good reason to go to England. My entire family, the British side, intended to spend the holidays together. Having my grandmother die while I was there didn't factor into my sobering-up plan. Her death from cancer after an eleven-day hospital bedside vigil left me emotionally wrung out. It had been ugly with intense suffering, and I couldn't wait to leave; I didn't even wait for her funeral. I returned to LA, where Kelly told me she was moving back home—to London. This meant the end of the Renegades. I wished her well; we had tried for two years to have something special together. I had chosen the coolest, best musicians I could find, and we'd worked as hard as any other band we were up against. The X factor is an organic endowment of chance. Bands without the magic make it too, but none I've ever been in. Showing up and trying is all I knew how to do, but now I wondered if I even knew how to do that right.

Looking ahead at an upcoming landmark birthday, I felt my twenties were like a wind tunnel: I had been flying high or uncontrollably blown around. The tempest ruling my life had no direction or conscience about where it might let go. A deep instinct surfaced, grasping for acknowledgment: thirty is a milestone, adult time. If I can't get my shit together and land myself, I could get dumped into a garbage heap or worse.

My friend Carlene Carter relocated to LA and moved in with her new boyfriend, Howie Epstein, the bass player in Tom Petty's band. She had been clean for a year. I hadn't seen her since she got sober and expected to find a completely different gal. Our history held a lot of fun, wild times, as well as the nightmare of the home invasion and robbery.

We met in the bar of a hotel lobby. I was sure Carlene wouldn't be okay with me ordering a glass of wine, but I asked, just in case. I really wanted a drink.

"Sure, whatever you want," she said.

My interest sparked. How could someone who used to drink hang out in a bar with an old friend who still drank and not be uncomfortable? After my glass of wine, and a second, I diverted our talking back to my curiosity.

"So, what do they tell you at AA?" I asked Carlene.

"Why don't you come to a meeting and see?" she countered.

The fact that she seemed like the same Carlene I had known left an impact. I looked for signs that she had changed into a robot zombie or lost her personality, but her demeanor hadn't been altered by not drinking. She laughed just as easily, joked around, seemed fine and dandy. I thought she would be desperately drooling for a drink, especially when she saw my chilled white Chardonnay in the crystal glass, but it was nothing of the sort. I filed the encounter away. *Good for her. Interesting, but not for me.*

The coming year, without prospects or possibility, looked as bleak as the winter. I had turned thirty years old, when most people were deep into their careers, but I didn't know anymore how to have the kind of life I wanted. With no band, no good songs, and no work for close to four years, I had plowed through my money and bankrupted my self-worth. I existed on a tipping point of fear and sadness, with drinking as the only tool to keep my balance. My sadness began when I was a child and grew alongside me with each passing year. Each fearful thought fell like fruit from the branches of my failures: I'm doing something wrong; my career is over; I have no future. And the worst thought of all, the one I could barely acknowledge: maybe I had no talent. Maybe my only talent was being in the right place at the right time.

I wanted nothing more than to duck and cover from any more incoming blasts of failure.

I accompanied Clem back to New York. The only rock 'n' roll on the agenda was an upcoming gig he had playing with Johnny Thunders. At a rehearsal, I sat on a couch pushed against a wall, enjoying the band a few feet in front of me. I loved watching Clem play, and Johnny ripped on guitar.

It got me thinking about trying again, finding some new people. I couldn't stop wanting to be in a band, no matter what.

Two nights later at a club downtown, Johnny Thunders and his band took the stage. I remember nothing. This counted as my second, and last, blackout from drinking.

I've been told about conversations I had with Johnny's backup singer that night. I've been told I left the gig and walked to a quieter bar in a restaurant nearby. I do remember being unable to walk. Clem carried me into his dad's house. I crawled to the bathroom and threw up, then crawled into the living room, passing out on the sofa.

Many alcoholics talk about hitting a bottom—often, it entails car wrecks, jail, devastation, and ruin. My first bounce on the bottom was physical. I couldn't move. Every nerve ending in my body felt simultaneously fried and raw, like a short-circuiting, exposed wire had wound its way through my being. Hugging a sofa cushion, sobbing and throbbing, I never wanted to feel like this again. It had to stop. The second bounce on the bottom entailed everything else. It all caught up at once: the sorrow, regret, shame, fear, abandonment, and betrayals. My rock bottom came with realizing my inability to change my life or my circumstances. I desperately wanted something to change. Anything would be a start. I had one thought: *If I stop drinking, at least one thing will be different.* Just one thing might be enough. The certainty and finality of the decision felt irrevocable; there was no turning back. I kept it to myself, a treasured sacrament. Telling anyone might dilute the power.

Upon waking the next day, a new knowledge filled my mind: I didn't drink anymore. Fear and doubt crowded it out. I had no frame of reference to imagine a life without alcohol. I would have to go back to the fifth grade to picture myself as a nondrinker. Physically, I already felt better. With each hour, second thoughts and misgivings replaced my hangover. *Maybe it's not the time to stop. I should wait until I get home.* But I hated to fail so soon after the momentous decision. Back and forth I waffled through the day, not realizing how crucial a space I had moved into. Had I decided to put off my sobriety, shrugging at the crossroads, untold doors and paths could have led to any number of fates. When comprehension blows through the clouds of the addicted mind, when the understanding is bound to an impulse to stop, it's like a mystical connection occurring— maybe even a divine intervention. Free will exerts its own power, but it's a far lesser choice when one can choose between that and the divine.

Ideas as lofty as mystical connections and enlightenments were nowhere near my conscious thoughts. Demoralized and utterly astray, with only the tatters of my ego to guide my actions, pride alone got me through the next two days. When I say I didn't want to fail, I mean sobriety felt like the only thing I had left that I could try. Everything else had been lost or broken, cheated or squandered. I went back to Los Angeles on the third day; I called Carlene on the fourth. I needed help. Someone, please, show me how to live without drinking.

42

COOKIES

In LA, I walked into an old wood-frame church, purchased for ten dollars in 1947 by the North Hollywood Chapter of Alcoholics Anonymous. The building is legendary to recovering alcoholics of the San Fernando Valley. At my first AA meeting, I had been sober for three days, hanging on, waiting to get home to start my new life.

The room was filled with people and smoke. At the front, a podium with a microphone stood center stage in front of rows of folding metal chairs. The demographic spread was wide: young to old with every shade of skin and hair, high heels to sneakers, business suits and dresses to sweats, jeans, and tees. They were standing tall and proud or bent and beaten down. You name it—alcohol had claimed it. For the next year, every single day, I came to this meeting to learn how to not drink.

I didn't want to be there. I didn't want to be like those people— not the sorry ones, not the together ones. And then a rock 'n' roller with muscled arms, spiky hair, defined cheekbones, and a huge smile turned around and locked eyes with me. It was a well-known virtuoso guitar slinger pal of mine.

"Kath! I've been saving a chair for you."

He sat in the front row, and I sat next to him; on my other side was another surprise—a musician from one of my favorite bands sat with my bud Carlene. *OK, I'm going to do this thing*, I thought. Would I have stayed without the musician friends in the front row? I don't know. It marked the beginning of a belief that sometimes, all is how it should be.

In the early days my worst qualities kept me sober—pride, perfectionism, obsession.

I'm going to be the best newcomer ever. I'll show them. I won't struggle, complain, or cry. With no idea how to live without drinking, I shrunk down into a small existence, sitting on my sofa eating cookies and watching TV or going to meetings. I lived in fear of doing anything or going anywhere else. As a drinker, every restaurant had a corresponding alcohol I enjoyed with the meals: margaritas with Mexican, Sake with Japanese, wine with European food, beer with Indian and Thai. I drank mimosas at breakfast and anything at parties, and I carried a flask for movies, bowling, or other nondrinking activities. I would even take a smooth bottle of Remy for my own elite consumption when I played seedy gigs like Al's Bar in downtown LA. I associated every good time, every happiness, with drinking alcohol.

When they told me to find a "higher power" and to pray, I took it as telling the higher power to show me I could still have a good time, and the sooner the fucking better. I kept my distance from people I didn't know, saying, "Yes, I'm fine, thanks," and moving along. Thirty days of couch sitting, cookies, and meetings later, I took an AA chip, an acknowledgment of staying sober for a certain length of time.

If my worst qualities helped me, what I thought were my best qualities nearly derailed me. Being strong and tough, being "OK" no matter what I really felt, didn't fly as a sober woman. A lady with seven impossible years of sobriety offered congratulations and asked how I was doing. "Fine, thanks," and then tears welled into my eyes. I turned away fast, hoping she hadn't seen, and ran to my car. I barely made it to the door of my home, sobbing and desperate to get inside. I couldn't stand and collapsed on the floor, my body wracked, gasping. A wave of sorrow, a deluge of sadness, as real as any undertow of nature pulled me into an ocean of despair. I couldn't stop it; I couldn't get my feet under me and felt my entire sense of self being obliterated. All identity and every idea of myself were being washed away like sand under a firehose.

The tiniest decision infiltrated my anguish: *Get off the floor and go lay in bed.* My room comforts me. Black carpet, purple velvet drapes, king-size bed with thick duvet. I curled into a ball, full fetal, heaving as I wept. The TV had been left on. An old show flickered on the screen. Through puffy, swollen eyes I squinted at it. *The Munsters*—I hadn't seen it in ages. Pulling a down pillow to my chest, I cried and mourned. Still shaking and sniffling, my face sticky with tears, I glanced again at the show. Grandpa gave Herman some potion to drink and it made him look normal. Herman marched to a mirror and reacted, horrified. I started giggling. Alone in my bed, I moved from wallowing in the abyss of despair to laughing at an old sitcom. Life is crazy. Sometimes you have to hang on until the magic moments come. Sobriety had unlocked the box, and every element of pain and hurt from as far back as I could remember, or not remember, had burst forth with a frightening force. The magnitude of it had engulfed me, and yet here I remained, wondering what, if any, parts were left intact. Without drinking, I wasn't sure at all who I would be now. Maybe my new starting place could be just a girl who laughed at *The Munsters*.

I had no religious upbringing, didn't believe in a dogma God, never thought about meaning-of-life stuff except on a cocaine-fueled all-nighter. The first stone in my spiritual path was humility. I hadn't entered AA thinking I was better than everyone else but didn't realize the things that would be asked of me. I did them all, took every suggestion, followed every instruction: Setting up or putting away chairs, making coffee for the group, washing cups, doing chores. Talking to people with less time sober—to someone with a day or a week, my couple of months could seem more relatable or attainable than the years some people had accrued. Answering the phone at the AA headquarters. Driving over to help a desperate alcoholic who had called for help. Going to halfway houses, rehab facilities, even jails, to speak and offer hope. I looked for similarities instead of the many differences between my story and the ones I heard. I always offered to help people. The second stone of my spiritual path was service. I didn't know humility and service are the essence of living in the light of God; I just wanted to stay sober.

If this all sounds angelic and pure, that's not the case. An ex-cop from Detroit—an irreverently funny, smart, and cynical hard-ass—was my favorite speaker. My thoughts were darker than my actions, but I saw the slogans and mottoes come true. I couldn't think my way into right actions, but I could act my way into right thinking. It didn't matter what thoughts went through my head or how I felt. Showing up and doing the damn work is what mattered. That is how it works, and that is how I changed.

Some sober people invited me to a party. *Oh great.* I stopped at 7–Eleven and picked up a six-pack of sodas. This would suck, for sure. But I would show up. At the party I sat silently, watching, listening. These losers were enjoying themselves. Someone said something funny and it made me laugh, and then I started enjoying myself too. Later, I got on my knees and thanked the higher power for showing me I could still have a good time.

The world called, and I felt ready to start being a part of it. With nearly three months of sobriety, I went to dinner at one of my favorite restaurants. I learned something there: there's more good stuff about eating a meal out than drinking alcohol. The atmosphere felt nice, being waited on was a great thing, the food tasted excellent, and not having to do dishes or clean up was sublime. Who knew? Apparently, tons of people knew.

Music came to my rescue. It always had: as a kid singing along in happiness, as a teenager saved by rock 'n' roll, as a musician discovering that playing took me out of myself, and as a song-writer. All these new sober feelings and thoughts, my experiencing the world in a brand-new way, had to be put somewhere. Picking up my beautiful, perfect Stratocaster, the one I had gotten in Austin fifteen years before, I proceeded to write a batch of the most hideous, Hallmark-card-worthy, sonorous, overwrought songs imaginable. At the time I thought they were great, and doing it served a purpose. The songs were simply excruciating. I will thank my higher power forever that I didn't have a publishing deal or record deal or band—no one heard these awful tunes, and no one ever will. Permanent cringe.

43

ULTRAS

I had never forgotten Charlotte's phone number. She had nearly five years sober when I called. This is considered serious time—some say it's a turning point because drunks are still sicker than shit the first few years. They say it quietly, so as not to discourage the newcomers. Don't believe it. Works in progress are the enduring and perpetual mainstays of self-improvement.

"Charlotte. It's Kathy. I've been sober four months." I blurted it out, right after she said hello.

In less than a minute we had a connection again. Her five years of sobriety, our years of separateness, were irrelevant dust, swept aside. The words spilled out, and I told her about my meeting, my sponsor, everything I could do, and the things I still wasn't comfortable with. We said nothing about the Go-Go's, or the past, or music. I could tell, even over the phone, that sobriety had brought Charlotte home to herself—her best self. She was kind and supportive, and she listened to me as I went on and on.

How cathartic to understand how sobriety had given her life back. My drinking spanned the ultras: sex, recklessness, all-nighters and all-dayers, songwriting, hangovers, making best friends, danger, great fun, regrets. It gave me a life of extremes. Charlotte's addiction had been a unidirectional force pulling her away from any meaningful life.

How strange to have her pick me up at my new home, the fourth place I had lived in as many years—she knew nothing about what I had gone through, and I thought her life had been a cakewalk. Char took me to a big meeting in the Valley, the musicians meeting. Hundreds of us: world-famous ones, obscure ones, locals, hired guns, virtuosos, entire bands. I preferred stock, off-the-rack AA, but going with her and being there together felt like a momentous occasion. I half expected people to notice and be aware of the significance taking place right in their midst, but the occasion went unnoticed. Only we knew, testing this foreign kinship that was the antithesis to hours spent drinking and getting high together.

How interesting to talk to my old bandmate about then, about now. We exhausted every topic, and then the terrible breakup couldn't be ignored. Only now could I understand how the toxicity of the band had felt to a brand-new recovering addict. Remembering how I could do nothing for three months but sit on the sofa in my house and go to meetings, I realized that the things expected of her when she got out of rehab would have been terrifying. The old stuff remained—the quips and flip sarcasm, the jokes and memories—but new elements expanded the base—an openness to seeing our changes. Not everything would be resolved, but something else came first now, a brand-new priority we shared.

We took things slowly as friends, but as sober women I knew we would be there for each other. I had work to do, meetings and AA commitments, bad songs to write, and major money problems. Selling the Sunset Plaza house I had rented out since the home invasion helped a little. I had used most of my profit to live off of for the past few years, refinancing and taking equity cash chunks like they were free money.

Sobriety is an instant makeover; I looked good. I joined a gym and made a habit of regular workouts, replacing the sporadic exercise and diet binges I had done in the past. I felt like a brand-new person and wanted to look as new and different as I felt. Dying my hair a platinum blond did the trick.

Sobriety strips the filters, lays bare what's underneath the bullshit. It can take a hatchet to relationships with no fundamental source of mutual friendship. All of mine stayed intact. A few friends, and more acquaintances, expressed surprise that I had stopped drinking, having not perceived any problem. This is something we functioning alcoholics do really well: trick people and make sure no one can tell how bad we are. If they knew, we might have to face it. I had good people in my life, sober and otherwise, and felt supported.

I had never lost touch with Gina. Belinda had contacted me one time in the years since the band had broken up.

"It wasn't because of you that I left," she said. "I'm sorry we did it the way we did."

She just wanted me to know that. It had helped at the time, not with my overall decline and the loss of my band, but with not holding a grudge or resentment. My fake bravado and pathetic sadness ratio had seesawed by then. I didn't have enough energy for a grudge.

I hadn't heard from or seen Jane since she left the band. The first startling event resulting from reconnecting with Char took place in the spring. Belinda invited everyone to sing backup vocals on a song for her new record. Being together, slightly forcing a naturalness we all wanted, we broke through the ice of our painful split. The dynamic, with Belinda's producer, her success, and her years-long partnership working with Charlotte, should have been awful. But it wasn't. Gina and Jane had drifted back into good terms, and the sobriety bond I had with Charlotte was strong. I appreciated the goodwill of Belinda's gesture. I appreciated being in the presence of the women I had grown up with. We were tentatively testing the waters. Never had the Go-Go's been so careful with each other.

I didn't see it coming. For the first time since our last show with Jane in October 1984, all of us sat together in a West Hollywood Italian restaurant and shared a meal. This time people took notice. Each of us in her prime, beautiful and self-possessed, the Go-Go's had never looked so collectively gorgeous. The chemistry and camaraderie could have blown the roof off the restaurant. The five-headed monster had returned, this time with very different heads on the same Go-Go body. It was simply wonderful. The happiness I felt being together had a purity and intensity I had never felt in our crazy wildness. With no booze, no drugs, and no expectations about the future, I celebrated a fragment of time where the joy of being together in the present was enough. Our history would always be there, but this communion, interlaced with gratitude, was a first. No plans for the future crossed our lips; the new connection relied on a tenuous balance between having let go and hanging on, to our past and to each other.

I didn't want to drink, nor did I struggle with not drinking. Working the twelve-step program meant I had amends to make. As a sober person, one of the biggest amends is a change of behavior, but most people have some wrongs to right. Working with a sponsor, I made a list. I've described some of my regrets and my shoddy behavior—if I remembered it now, I remembered it then. And if I remembered it, I needed to address it. With this in mind, I began the process. In person, on the phone, or with a letter, I expressed sincere regret to those I hurt. I sent money where I needed to—recalling how I left June and Johnny Cash to foot the bill at the Sunset Marquis after the robbery, I estimated my share and sent a large check. The letter Johnny wrote back to me is a treasure. The gifts of doing the right thing, when they came, were blessings. If I couldn't make the amends, I tried to ease my remorse by doing more service, donating to causes I thought might help someone else.

I found a therapist and began to unwrap and reveal the deep complexities of my relationship with my mom, and the absence of one with my dad. Mom still drank and drugged, and several visits had ended terribly after full-throttle fights fed with lies, anger, entitlement, and resentment. Sobriety didn't let me cover up, lock down, hide, or stuff away how I felt anymore. Yet I loved my mom, the only family I'd ever had. I hoped for a day we could have a healthy connection.

Sobriety means finding out what's real. I had been so afraid that I'd lose who I thought I was and wouldn't know, or wouldn't like, the "real" me. I needed to be on my own; I didn't want to be in a relationship anymore. The ground had shifted and over-turned, I stood somewhere else, and there were parts of my life I couldn't hold on to anymore. My first undiluted, unmedicated pain came from breaking up with Clem. I felt like the worst person in the world. The hurtful things I had done in the past couple years of our five-year relationship stacked on top of the hurt I inflicted by wanting to be single now. He had endured my worst years of drinking and misery and deserved this better version of me, but I couldn't handle anything else. Staying sober had to be the center of my life. Maybe we could have a future, but—cliché warning—I had to learn to love myself first.

44

THINGY IN THE SKY

The Whisky a Go Go marquee read "Klamm." Surprise, surprise, Klamm was actually the Go-Go's, who were playing an unannounced secret show. Word had gotten out, and the sidewalk had been mobbed all afternoon with folks dying to get the hottest ticket in town. Most had been allotted to friends, family, and associates. The name we had actually dreamt up was the Clam Family, but something had gotten lost in translation. It was a typical screwup, proving some things never change in Go-Go-land—in this instance, an in-joke gone astray. An assortment of "hair" bands had taken over the Strip over the years, and part of our joke was to pay tribute by coming out in big, teased-out, ridiculous wigs, headbanging and making grimacing, wide-mouth guitar face. It was too silly for us even, and after a few songs the wigs came off and we slammed through a set of hits and favorites, right on the very stage where my journey with the band had started. The Clam Family/Klamm gave us a chance to do what we still did best: goof off, have a great time playing, and make an audience really happy. It also served as a warm-up show before the big one happening the next night—the real thing.

Belinda's manager had presented the Go-Go's with an opportunity for a reunion concert. It was perfect: a benefit to help raise money for the California Environmental Protection Initiative. Doing it for a cause we all believed in took the pressure off, no expectations, just the present-day, grown-up and responsible Go-Go's doing our part. Jane Fonda was an organizer working to get the initiative on the ballot. Thrilled to have us involved to raise money and awareness, she had us over to her house to discuss the initiative. A splashy press conference with her, and just like that, the limelight shined again. All the fangirling between Ms. Fonda and the band was one of those completely unexpected dividends that came from being in the Go-Go's.

The afternoon of March 28, 1990, a limo picked me up at the Studio City house I still lived in. Clem's house. We had stayed broken up but were trying to transition to a new relationship, one of friendship. It had been rough going, but he would forever remain a part of my life. Riding the short distance to the Universal Amphitheater, I sat alone in the middle of one of the leather seats. It had been a long time since I had taken a limo to a gig. All through the sound check, hanging in the dressing room, being with the Go-Go's, I was acutely aware of how it felt: strange and wonderful and terribly frightening. I had fourteen months of sobriety and did what I had learned to do: find a quiet place to get centered. Wandering down the backstage corridors of the clean, modern venue, I found an empty bathroom. In one of the stalls, I got on my knees. In the old days I might have been snorting coke. Or vomiting.

Holy fuck, I'm praying!

"God, or whatever, mysterious universe energy. Vague higher power thingy in the sky. Thank you. I can hardly believe I get to do this again. I'm so afraid. Please make me a channel, so that I may bring joy through music with my band tonight."

That seemed good enough. It's the action that counts, the willingness to be humble and appreciate what is given. What had been given to me that night was the first Go-Go's show— not counting the Clam Family—in five years. Being grateful for that was a lot nicer—a lot less buzzy, messy, and negative—than being fucked up.

Leaving my sanctuary, I found Charlotte wandering too. We ducked into a spare dressing room. Talking about how we both felt in that moment helped—it only takes two alcoholics to have a meeting.

An hour later I ran onstage to thousands of people, already out of their seats and on their feet. It felt like the most natural thing in the world. Every emotion was unfiltered and full strength. The joy was overwhelming. But so was the confidence. I had never been more certain of who I was in that band and owned every moment. Tears welled in my eyes and, before they could fall, morphed into exhilaration. I wasn't on the ride; I *was* the ride.

I was seeing, really seeing, the band—everyone in their prime. Looking out in the audience, I made eye contact with different people. Each face made me smile more. A whole new way of being a Go-Go had opened up for me. At one point, Jane Fonda was onstage playing tambourine with us. In the front rows and on the side of the stage were our friends from the height of our careers, including Jodie Foster and Rob Lowe, both huge stars now.

After the encore, the whole band ran down the backstage hall to our dressing rooms, exuberant and screaming.

"Who wants to go on tour?" Belinda yelled. We whooped and hollered, and it was like nothing bad had ever happened to the Go-Go's, ever.

I wasn't prepared for the manic aftermath of a show. Without being high and drinking, it was hard to keep up, hard to be pulled in different directions, to greet and talk to everyone. Everyone came—all the people who had helped build the band—celebrities, family, and friends from each of our lives that we had all come to know over the years. I felt a wave of melancholy at not sharing the night with Clem, and I had to accept it and let it be part of the night. For the first time, I left way before the party was over. Riding home alone in a stretch limo, just me and a shitload of feelings, all without buffering, enhancing, numbing, or burying. Being real was the toughest, most rock 'n' roll thing I had ever done.

The flurry of Go-Go activity and the warm fuzziness of reconnecting was a spectacular and unexpected gift—but it was like some fancy art piece that you have to put on the shelf because as great as it is, there's not much you can do with it. Despite the triumph of our show and Belinda's impulsive "Who wants to go on tour" shout-out, I didn't dare expect anything more. Her third solo album was still dropping singles and she had attained international stardom, far beyond what the Go-Go's had ever accomplished. Jane had also released a third solo album on a major label and would be touring in support of it. Both Charlotte and Gina had formed bands and gotten record deals. I was too cautious to expect more, and I had come too far to want more. Sobriety was a current, electric and transformative for me. I was grounded. Staying that way would remain the foundation of my life.

An alcoholic/addict isn't in the clear or cured with abstinence. I took each day as a reprieve and continued to follow the advice of people who knew how to live without booze or drugs. That meant doing all the service, speaking at facilities, helping newly sober women, and sticking with therapy. And finally, all the music I had been writing and working on started to take a shape. Not the best shape, but good enough to do something with. Even this new, spiritually improved version of me had the same core desire I'd always had: to play guitar in a band. Old friends from as far back as Charlie Quintana from the Plugz, who had gone on to play with Dylan; my roommate Craig Ross, soon to join Lenny Kravitz; and my old bandmate Jebin Bruni, an in-demand session and band player, came together to help me figure out what I was trying to do next musically. As I had always found, the guy musicians in my life had my back. It would be a while longer before I acquired a confident direction in my post–Go-Go's music career, but starting over is always going to crush giving up. The idea of not playing, not writing, and not performing is unimaginable. I don't know if that's a good thing or not; it's just how I'm wired. That thing happens in music, where time stops and I'm in that moment without a thought or a care or a feeling or a need. Just alive.

It seems like when I take care of myself, show up, do the work—even if the work is about letting go and moving on—that good stuff comes up behind me. There are all kinds of mottoes and proverbs that say just that, but seeing it happen again and again in my life is a powerful tool.

Within a couple of months of the last Go-Go's concert, IRS Records announced plans to release a greatest hits record. Since we didn't have enough hits to make an entire album of hits, they canned the "hits" part and just called it *Greatest*. It was a record of all the songs that might have been hits if we had milked the first record more or hadn't imploded. We didn't have much say in the tracks they chose, but we had the idea to record a new, modern version of "Cool Jerk." Miles Copeland, again doing a great job of matchmaking, got David Z on board to produce the new version. David Z worked extensively with Prince and had produced a fantastic hit for another IRS band, the Fine Young Cannibals, called "She Drives Me Crazy." I thought the new sound would be interesting—who knows, maybe even launch the Go-Go's again. And recording a cover song meant no songwriting Go-Go would make more money than someone else. We were trying. No one wanted any of those old problems to fuck up our vibe.

Our record company had flourished after the success of *Beauty and the Beat*, and it could afford a snazzy video to go with the new song. Everyone had grown into women, so there was nothing girly or cute about this reboot. I had kept the platinum blond hair; it was so shiny and perfect that it looked like a wig, but for me it marked my reincarnation.

Jane had become an animal rights activist and asked us to help launch a new marketing scheme for PETA—People for the Ethical Treatment of Animals. We were the first to pose in what would become their most well-known campaign, We'd Rather Go Naked Than Wear Fur. There was press around that and our new video and single, the *Greatest* album was released, and then a tour was booked. Twenty-five cities across the United States. Only then did I know that everything I had lost had come back. And it did—I got to do it all again: record, perform, travel, meet fans, be on TV. This time, I knew I wouldn't lose track of myself. Never again.

The single, ironically, charted in England, where we had never had a hit, and flopped in the United States. The album failed to generate much excitement either. It seemed our time had passed, but for a musician like me, a girl who wanted to play in a band, none of that mattered. I had never taken any of it for granted. Not the hits, the shows, the touring, the songs and albums—my success was the sweetest glory, taking me beyond where I hoped to go. The truth is that at any point, any pinnacle of success, I would have been happy if that was as far as we got. Getting to join a fun band with fans who showed up? Great! Getting to make a record in NYC? Perfect. Going on tour in a tour bus, traveling all over the country? Amazing! Wait, now Europe and Japan, and Australia? Unbelievable. Each phase was a prism of fantasy and raw need. It could have stopped any-time, because what I wanted was to feel like I belonged. Once I felt that, it became my everything. I hadn't taken any of it for granted except one essential part: my bandmates.

In the decade since we had come together, my relationship with the band had been like the dual nature of light, slipping from allies to antagonists, from coconspirators to traitors, from friends to enemies. They had inspired me, disappointed me, protected me, and threatened everything I valued in my life. More than anything, I had seen them as my sisters. The Go-Go's had given me the family I'd longed to be a part of—except I didn't know how to be in a family. Families look out for each other, or they're supposed to anyway. I only knew how to take care of myself, like I had always done, in the only way I knew how.

Not drinking—the one thing I didn't think I could do—had shown me that I could accept all the sadness, grief, and loss I had buried from my childhood through my adolescence, and anything else life would throw at me. I had to lose—be forced to let go of—the things I thought defined me in order to find out what parts were real. I look back sometimes and add up my sober time with the time spent playing in the biggest band I would ever be in, and the best part is how all the years have made me a better person in every way. A better friend, daughter, wife, bandmate, girlfriend, and mother. Those are well-lived years.

EPILOGUE-A-GO-GO

The gifts kept giving. My mom got clean, too, after a few years of us fighting and her needing to lose everything before realizing she had a problem. She's a grandma now, and I still protect her—I'm the magic cloak now. My dad and I became close, super close, in the last eight months of his life. It healed and broke my heart all at once. Clem is the brother I always wanted; we are family. Saul Davis and Carla Olson from my Textones days are too. With so much life lived between Austin and Los Angeles, perhaps it's fitting that I moved back to Austin for another chapter with my very own "real" family, one with a mom, dad, and little girl—who is now the teenager in the introduction of this book.

Jesse Sublett and Lois Richwine, who have known me since I first started out, are still a part of my life. Catherine Sebastian has continued to capture key points of my life, and I cherish those photos along with our friendship. I'm grateful to still keep up with tour manager Bruce Patron, band manager Ginger Canzoneri, and first boyfriend Danny Harvey. My guitar God friend Craig Ross became a longtime bandmate of Lenny Kravitz's— whom he met because I had met Lenny on the steps of A&M way back during the *Vacation* recordings. And after forty years I heard from Marilyn, the friend I had started my first band with. A few cherished musicians I introduced in this story are gone now from cancer, most notably Chrissy Amphlett, Kelly Johnson, and the sweet World's Cutest Killer drummer, Craig Aaronson.

I always play in a band, knowing that it's too much of my identity to ever let go of. Somehow, at sixty years old I still feel the same when I play as I did when I was twenty. And somewhere along the way I became very sure, comfortable, and happy with the knowledge that I'm a really good musician, songwriter, and yes, even singer.

And the Go-Go's? There's a lot left to that story. This one detailed the phenomenon of five women who formed a sisterhood and did something together that hadn't been done before. We're still predictably manic and unpredictably sensitive, and even though everyone is the same person she is in or out of the band, being together changes everyone slightly. Just enough to bring out the best and the worst in each other. We managed to record more, tour more, and break up more, all the way up until 2012. During that year, the wrong history repeated itself and I became the fired bass player. It was undoubtedly the worst and ugliest era in this decades-long five-way relationship. But in usual Go-Go's fashion, the split couldn't stick and we returned intact with homecoming shows, a Broadway musical, and a documentary film. In short, we've had more than enough betrayals, breakups, and backstabbing as well as public fallings-out and private knockdowns. We've also grown up together, helped and supported each other, learned from each other, and accepted and changed with each other. Dysfunction is in our DNA, but it's a tendinous and strong imperfection that seems to also keep us connected. I see a future in which we have the tools to better manage it. Maybe.

Not the End

ACKNOWLEDGMENTS

I am so proud to be associated with the University of Texas Press, and I cannot begin to think of words that convey what it has meant to me to be given the chance to write this story. Gianna LaMorte and Casey Kittrell, you have made a reality out of a far-flung hope I could barely see on the horizon. I know I would have nothing but endless starts and fantasy finishes without the vision you lent me.

I relied on Christopher Schelling's advice as a representative and was incredibly lucky to have access to his knowledge. Karen Valby seemed to intuit exactly what encouragement I needed, and her kind but firm judgment kept me on schedule and kept my story from straying all over the place. To my friends who read portions and offered validation and feedback, you helped more than you know: Raoul Hernandez, Jon Wurster, Wendi Aarons, Abby Ellin, Kristy McInnis, Steven and Mikel—thank you.

I cannot imagine the life I would be living without Steven Weisburd; I'm eternally grateful to have cocreated the love of our lives and for his gifts to me: the family and purpose that gave me true fulfillment, not to mention always being my number-one supporter. Clem Burke knows how much I love him, but I'll say it here, too. Denny Freeman, you changed everything for the better. Carla Olson and Saul Davis, I'm blessed for our lifelong friendship, along with the friends who walked alongside me as I grew up: Marilyn Dean, Jesse Sublett, Lois Richwine, Eddie Munoz, Catherine Sebastian, Carlene Carter, and Holly Knight. To my Go-Go's sisters: Char, Jane, Belinda, and Gina—we might have ruled the world, but I'll settle for having had the time of our lives. I smile every time I think of us. Colette Brooks and Marina Muhlfriedel, you were not forgotten: I cherish our history, our bonds, and our friendship. I'm grateful for Melessa Cowan, who has become part of my family. Dominique Davalos, you are a rock in my life, and we've made some of the best rock 'n' roll that ever took place. Eve Monsees, I'm so proud to share a stage and a song with you. Last but not least, in a league of his own: Mikel Rouse, thank you for opening up my world in so many ways and for showing me every day that laughter, love, joy, courage, art, and music are still the best things in life any time, at any age.

A NOTE ON SOURCES AND IDENTIFICATIONS

I relied on journal entries, personal essays, band itineraries, years of leather-bound Filofax calendars (I keep everything!), and my own memory to write this work of nonfiction. Part of my preproduction work entailed creating playlists, organized by year and comprising multigenre chart hits, AM/FM radio staples, album releases, and tracks culled from my record collection. The music made the past come alive in the present and never failed to stir the feelings and thoughts I experienced when those songs were the unofficial mixtape of my life.

I turned an unfortunate inclination for procrastination/writing avoidance into a productive fault by spending hours and days doing extensive research to ensure an accurate and factual timeline. However, even with these searches, authentications, documents, and prompts, memory is a slippery abstraction. It tends to take the shape of whoever is doing the remembering, so it's entirely possible that another person at the same place and time might have a perspective different from my own.

Interspersed with the real and actual, several names and physical descriptions have been changed or invented. I did so at my discretion or at the subject's request, to protect the privacy of friends, family, and significant encounters I have written about.

INDEX

INDEX *283*